The Rep........

And their connection with Egyptian history

Fanny Corbaux

Alpha Editions

This edition published in 2019

ISBN : 9789353802592

Design and Setting By
Alpha Editions
email - alphaedis@gmail.com

THE REPHAIM,

AND

THEIR CONNECTION WITH EGYPTIAN HISTORY.

BY FANNY CORBAUX.

[Reprinted from the JOURNAL OF SACRED LITERATURE, Vols. I, II, and III,
New Series.]

[Reprinted from 'Kitto's Journal of Sacred Literature,' for Oct. 1851.]

CHAPTER I.

State of Palestine during the Patriarchal period.

BEFORE we can hope to understand fully the political condition of Egypt and that of Israel, at the momentous epoch when the latter were " brought out of the house of bondage" to be made a nation among nations, we must ascend the stream of time some five centuries, in order to study the revolutions wrought during that interval in the condition of those people of Palestine who were the precursors of Israel in the land; and who, under the appointment of an overruling Providence, were the principal agents in working out—indirectly, the destinies of Israel,—and directly, those of Egypt. The two centuries preceding the Exode are a point in time when the history of these two nations unites; and we must look to Palestine for the connecting link between them.

Why—when Joseph's family entered Egypt (Gen. xlvi. 34) —was every shepherd such an abomination to the Egyptians, that the relatives of the king's greatest benefactor were objects of suspicion to his people from their manner of life and occupation? Why was the land of Goshen the only spot in all Egypt where they could be tolerated by the population? What revolutions subsequently brought on such a change of feeling towards the blameless and harmless Hebrews, that nothing short of their extermination could make the Egyptian monarch feel sure of his kingdom's safety? Why was he afraid that if they left the land, they would join his enemies? (Ex. i. 8—10.) And finally, *who were those enemies?*

Many and various solutions of these problems have been put forth from time to time; but nothing more definite than detached and imperfectly supported conjectures, has hitherto been offered in answer to the last and chief question of all—the key to the rest—Who were those great and formidable foes of Egypt

---

[a] In the *Biblical Intelligence* of the last number of this Journal, we noticed a paper on the Rephaim, and their connexion with Egyptian History, by Miss FANNY CORBAUX, which had been read before the Syro-Egyptian Society, and a brief abstract of which appeared in the *Athenæum* for March 15. This lady's close acquaintance with the class of subjects to which this enquiry relates, is well known through her able and interesting communications to the Society just named; and it is therefore a peculiar satisfaction to us that our notice of the above paper has procured us the opportunity of laying the whole of this ingenious and valuable disquisition before our readers. What we now offer is the first portion of it.—EDITOR *J. S. L.*

whose power the Egyptian monarchs so greatly dreaded, although upwards of a century had elapsed since they were beaten out of the land?

It is very clear that the brief and mutilated fragments of Manetho which have survived the wreck of ages, appear to connect these aggressors of Egypt with Palestine. I trust I shall succeed in producing sufficient data to demonstrate that it is indeed to the history of a very remarkable, but hitherto disregarded primeval race, once extensively spread over that land, and called in the Bible the REPHAIM, that we may look with confidence, both for the solution of the great problem in Egyptian history—and for a test of the great chronological problem in Scripture history, the synchronical connexion of Egypt and Israel by equally authentic accounts of corresponding events, described by the great Theban conquerors in the monumental records of their triumphs, on the one hand; and by the patriarch of history in the sacred annals of his people, on the other.

The historical fragment which forms chapter xiv of Genesis, inserted by Moses into the biography of his ancestor Abraham, introduces us to this people; and exhibits at the same time in so striking a light the political condition of Palestine at the epoch of his settlement in the land, that it will be desirable to have the narrative entire before our view for consideration.

GENESIS XIV.

"¹Now it was in the days of Amraphel king of Shinar, Arioch king of Ellasar,[b] Chedorlaomer king of Elam, and Tidal king of Goïm; ²they made war with Bera king of Sodom, and with Birsha king of Gomorrah, Shinab king of Admah, Shemeber king of Zeboim, and the king of Bela, which is (now) Zoar; ³all these were confederate in the vale of Shiddim,[c] which is (now) the salt sea.

---

[b] אֶלָּסָר *Ellasar.* In a very interesting paper read before the Geographical Society on the 14th April, Col. Rawlinson identified this name with the Λαρισσα of Xenophon, which he takes for Resen; and considers the mounds of Nimrúd, named in the inscriptions Rebekha, to be the רְחֹבֹת Rehoboth of Gen. x. 11, and only a suburb of "the great city" Resen or Larissa = Ellasar.

[c] שׂדים In etymology, and especially in the identification of proper names written in one language, with their corresponding forms in another, a close adherence to the original orthography is of great importance. On this account I shall always render the Hebrew names of places to be hereafter identified, by their radicals, without regard to the Masorite pointing, whenever a more ancient and authentic orthography of the names is found extant in the Egyptian records, to prove that the points give a wrong pronunciation.

In the present instance, I read *Shiddim,* the variation of שׂ from sh to s being unknown in early times. The same observation applies to my reading of שׁלם Shalem. Had Shiddim and Shalem been originally pronounced Siddim and Salem, Moses would have written them with a ס. Vide the two orthographies of the test-word *Shibboleth,* in Judges xii. 6.

[4]Twelve years they served Chedorlaomer, and in the thirteenth they rebelled. [5]And in the fourteenth year came Chedorlaomer and the kings that were with him, and smote the REPHAIM in Ashtaroth-karnaim,[d] the ZUZIM in Ham, and the EMIM in Shaveh-kiriathaim, [6]and the HORIM in the mountains of Seir as far as El-Paran[e] (Elath), which is near the desert. [7]Then they turned, and came to Ain-mishpat, which is (now) Kadesh, and smote all the country of the AMALEKITES, and also the AMORITES who were settled[f] in Hazazon-tamar.

[8]Then went forth the king of Sodom, the king of Gomorrah, the king of Admah, the king of Zeboim, and the king of Bela (now Zoar), and arrayed themselves in battle in the vale of Shiddim [9]against Chedorlaomer king of Elam, Tidal king of Goïm, Amraphel king of Shinar, and Arioch king of Ellasar, four kings against five.

[10]There were pits of bitumen in the vale of Shiddim. The kings of Sodom and Gomorrah fled, and fell there, and the remainder fled to the mountain. [11]And they *(the enemy)* took all the riches of Sodom and Gomorrah, and all their provisions, and went their way; [12]they also took Lot, son of Abram's brother, and his riches, and departed; he was settled in Sodom.

[13]A fugitive came and told Abram the Eberite;[g] he was then dwelling in the terebinth-grove of Mamre the Amorite, brother of Eshcol and of Aner; these were in alliance with Abram. [14]When Abram heard that his kinsman was taken captive, he led forth his trained servants, born in his own house, three hundred and eighteen in number, and followed (the enemy) as far as Dan. [15]He stole[h] upon

---

[d] עַשְׁתָּרֹת קַרְנַיִם *The two-horned Ashtaroth*, to whom this city, metropolis of Bashan, was dedicated.

[e] אֵיל פָּארָן *El-Paran*, Elath. The Septuagint version, though in some parts made from a faulty text, happens in this place to give us the key to a valuable emendation of the Hebrew reading, pointing to the identity of El-paran and Elath, by shewing that the Hebrew must have originally read אֵילַת פָּאן the terminal ה of which has been accidentally dropped. They translate ἕως τῆς τερεβίνθου τῆς φαράν "unto the terebinth-tree of Pharan," having evidently mistaken the final ה of the proper name Elath for the feminine constructed form of Elah, *a terebinth-tree*. And thus their translation—albeit an evident misinterpretation—proves the original reading *Elath*, and establishes the high antiquity of this important maritime city, ascending to an unknown period before the migration of Abraham. The situation of Elath confirms this reading; for the Israelite host passed this place and the contiguous fortress of Eziongaber, when they turned back from Kadesh to compass the mountains of Seir. Hence their route was the same as that of these Assyrian invaders, only reversing the direction.

[f] "Settled" seems to render more precisely than *dwelt*, the radical idea of ישב to sit down, settle, take up a *fixed* residence, as opposed to גור to sojourn, take up a *passing* residence, *Dwell* is ambiguous; it covers both these ideas, which the Hebrew distinguishes.

[g] הָעִבְרִי The Shemite descendants of Eber were known by this name among the Hamite races of Palestine and Egypt, to distinguish them from the Aramite Shemites their neighbours. It is remarkable that the Egyptians—and long afterwards the Philistines—invariably speak of the Israelites as the Ibrim or Eberites—*Hebrews*.

[h] וַיֵּחָלֵק עֲלֵיהֶם This expression has given rise to much variety of opinion as to its

them by night, he and his servants, smote them, and pursued them as far as Hobah, which is to the north[i] of Damascus: [16]he brought back all the riches, and brought back also his kinsman Lot, and his riches, the women, and the people.

[17]The king of Sodom went forth to meet him, after his return from smiting Chedorlaomer and the kings with him, in the valley of Shaveh, which is the royal valley; [18]and Melchizedek king of Shalem brought forth bread and wine, (he was priest of the Supreme God,) [19]and blessed him, saying,

'Blessed be Abram of the Supreme God,
Possessor of heaven and earth ;
[20]And blessed be the Supreme God,
Who hath delivered thine enemies into thine hand.'

And he *(Abram)* gave him the tithe of all.

[21]Then said the king of Sodom, Give me the persons, and take the riches for thyself.

[22]Abram replied to the king of Sodom, I have lifted up my hand unto Jehovah, possessor of heaven and earth, [23]not to take of aught that is thine, from a hair-fillet even to a sandal-tie ; for thou shalt not say, 'I have enriched Abram; [24]excepting what the youths have consumed, and the share of the men who went with me, Aner, Eshcol, and Mamre, let these take their share."

However unconnected with the remainder of the sacred history this chapter may appear, in its relating events which befell nations we never hear of again until we hear that they have ceased to exist as nations, its import becomes of inestimable value when we turn our attention to the circumstantial character of the account. Then, each incident included in this precious fragment of primeval history becomes doubly significant by the consequences it draws after it in the way of inference.

Firstly: We see a group of nations, whose settlements extend from the foot of Mount Hermon to the head of the Elanitic

---

precise signification. *To be smooth* or *slippery* seems the radical sense of חלק. Compare Gen. xxvii. 11, "My brother Esau is a hairy man, and I am a smooth man:" also Ps. xii. 2, "flattering lips;" Prov. vi. 24; Isa. xxx. 10, "smooth things," *i. e.*, flatteries: and in a reduplicate form, Ps. xxxv. 6, and Jer. xxiii. 12, "slippery ways." In Jer. xxxvii. 12, the marginal correction of the common translation, *to slip away*—instead of "separate himself," which has no sense—is very appropriate ; the prophet was endeavouring to return by stealth, unperceived, among his people, and was accordingly accused of "falling away" (or deserting) to the Chaldeans. In the present passage, the sense of this expression is the same; the writer seems to imply that Abram *slipped in*—glided by stealth on the enemy during the night, to take them by surprise. "He stole upon them."

[i] מישמאל לדמשק The quarters of the compass are conventionally referred by the Hebrews to the position of a spectator fronting the rising sun. Since קדם *the front*, is the east, and ימין *the right hand*, is the south,—שמאל *the left*, must be the north, and אחר *behind*, the west.

Gulf, at open war with another group of nations resident beyond the Euphrates, among whom the king of Elam takes the lead. Thus the power of Shinar, precursor of the great Babylonian empire, was at that time so inconsiderable, that its king acts here only the secondary part of subsidy to the state of Elam.

Secondly: We see that although the Emim were no more than a section of this national group, the confederate princes of their five chief cities formed at that early period a sufficiently powerful body of people to withstand these four Asiatic kings, and to be evenly matched against them. This speaks very decidedly in favour of their power and importance relatively to their adversaries.

Thirdly: We learn from the part taken by the king of Sodom in the proceedings after the victory, that this city was the metropolis, for its site is called " the Royal valley ;" and he himself must have been chief among the confederate Emim princes, for he claims the persons of the captives rescued by Abram, as his subjects; and takes upon himself to dispose of the recovered booty, by his munificent offer of the whole to the deliverer of his people. Such a claim and exercise of authority can only be the privileges of one whose supremacy is admitted : the metropolitan chief and head of the tribe.

Fourthly—and what appears very extraordinary—the king of another district leaves his metropolis in the centre of Palestine, and goes forth to the land of the Emim, to meet Abram and his people, who were escorting home Lot and the other rescued captives. Brief as are the terms of the record, the transaction in question obviously refers to a solemn public ceremony of thanksgiving, at which this king officiates in a sacerdotal character, and fulfils religious rites of which he and Abram partake in common. He not only prays for the Divine blessing on Abram, but returns thanks to God for his victory ; although it does not appear, as far as that narrative shews, that his own immediate subjects had either been endangered or implicated in the war. What then could his relation be to the people in the Royal valley of Shaveh, whom the danger and the deliverance so nearly concerned?

But, what is more extraordinary still, and certainly implies that this king of Shalem did stand in some acknowledged relation of superiority to the people of Sodom, is, that he receives as a matter of course the tribute of a tenth of the spoil recovered from the enemy. He receives it, as St. Paul very clearly intimates (Heb. vii. 1—7), in virtue of a prescriptive right analogous to that under which the Levitical priesthood afterwards received their tithe. For mark : " Abram gave him *a tithe of all,"* immediately after the religious ceremony; this was before *all* the spoil had been offered to himself by the king of Sodom. So that at the time he is said to have given *"a tithe of all,"* it was not yet his own to present as a *personal* gift. We can hardly avoid inferring from this, that Melchizedek must have received it through the hands of Abram, in virtue of a sacred pre-existing right, acknowledged by all parties present, and by the king of Sodom the very first. This duty fulfilled, the residue is to be divided. A share of it was in justice due to Abram and to his allies, in return for the benefit they had rendered to the people by its recovery and the rescue of their captives. The king of Sodom offers him the whole without reserve: "Give me the persons, and take the riches for thyself." But the patriarch, unwilling to place himself under obligation to a people with whom he did not wish to keep up any personal intercourse, declines any share of the wealth for himself; and that in terms which admit the right of the giver: "I will not take of aught *that is thine."* He only avails himself of the Emim chieftain's generosity to secure his Amorite friends a just reward for their personal assistance.

What then was the position of this king of Shalem towards the Emim tribes, that such a right should exist on his part, and that the others should so scrupulously fulfil its claims? And finally, on considering over these circumstances, we ask ourselves, What were these nations whom we find spread over so large a part of Palestine at this early age, occupying so conspicuous a position in its political affairs; united by so striking a bond of federal discipline, which implies a systematic national organization of no short standing; and yet of whom we hear no more in Scripture, until Moses informs us that they have almost wholly disappeared? (Deut. ii. 10, 11, 19—21; iii. 1—11.) What was their origin—their history—their end?

The reversion of their lands to Abram's posterity was prophetically announced to the then childless patriarch, just after these events, when they were yet "a great, numerous, and haughty people;" when the land was full of them, and they were its lords. Where shall we read their whole history, so as to follow up the succession of events whereby, under the inscrutable dispositions of Providence, the fulfilment of that promise was finally accomplished?

Not in the sacred annals alone. But these give us the key to that history. They give us the names of this people—of their tribes—and of their cities; we can thereby learn their geographical distribution. In the opening of the Mosaic record, they are displayed once to our view, while in the plenitude of their power. At its close, they are mentioned again as fallen—dispersed—lost!

But the monumental records of ancient Egypt abundantly supply the missing links of this broken chain. I propose to shew how, in these, we not only may recognize the same names, and trace them to the same lands; but also how the very people live again before our eyes, their appearance, their costumes, their arms, their gods, depicted on her sculptures; their deeds recorded on her tablets. These tell the tale of a long, inveterate national struggle between the two giant powers of primeval antiquity. In these we may learn how and when this ancient people of Palestine were cast down from their lofty position as conquerors and rulers of Egypt—pursued into the heart and to the very recesses of their native domains—and there cut up piecemeal, tribe by tribe, during a fierce conflict of three long centuries; till they were at last brought so low in the scale of nations, as to yield before the conquering Hebrew host and be scattered to nothing in a single battle, even before these had crossed the Jordan to enter the land of Canaan.

CHAPTER II.

Geographical distribution of the Mizraim.

It is now generally received among ethnologists that the original settlers in the valley of the Nile were an Asiatic race. The final establishment of a large tribe in the remoter regions of a newly colonized country is always a work of time, the natural effect of a gradual advance from the starting-point, according to the necessities of an increasing population. We therefore must not be surprised at an attempt to trace, in the various tribes comprehended under the name of REPHAIM in the most ancient parts of the Bible records, and resident in southern and eastern Palestine, a people identical with or nearly related to the primitive colonists of Lower Egypt, who are included in those records under the general denomination of Mizraim.

Two Asiatic races, both Hamitic families, would appear to have established colonies in the valley of the Nile, simultaneously, but advancing from opposite directions. The Cushites of northern Arabia, after forming a line of settlements along the shores of the Persian Gulf and Indian Ocean, entered the African continent that way, and founded an empire in Nubia; from thence extending far into Upper Egypt. For all these lands are denominated "Cush" in the Bible. Meanwhile, another Hamitic family, the Mizraim, having entered Lower Egypt through the intermediate tract of eastern and southern Palestine, ultimately extended their settlements up the Nile.

How far southward the Mizraim may have reached before they came up with the Cushite colonies, and to what extent the ancient Egyptians of the Thebaid may be considered a mixed race, must remain a matter of conjecture. Where such a mixture has taken place, whether from gradual and peaceful amalgamation of two neighbouring stocks, or whether from subsequent conquest, it becomes very difficult to draw the exact line of demarcation between them, from their physical peculiarities. But a record of the original boundary between these two ambitious rival races of Egypt seems preserved by the Biblical names of their lands. Migdol and Syene are quoted in Scripture[j] as the "Dan and Beersheba" of Mizraimite Egypt, its two opposite extremities; beyond this, Cush or Ethiopia begins; and all this country is generally included under the designation of Mizraim, whether the whole remained under the dominion of the Mizraimite race or not.

The religious institutions of ancient Egypt shew evident traces of having resulted from the blending of two races originally as distinct in their religious ideas as in their physical peculiarities. Their pantheon exhibits a tendency to separate each tangible manifestation of a Divine attribute, or of a power in nature, and to set apart each of these impersonations as a distinct object of reverence and as a peculiarly local deity; the cosmogonic system thus framed being found strangely blended with another system of astronomical worship quite inconsistent with it, though very consistent in itself. This mixture is as old as the Egyptian nation known to us by its traditions and monuments since the era of Menes. The Sabean[k] or Cushite form of star-worship, in thus adapting itself to the indigenous religion of Mizraim, betrays both its originators and its relative age. It has all the appearance of being the after-idea arising out of a previously-formed methodical system, and superimposed on ano-

---

[j] Ezek. xxix. 10: "I will make the land of Mizraim utterly waste and desolate מִמִּגְדֹּל סְוֵנֵה וְעַד גְּבוּל כּוּשׁ from Migdol to Syene, and to the frontier of Cush." *Migdol* is the Magdolum of the Antonine itinerary, a frontier-fortress twelve Roman, or rather less than ten geographical miles, south of Pelusium. Syene, now Asouan; the Masorites were sorry geographers; and here, they have pointed סְוֵנֵה *Seveneh*, as though the ה were a final of the proper name, instead of the determinative particle of direction, "to Suan." *Syene* was the separation of Upper Egypt and Ethiopia or Cush.

[k] For some highly interesting and judicious remarks on this subject, consult Sir Gardner Wilkinson's *Ancient Egyptians*, part ii., vol., i., chapters xii. and xiii. This author, however, supposes that the Sabean may have been the fundamental system. But the local character of the Egyptian Gods would rather indicate the contrary hypo-

ther whose parts had been casually brought together.[i] It may be regarded as the recent addition made by the powerful hierarchy of a dominant race, under whose sway were first united the detached tribes of the older possessors of the land, and their distinct, though analogous, objects of local worship; and it argues that this race did not actually displace those whom it superseded in power, but rather sought to conciliate them and amalgamate them with itself.

Manetho gives seven dynastic lines representing " the hereditary chiefs who held authority in Upper and Lower Egypt after Menes, either conjointly or separately. These are the Thinites, Memphites, Elephantines, Heracleopolites, and Thebans, referable to Upper Egypt and the Heptanomis; and the Xoites, and Phœnician, and other shepherd kings, referable to the Delta and the provinces beyond the Egyptian frontier. Moses (Gen. x. 13, 14) likewise gives the names of seven tribes descended from the original family of Mizraim. From this coincidence in numbers, various attempts have been made to identify the two lists, and thereby assign to the primitive tribes of Moses a definite geographical position in the valley of the Nile. But in these attempts, one main main feature of the case was overlooked; that the period of Cushite ascendancy, with which Manetho's lists and the empire probably begin, put an end to the former state of things; that in those parts of Upper Egypt where an amalgamation of the two races may have taken place, this union must have blotted out the names of the submissive one as rulers or heads of dynasties, even though it left the mass of the primitive population standing; so that in fact, one list ends where the other only begins; and that on this account, a full identification of the two lists must be as much out of the question, as to identify our list of Norman kings of England with the petty rulers of the Anglo-Saxon heptarchy who preceded them.

thesis. It is very remarkable that in Eusebius's version of Manetho, Menes is represented as a conqueror ; and moreover, according to a tradition reported by Diodorus Siculus, b. i., c. 45, he is said to have changed the simple customs and the religion of the Egyptians.

[i] The incongruous pedigrees and relationships of the Egyptian divinities strongly illustrate this. The subject has never been more fully and ably set forth than in the excellent analysis of the Egyptian pantheon, in the Chevalier Bunsen's *Egypt's place in Universal History*, to which the reader is referred (vol. i. sect. vi.). All the gods appear ultimately resolvable into Osiris and Isis, and were probably only so many local forms of these two primitive impersonations—of various degrees of antiquity—afterwards subdivided into new forms, on the formation of new tribes; and subsequently reunited into a genealogical system as these tribes gradually merged together into larger states; their respective divinities being then represented as parents of the new local gods appointed to preside over the newly-formed states.

It being thus premised, in order to avoid confusion hereafter, that under the name of MIZRAIM, as a land, in Scripture history, we are to understand the land originally colonized and civilized by the Mizraim, whether they continued under the government of rulers of that race or of any other,—we may now endeavour to ascertain the extent of the primitive Mizraimite settlements, with the help of the few casual references to them which the Bible affords. This will so far be useful to our present history, that some of the genuine Mizraimite nations survived the subjugation of their kindred, long after the formation of the Memphito-Theban kingdom; earnestly contending for their independence, and successfully maintaining it during many centuries. The tribes whose destiny I propose to trace out, will be found to constitute a highly important member of the series. So that by distinguishing which were the Mizraimite tribes belonging to Egypt proper, and which may be those referable to the country beyond, a material progress will have been made in our present enquiry.

1. The Ludim, לוּדִים. — These are associated by Ezekiel (chap. xxx. 5) with Cush and Phut, the Egyptian Ethiopia and Lybia, as among the multitude of Egypt who were to be taken away. Jeremiah (chap. xlvi. 19) likewise mentions these three nations as allies or subsidiaries to Pharaoh-Necho. Thus—although not a leading tribe—they still formed, in the time of the prophets, a distinct family in the compound Egyptian nation. This gives us no clue to their geographical position.

2. The Lehabim, לְהָבִים.—The original location of this tribe is equally obscure; and as it is never mentioned again in Scripture, its destiny remains unknown.

3. The Anamim, עֲנָמִים.—From the very slight resemblance between this and the royal family name Amenemha recurring in the 11th and 12th dynasties of Manetho, some incline to recognize in this tribe the original stock of the Thebans. If the remote verbal coincidence be more than accidental, it might suggest the original location of the tribe governed by a line of rulers who assumed the older tribe name in token of their supremacy; but this is too doubtful to be worthy of much attention.

4. The Naphtuhim, נַפְתֻּחִים. — This name very satisfactorily identifies the tribe that bears it with the original Memphites, whose capital, "the dwelling of PTAH," Na-Ptah, is contracted by the Hebrew prophet into Noph. After the failure of the first Thinite line of Manetho as sovereign rulers of Thebes and Memphis, three successive Memphite dynasties occupy the supreme position in the empire.[m] The Thebans only succeed

---

[m] This point is clearly demonstrated by Chevalier Bunsen's ingenious collation of

to these. We thus obtain a tolerably long intermediate period of genuine Mizraimite supremacy in Egypt, which includes the era of the pyramid-builders, and only terminates with the accession of the 11th and 12th dynasties of Thebans, when the southern race resumed a temporary ascendancy.

The Pathrusim, פַּתְרֻסִים.—The original location of this tribe in the valley of the Upper Nile is placed beyond a doubt by the prophetic references to the name. Ezekiel, in particular, points out their position by the alternate parallelism of ch. xxx. 14, which would seem to make Pathros equivalent to Upper Egypt:

> " I will put fear in the land of Mizraim,
> And make Pathros desolate:
> I will put fire in Zoan, (capital of Lower Egypt)
> And execute judgments in No. (Na-Amun, the dwelling of
> Amun, Thebes, capital of Upper Egypt.)

The Casluhim, כַּסְלֻחִים.—We cannot assign a place to this tribe from the etymology of their name. But we are further informed that " out of them came the Pelishtim," and since this fixes the origin of the Philistines as a member of the Mizraimite nation, it may assist us in determining the original location of the family to which they belonged.

The Caphtorim, כַּפְתֹּרִים, were most probably a family settled in the Delta. In treating of the Philistines hereafter, we shall have occasion to refer in greater detail to the migration of a people from Caphtor (Deut. ii. 23), who settled near them in southern Judea, and joined them in extending their possessions northward at the expense of their weaker Canaanite neighbours. The district thus occupied is called in the conquests of Joshua " the land of the Goshen," (Josh. x. 41; xi. 16; xv. 51;) which was also the name borne by the eastern part of Lower Egypt in the time of Joseph, and before. The people expelled from Lower Egypt by Amosis, who took refuge among their kindred of Palestine, would appear by this to have brought with them into the land in which they settled, the name of the land they had left.

---

the chronological list of Theban kings given by Eratosthenes, with the early dynasties of Manetho; whereby it appears that the third dynasty of Memphites follow—as kings of Thebes, and consequently as supreme rulers over all the Egyptian states— immediately after the four successors of Menes, whose Thinite descendants continue in the subordinate position of local sovereigns until the eighteenth dynasty of Thebans, save a short interval of supremacy in the beginning of the twelfth. It is remarkable that the pyramid-builders, and after them the conquering shepherds, who fill up this interval, are traditionally stated to have again disturbed Egypt by innovations in religious matters.

We may then sum up our comparison of the Mosaic tribes
of Mizraim with the more recent Manethonic dynasties, as follows: Out of seven we can identify three whose national institutions and rulers remained comparatively unaffected by the super-
seding power of the south, and this advantage they owed to their
more northern situation. The Naphtuhim are referable to the
Memphites, the Caphtorim may be represented by the Xoïtes
and shepherds of the Delta, and the Casluhim by the foreign
Phœnician shepherds. We can find a place for the Pathrusim,
but only as permanently subject to the Thebans. The original
place of the Ludim and Anamim remains extremely doubtful,
and that of the Lehabim is entirely lost.

CHAPTER III.

Geographical distribution of the Canaanites and Rephaim.

Before we endeavour to ascertain of what stock the Rephaim
were, it is desirable to be well satisfied as to what they were not.
For the destiny of this primeval nation has arrested but little
attention on the part of biblical commentators; and a general
idea concerning them, that they were a gigantic tribe of Canaanites, has thus passed current without awakening either doubt
or enquiry. Their very existence, as a distinct nation, would
seem to have been doomed to oblivion by the stratum of gratuitous error that has been permitted to overlay the scanty historical records yet extant of their fate; for although, in various
parts of Scripture, there are many passages referring to them
by their proper name רְפָאִים—the REPHAIM, that name has almost invariably been mistranslated by *giants.* Certain individuals of this nation are incidentally quoted as exceptional instances of excessive bodily strength and stature, namely, the
king of Bashan, and the Philistine champions slain by David
and his kinsmen. Hence arose the strange mistake, originated
by the Alexandrian Jews who translated the Septuagint, and,
on their authority, perpetuated in our modern lexicons, that
because some particular individuals of the Rapha race were of
gigantic stature, a Rapha must necessarily mean *a giant.* But
although our common English version has reproduced this mistake of the Septuagint, the two are sometimes at variance as to
where it should be corrected; for in Gen. xiv. 5, the Septuagint
has γίγαντες, *giants,* where the English, for once, has retained
רְפָאִים correctly as a proper name, REPHAIM; while in Deut. ii.,
the Septuagint has throughout the chapter rendered the proper
name by 'Ραφαΐν, as it should be, where the English version

has put down *giants*. In this way, the historical value of the scattered notices referring to this ancient people has been disguised to the reader or commentator who merely follows these translations.

There is no etymological support whatever for the rendering of רְפָאִים by *giants*. If this word be taken for a Hebrew appellative, its root רפא, is, " to restore to a former state," "to heal ;" hence, the noun denotes a *healer* or *physician*[n]—an idea which has no connexion or affinity with that of great personal stature, and therefore could not possibly have been employed to express *a giant*, in Hebrew.

This correction made, we shall find little difficulty in disposing of the common inference that the nation called Rephaim were Canaanites.

Firstly, we have direct though negative evidence to that effect, in the ethnographical sketch of Moses, Gen. x.; for no tribe of that name is included in his Canaanite list. This primeval record states (ver. 15) that "Canaan begat his first-born Zidon, and Heth ;" and afterwards enumerates the nations that sprang from these two sons of Canaan, by their tribe-names, as "the Jebusite, the Amorite, the Girgashite, and the Hivite," who, from the subsequent notices of their position in Scripture, were the southern and inland tribes, and probably descended from Heth; and "the Arkite, the Sinite, the Arvadite, the Zemarite, and the Hamathite," who were the northern tribes, and probably all descended from Zidon.[o]

Now—had the Rephaim been Canaanites—if Moses enumerates, as separate nations, such unimportant tribes as the Girgashites and Perizzites, who never appear otherwise than by name once or twice in Scripture, is it likely that he would have excluded from the above list a tribe so considerable and power-

---

[n] רֹפְאִים. Participial form of the same root, has that sense in Gen. l. 2: " Joseph commanded his servants, the physicians, to embalm his father." In Egypt, the apothecaries were both physicians and undertakers. Herodotus, in *Euterpe*, chap lxxxv. to lxxxix. gives a full account of the processes they employed.

[o] The settlements of these tribes are well recognized and laid down in the best maps of ancient Palestine; this is far from being the case in the locations assigned to the Hittite tribes, which, on that account, I shall more particularly define. The Arkites עַרְקִי, Arvadites אַרְוָדִי, and Zemarites צְמָרִי, are represented by the known sites of the ancient Arka, Aradus, and Simyra; the Sinites, סִינִי, occupied the mountain district still called Jebel Sunnîn; and the Hamathites חֲמָתִי, the tract lying between the Lebanon and the Anti-Lebanon, watered by the upper Orontes. The river Leontes appears to have been the original boundary of the Zidonians and Hittites, and after their respective families were spread abroad, northward and southward, the elder branches retained their central and primary seats, as the juniors moved on to found new settlements.

ful, that for more than five hundred years before his time, they
had occupied, in central Judea and the transjordanic provinces,
as extensive a tract of land as that of all the children of Heth
put together? This circumstance alone should have made us
pause to consider, before we so readily took this people's Canaanite extraction for granted. But when, in addition, we come
to examine the geographical boundaries assigned to the Canaanites by Moses, both directly and indirectly, we shall soon
convince ourselves that, whatever other origin we may ascribe to
the Rephaim, the supposition of their being branches of the
Canaanite stock must be entirely set aside. For his description of the Canaanite's limits, as existing in his time (Gen. x.
19), particularly avoids the country occupied by the Rephaim.
"The border of the Canaanite was from Zidon, as thou goest to
Gerar, as far as Gaza:" this gives the western limit. And:
"As thou goest to Sodom, Gomorrah, Admah, and Zeboim, as
far as Lesha," (afterwards Dan, near the sources of the Jordan:)
this gives the eastern limit—a line drawn by the western coast
of the Dead Sea, and the river Jordan. The frontier thus described evidently leaves the southern boundary of Canaan unde-
fined. We shall consider hereafter, in its proper place, how far
the mixture of the Rephaim of Anak among the Amorites of
this region, either as co-settlers or as conquerors, may have been
the motive of this omission; the eastern frontier line is the
geographical datum which most particularly bears on the question we are now discussing; and this is given in very precise
terms.

Not less positive is the conclusion, deducible by inference
from other passages in the history of Moses, that he entirely
excludes the lands originally possessed by the Rephaim from all
claim to be regarded as Canaanite ground. For instance, in
Num. xxxiii. 51, he says: "The Lord spake unto Moses in the
plains of Moab, by the Jordan near Jericho, saying, When ye
are passed over Jordan into the land of Canaan;" ... which
clearly implies that the land the Hebrews were in at the time
was not reckoned "the land of Canaan." Again, in Num.
xxxiv. 11, 12, he defines the eastern frontier of Canaan more
particularly by "the sea of Chinnereth, the Jordan, and the
Salt Sea," which gives the same boundary line as "from Sodom
to Lesha" of Gen. x. 19, and absolutely excludes the transjordanic provinces. Finally, in Deut. xxxii. 49—51, he says: "The
Lord spake unto Moses, saying, Ascend this mountain of the
Abarim, Mount Nebo, which is in the land of Moab, opposite
Jericho, and behold the land of Canaan: ... thou shalt see the
land before thee, but thou shalt not go thither into the land

which I give the children of Israel." Now considering that the country he was in, when this was spoken, had been occupied by Rephaim, not only since the days of Abraham, but how much earlier than that we cannot know, this passage would be a singular contradiction of facts, if these Rephaim had been a Canaanite people. For Moses would actually have been standing on Canaanite ground at the very time he was being told that he should *see* the land of Canaan, but would not be permitted to *enter it !*

The same exclusion is implied in Gen. xiii. 12 : "Abram settled in the land of Canaan, and Lot settled in the cities of the plain, and pitched his tent in Sodom ;" and in the evident distinction made in Jud. xxi. 12, between "Shiloh, which is in the land of Canaan," and Jabesh-Gilead in the transjordanic provinces.

So determined an exclusion of these provinces from any right to be regarded as Canaanite territory is the more remarkable, that full a century before that time, the Amorites, who originally occupied Southern Judea jointly with the Anakim, had also formed a settlement among the Rephaim of the eastern district ; and they ended by taking advantage of this nation's decay to seize on the portion of their lands lying between the rivers Jabbok and Arnon (Numb. xxi. 26). Yet, neither this earlier settlement of the Amorite colonists, nor their subsequent seizure of the land by force of arms, are permitted to affect the strict principle of ethnographical definition that guides the sacred historian. This forcible occupation of the Rephaim territory by a Canaanite tribe is so evidently regarded as a passing usurpation, as to constitute no more valid a claim to the land, on their part, than a similar forcible occupation of five Canaanite provinces by the Philistines had entitled these to have that part of the country "counted to them" (Josh. xiii. 2, 3). The original and lawful boundary of Canaan, eastward, was "from Sodom to Lesha ;" therefore the subsequent encroachments of the Amorites beyond that line—though noticed *historically* in their proper place—are geographically and ethnographically disregarded here. The original and lawful boundary of Canaan, westward, was the coast-line extending to Gaza ; therefore the five principalities of the Philistines and their allies of Goshen,—Gaza, Ashdod, Ashkelon, Gath, and Ekron,—are geographically and ethnographically "accounted to the Canaanites" whom the Philistines had subjugated.

The divine promise to Abraham concerning the ultimate extension of his posterity, and of their settlements, in the land of his migration, was to this effect :—

GENESIS XV.

" ¹⁸Unto thy seed will I give this land, from the river of Mizraim to the great river, the river Euphrates:

¹⁹The Kenites, the Kenizzites, the Kadmonites,

²⁰The Hittites, the Perizzites, the Rephaim, the Amorites,

²¹The Canaanites, (the Hivites,) the Girgashites, and the Jebusites."

The primary disposition of some Canaanite tribes prior to the age of Joshua, may be gathered from a few incidental notices in the earlier portions of sacred history. Some others are not referred to, and there is accordingly a little difficulty in defining their place of settlement.

By the HITTITES, generally, we should understand all the junior branches of the two great Canaanite stocks ;[p] but when the Hittites are mentioned in conjunction with the other branch tribes, we must then understand more particularly by that designation the elder tribe of the children of Heth, retaining its distinctive patronymic, according to patriarchal usage. Just as the general term, "the Canaanites," includes all the children of Zidon and Heth collectively ; although when the name occurs among others as denoting a particular tribe, it should be taken as standing for the elder branch of the Zidonians. The elder Hittites would appear to have at first occupied the lands west of the sea of Chinnereth (Lake Tiberias) to the Mediterranean coast. The junior branches extended themselves from thence, southward, as far as the Mosaic limits of Gaza and Sodom.

The PERIZZITES, in the time of Abraham (Gen. xiii. 7 ; xxxiv. 30), and afterwards under Joshua (Josh. xvii. 15), are found established in the region west of Bethel.

The AMORITES occupied chiefly the western side of the mountain tract of central and southern Judea. Most of their cities, in the time of Joshua, lay in that part. But they also had settlements on the other side, as far as Hazazon-tamar (Engedi) by the Dead Sea, eastward, and Arad on the border of the desert, southward.

The name of the HIVITES is accidentally lost from the Hebrew text in this enumeration ; but the Samaritan and Septuagint retain it. They were a very large tribe. They dwelt from "the land of Mizpeh under Mount Hermon," which appears to

---

p The sub-tribe of Hittites settled about Hebron were clearly Amorites, from the notice of Gen. xiv. Yet in Gen. xxiii., they are called "children of Heth." The Hivite wives of Esau are also called "daughters of Heth." Thus the Reubenites, or the Benjamites, would be equally called, in speaking generally, "children of Israel."

have been situated on the western flank of this great mountain, near the sources of the Jordan[q] (Gen. xxxiv. 2), extending their settlements southward as far as Shechem and Gibeon (Josh ix. 17), along the ridge of high land which forms the watershed of Palestine.

The GIRGASHITES are merely named, in the Old Testament; no indication of their locality is given. In Matt. viii. 28, the lands on the east side of lake Tiberias (the sea of Chinneroth) are called "the country of the Gergesenes." The mountain ridge extending southward from Mount Hermon, and enclosing the northern and eastern side of the lake-region, appears to have separated them from the land of Bashan belonging to the Rephaim. But they ultimately extended themselves in that land also. The parallel passage in Luke viii. 26, defines the scene of the miracle as "the country of the Gadarenes;" and Gadara, on the river Hieromax, the chief river of Bashan, is quite beyond the Mosaic limits of the Canaanite territory. This extension of the Girgashites, therefore, like the Amorite settlements in Gilead and Heshbon, must be regarded as an encroachment by the Canaanites on lands originally and properly belonging to another nation.

The JEBUSITES are only heard of—for the first time—under Joshua (Josh. x. 1 ; xv. 63), as in possession of Jerusalem ; but it is very doubtful whether that was originally Canaanite ground, being part of the land of the Rephaim. This branch of the Hittite stock appears to have been very recent at that time, and inconsiderable as to numbers and extension.

All these Canaanite lands passed over by conquest to the power of Abraham's descendants, as also did the domains of the REPHAIM mentioned with them. As for the KENITES, KENIZ-ZITES, and KADMONITES, which open the list, the race of Abraham succeeded the original tenants in the more peaceable but not less sure way of gradual substitution.

The KENITES, whose history will be given hereafter in its place, were a people whose lands afterwards formed part of the Edomite kingdom. Thus the fulfilment of the promise made to Abraham, in this respect, is very satisfactorily found. The

---

[q] Josh. xiii. ; compare ver. 3 with ver. 8, and with Jud. iii. 3. This remark is important, because, generally, the Bible-maps place these Hivites on the other side of Hermon, in the land of Bashan. Unless the " valley of Mizpeh " had been west of mount Hermon, Joshua's army could not possibly have pursued the flying Canaanites thither, and " to the great Zidon," in the same expedition. The description in Jud. iii. 3, " the Hivites who dwelt in mount Lebanon, from mount Baal-hermon unto the entrance (or pass) of Hamath," confirms this. Hermon, הֶרְמוֹן, " the separation," divided the Canaanites from the Rephaim.

KENIZZITES are unknown, as they are not mentioned again in sacred history.

The land of the KADMONITES, or "children of the East" (Job i. 3; Jud. vi. 3), seems an indefinite geographical term for as much as Abraham knew of the extensive pastoral plains, or *wilderness* of uncleared and uncultivated lands that border on the great Syrian and Arabian deserts. This tract is tenanted exclusively by nomads during the grazing season, but has no fixed habitations. As Abraham "gave gifts to the sons of his concubines, and sent them into the east country" (Gen. xxv. 6), where they rapidly grew into a numerous and powerful body of independent and industrious nomads, we also recognize without difficulty the full accomplishment of the divine promise.

Thus only the territory of the REPHAIM remains to be defined, and its primeval occupants traced to their original stock, before we can see how completely, in this respect also, was the prophecy fulfilled,—when the posterity of the Father of the faithful extended their dominion "from the river of Mizraim to the great river, the river Euphrates."

The different tribes ascribed to the race called "the RE-PHAIM in the Pentateuch," are ultimately referable to three great geographical divisions forming as many distinct states; each state consisting of several minor provinces.

Firstly: The Rephaim of the northern district beyond Jordan, the ZUZIM, called by the Ammonites Zamzummim. The chief or royal tribe occupied the district of Bashan; the southern region of Argob was called Gilead by the Hebrews. The children of Ammon, who settled on the south-eastern border of the Zuzim, may be considered as part of this nation, but only politically and by adoption.

Secondly: The Rephaim of the western district—THE CHIL-DREN OF ʿANKᵣ, (Anakim). These dwelt in the mountains of Judah and of Ephraim. The question whether they were the original possessors of the land they occupied, or whether—like the Philistines—they were only an intrusive race among the Canaanites, will be fully discussed hereafter in their history.

ᵣ ‏עֲנָק‎. The orthography and etymology of this name are important. I here write the Roman equivalent of the Hebrew ‏ע‎ with an accent over the Â to indicate a peculiar pronunciation, something between an a and an o, like the a in fall, ball, &c., which seems to have been its original value, before the vowel-points changed it to a variety of other vowel-articulations. When initial or final in a word or syllable, this letter has a peculiar guttural force, which the Septuagint endeavour to render in Greek by a γ or a κ, and which I shall express by prefixing the sign of rough breathing, wherever, for etymological illustration, it becomes necessary to indicate this orthographic peculiarity in the proper names hereafter to be analyzed.

Thirdly: The Rephaim of the southern district beyond Jordan—THE CHILDREN OF SHETH (Shittim), whom the Moabites called Emim. In the subsequent account of this powerful state, I will explain the reasons for inferring that, besides the chief tribe, it comprehended also the Kenites of Petra and the Amalekites of Paran as kindred tribes. This people further included, among their political dependencies, the adopted colony of Moab, and a vast body of later settlers, Edomites and Midianites, who resided on their borders and were in close and friendly alliance with them.

Finally, there is monumental evidence that all the land of ARAM was under subjection to the Rephaim during the period comprehended in this history; Aram-Naharaim, or of the two rivers; Padan-Aram, or Aram of the plains; and the Horite district, or Aram of the mountains. By this preliminary sketch, some idea may be formed of the immense extension of power achieved by the ambitious race whose history we are about to trace; in which the Egyptian records supply the political, religious, and personal details that abundantly fill out the rapid but decided outline of their condition and destiny afforded by the patriarchal records of Moses.

CHAPTER IV.

Origin of the Rephaim.

In the geographical classification of the Mizraimite families, we found the "Pelishtim" mentioned as issued from the tribe named "Casluhim" (Gen. x. 13). We will now examine how far this statement may assist us in identifying the original settlement of the parent tribe.

In an account of the victories obtained by David and his brave kinsmen over certain Philistine champions noted for their gigantic stature, it is stated that they were sons of a certain Rapha of Gath, and brethren of the celebrated Goliath (2 Sam. xxi. 16—22). From this, it appears that a whole family bearing the generic name of REPHAIM are pointedly included under the particular denomination of *Philistines*.

This remarkable circumstance gives us a clue to the probable origin of all the Rapha race. Coupling it with the geographical position of the Philistines, with the part we subsequently see them bearing in the political movements of Palestine, and with the little we shall be able to recover concerning their local religion,—all these, taken together, are indications pointing to the conclusion that the primitive Philistines of Gerar and Beersheba themselves were only a junior branch of the powerful tribe of Rephaim called Anakim, whose lands were immediately contiguous to Pelesheth.

Now the original affinity of the Philistines to the Mizraim of Egypt proper is placed beyond a doubt by their pedigree, as given by Moses. He states that "the Pelishtim came out of the Casluhim." Accordingly, if the Philistines are to be considered Rephaim, from the qualification of the Philistine champions of Gath, it follows that all the other Rephaim are likewise Casluhim tribes; that this Mizraimite family, for whom we cannot find a place in Egypt itself, may claim to be the original stock out of which branched out in succession the Rephaim of Bashan, elder and royal tribe, and its junior scions, enumerated, according to their geographical divisions and tribe-subdivisions, in the preceding chapter.

It may be urged against this hypothesis, that the qualification of Rephaim conferred by the sacred historian on the Philistine champions might be explained in another way, viz., they perhaps were only descendants of Anakim fugitives expelled by Joshua and Caleb from the mountains of Judah; and they might thus have been Rephaim without being necessarily Philistines. But why then should they be called Philistines in this account? why is Goliath of Gath also invariably mentioned as "the Philistine?" If the particular tribe-name of men who attracted so much attention in their day, must be stated by the historian, as well as the generic name of Rapha, why the wrong one? If the specific name of Anakim—once so familiar an object of popular awe to the Hebrews, as to be held up by Moses (Deut. ii. 10, 11 ; ix. 1, 2) for an example of what the other lost Rapha tribes had been—was so thoroughly lost sight of in the time of David, when the race had disappeared, can we suppose that the generic and unfamiliar name of Rapha would be preferred by the Hebrew annalist to distinguish supposed Anakim champions?

It seems much more natural to take the account as it stands, than to try to explain it away. The probability is much rather that the Philistine champions were called Rephaim, because the Philistines really were Rephaim by descent; and that, being the only people of this ancient race who retained their political standing in the days of Saul, they asserted the name as the ostensible ground of their bitter animosity against Israel, who had dispossessed their kindred, and now occupied their lands.

But such a supposition, that these champions might be refugees of Anak, is altogether gratuitous. For it is nowhere said that the Anakim, when expelled from the mountains of

Judah, fled to Gath, Gaza, and Ashdod. The statement is,
that "they were cut off from the mountains of Judah and
Israel;" that "there were none left" in the lands conquered by
by Joshua; that "only in Gath, Gaza, and Ashdod, some remained" (Josh. xi. 21, 22)—the lands which the Hebrews were
not able to take; and the form of expression, "*some remained,*"
seems rather to imply the previous settlement of the children of
Anak in those cities, than their subsequent flight into them.
Now Gaza, Gath, and Ashdod, are among the five Canaanite
cities of which the Philistines had become rulers in the time of
Joshua, but which are geographically accounted to the Canaanites, their original possessors.

The easiest inference seems therefore to be, that the Philistines were at first a sub-tribe and dependency of the children of
Anak, and thus Rephaim by descent; who, when they had grown
sufficiently numerous and powerful, formed for themselves an
independent settlement on the sea-coast at the expense of their
weaker neighbours: that when Moses wrote, all the Mizraimite
nations of Palestine were nearly exterminated, save this junior
scion of the Casluhim parent stock, now in the ascendant; and
that, on this account, the historian specially records their extraction from that nearly extinct family, "the Casluhim, out of
whom came the Pelishtim," so well known to the Hebrews since
the days of Abraham and Isaac, and with whom their fathers
had so long been on friendly terms.

The very name of REPHAIM, borne by this family of Miz-
raimites, bears witness to an Egyptian origin. By referring it
to the Hebrew or Canaanite homophonous root רפא, it would be
rather difficult to give a satisfactory explanation of it from its
sense, "a healer," as we can of the descriptive epithets *Emim*
and *Zamzummim* applied by their Eberite neighbours of Moab
and Ammon to the two eastern tribes of this great nation. The
fact is, that the resemblance between the name RAPHA and the
Hebrew root רפא rpa, is accidental, and therefore unmeaning.
RPA is the purely Egyptian form of a very ancient word common to all the Hamitic languages, and denoting a chief, prince,
or superior. In the Hebrew dialect, this word occurs also, but
with the vowel transposed, both in the name of Abraham's royal
ancestor, Arpa-Chasd אַרְפַּכְשַׁד, "the chief of the Chasdim," and
in the Hebrew radical אלף, to take the lead, guide, etc., from
whence are derived Aleph, *the leader*, first letter of the alphabet,
and the title אַלּוּף Allouph, leader, governor, by which the Edomite
heads of families are distinguished in their pedigrees.

The remarkable evidences in favour of the Mizraimite descent of the Rephaim, deducible from their local pantheon, will

be fully set forth when we enter on the separate account of each tribe. We shall then find how strikingly the fragmentary indications of their worship which still survive, bear witness to the fact that what is common to the Rephaim and to the Mizraim of Egypt, in their religion, is fundamental to the system of both nations; what is different in both, has been engrafted from individual or foreign sources on the ancient and common foundation.

F. C.

LONDON:
WALTON AND MITCHELL, PRINTERS, WARDOUR-STREET, OXFORD-STREET.

THE REPHAIM, AND THEIR CONNEXION WITH EGYPTIAN HISTORY.[a]

[*Reprinted from Kitto's 'Journal of Sacred Literature,' for January,* 1852.]

CHAPTER V.

The Zuzim.

FROM the notable circumstance that the Rephaim of Bashan are not distinguished by any other particular tribe-name, and from their proximity to the primary starting-point of that prolonged line of colonization which only terminates on the borders of the Thebaid, we may infer that they were the original stock from which the junior Rapha tribes branched out in succession. Their being named separately from the Zuzim, in Gen. xiv., does not necessitate our considering them as two distinct nations. By the evidence of the Egyptian historical monuments, we learn on the contrary that the Zuzim were the body of the nation, but that the title of supremacy borne by the elder tribe of Bashan, whose chief was sovereign over the other provincial chieftains, was disregarded by the Egyptians. They designate the nation collectively, the SHAS·U, which corresponds to the Σως of Manetho, and the זוזים Zuz-im of Scripture. Manetho alone has preserved the royal prefix 'Υκ *Huk,* by which the elder tribe distinguished its chief, who, as head of the whole Rapha people, took the lead in the invasion of Egypt. He says these people called themselves 'Υκ-σως, which he interprets "*Royal Shepherds,*" because 'Υκ signifies a king, and Σως, a shepherd. This epithet, 'Υκ, appears in Scripture as the title of the sovereign of Bashan, chief of the Zuzim, Σως or SHAS·U; for the Hebrew עוג *ʼHoug* (Og)[b] is a very fair attempt to imitate the native word, which Manetho endeavours to render in Greek letters by 'Υκ *Huk.* It is evidently allied to the Egyptian Hâk, *a ruler,* of which the reduplicate Agag אגג of Amalek may be taken as a variant. Like the Egyptian Phrâh (Pharaoh) פרעה *the sun* or *the king,*—and like the Philistine Abimelech, *royal father,*—or Rab-shakeh, *great cup-bearer,*—it is a title of dignity

---

[a] This article, devoted to the Zuzim, is a sequel to that, under the same general head, contained in our last number. To facilitate reference, all the Egyptian forms of proper local names occurring in this dissertation, will be given in small capitals, to correspond with the same in the tabular list.

[b] In the pointed Hebrew text, the guttural articulation of the initial ע is lost, and the value of the radical vowels altered.

A

or of office; and these are often given in the Bible as proper names.

Everything among the Rephaim of Bashan indicates a very ancient as well as powerful settlement. At the time of the Hebrew conquest, this kingdom contained "threescore cities, all cities fortified with high walls, gates and bars, besides unwalled villages a great many." (Deut. iii. 14.) This statement is amply borne out by the present state of the country. The Arabic lists of the Rev. Eli Smith[c] contain nearly five hundred names of places either inhabited or in ruins, within the area of this ancient kingdom. Among these are a great number of *tels* or mounds with ruins, relics of the fortified cities that once reared their crests on high, to overlook and defend the village dependencies of a vast agricultural and pastoral population.

The names of a few among these, known to classical antiquity, and still extant, enable us to determine how extensive were the domains of the sovereigns of Bashan. Besides the metropolis, Ashtaroth, in the centre of Bashan proper, they included the royal city of Salchah, now known as *Salkhad*, on the south-eastern confines of the Jebel-Hauran; and the Levitical cities Golan and Beeshterah, in the lands allotted to the Manassites. (Deut. iv. 33; Josh. xxi. 27.)

Both are known sites; the province of *Jaulan*, on the east side of Lake Tiberias, still retains the name of its former district capital; and Beeshterah, which, without the disguise of vowel-points is בשתרה Bôshtrah—the ancient Bostra letter for letter, now called *Esky-Sham* (old Damascus)—is found just south of the Jebel-Hauran. Burckhardt[d] describes the remarkable remains of this city; but he and others were led by the similarity of the name, into mistaking it for the Edomite Bozrah. Finally, the royal city of Argob points out the extent of this kingdom towards the south, as the name of this district capital is still extant in the torrent and village of *Rajib*, the Regaba of Josephus. (Ant. xiii., ch. xv. 5.) All the mountain region eastward of Argob was called Gilead by the Hebrews, because of the גלעד *Gal-ed, mound of witness* of Laban and Jacob, erected on the highest summit of the mountain tract of Jebel-Ajlûn. The southern peak of this hilly region, which alone retains the name of Jebel-Jelâd, was the limit of the king of Bashan's dominions.[e]

---

[c] *Biblical Researches in Palestine*, by E. Robinson, D.D., and the Rev. Eli Smith, (Appendix).

[d] Burckhardt, *Travels in Syria*, pp. 224—226.

[e] All biblical critics have felt the difficulty of defining the limit of this region, from the obscure wording of the few Scripture notices relating to it. The recent names

The homestead of the Rephaim is one of the finest countries in the east. The western part of Bashan is mountainous, and chiefly pastoral. The elevated undulating plains of the eastern province, irrigated by numerous winter torrents, are a particularly fertile arable tract; it is called "the granary of Damascus." The rocky region of the Kelb-Hauran, and the Lejah, beyond this, form another pastoral district inhabited by nomads. Its cattle, the bulls, kine, and rams of Bashan, are a frequent object of poetical comparison in Scripture; and the value of the oak timber grown on its mountain slopes, for ship-building, is particularly alluded to by the prophet Ezekiel. (Ch. xxvii. 6; compare Isa. ii. 13; Zech. xi. 2.)

The few modern travellers who have visited the region of Argob and Gilead, speak of it as a land equally favoured by nature. The Rev. Eli Smith describes it as a singularly picturesque tract; its heights are crowned with forests of evergreen oak; and its valleys, clothed with the most luxuriant herbage. It was thus an eminently pastoral country; it is therefore a circumstance of some interest, as strengthening the identity of its inhabitants with the Sôs of Manetho and Egyptian SHAS'U, that we should find them designated in Scripture by a name which is interpreted *a shepherd.*

When the descendants of Lot's second son, Ben-Ammi, had become sufficiently numerous to form a separate tribe, they established themselves on the south-eastern frontier of the Zuzim. Their first settlement and metropolis, Rabbah, was built among the hills, near the source of a small mountain stream, a tributary of the *Wady Zurka*, the Scriptural Jabbok. That stream still bears the name of *Moiet-Ammân* (Water of Ammon). The circumstance mentioned in Deut. iii. 11, that the iron couch of the last gigantic chieftain of the Rephaim

---

of the sites are our safest criterion, that Bashan proper was *El Bathanyeh, north* of the river Mandhur; and Argob, the region about *Rajib, south* of it. The author of 1 Kings iv. 13, places the Havoth-Jair in Gilead; and the Hebel-Argob, with its sixty cities, is appropriated to Bashan. Yet Moses, Deut. iii. 13—15, gives the Hebel-Argob to Jair, and Gilead to Machir. How can we reconcile this, except by supposing Argob the native, and Gilead the Hebrew, names of the same land, now called *Jebel Ajlûn;* and synonymous terms, though more particularly applied to denote—the former, the Jordanic—and the latter the hilly region?

Hébel הֶבֶל, *a line* or *band*, might mean a line or chain of frontier cities, extending from Argob or *Rajib*, northwards all along to the Aramite border of Geshur or Gether (*Jeidur*). In this way the line of Argob, given to Jair, might be partly in Gilead (*Jebel Ajlûn*), partly in Bashan (*El Bathanyeh*); by including the Golanite province (*Jaulan*). As the Gadites had the Arabah up to the sea of Chinneroth, the frontier lines of the tribes must have been inclined much more north by south, than they are generally made in Bible maps.

was preserved in their capital, is an interesting incident shewing how far southward his sway was acknowledged. As the indigenous population disappeared, the Ammonites gradually replaced them; so that their settlements ultimately extended northward to the banks of the Upper Jabbok, and westward to the river of Ammon. The political extinction of the aboriginal race is thus noticed by Moses, Deut. iii. 19—21 :—

> "When thou comest nigh unto the children of Ammon, distress them not, neither contend with them; for I will not give thee of the land of the children of Ammon any possession, because I have given it for a possession to the children of Lot. It was also accounted the land of the Rephaim: the Rephaim formerly settled there, but the Ammonites call them *Zam-zummim;*—a great, numerous, and haughty people,/ like the Anakim; but the Lord destroyed them from before them, and they dwell in their place."

The characteristic tribe-name of the Rephaim who originally occupied the Ammonite district appears to have been handed down to us in the first notice of them, Gen. xiv., as the Zuzim; the name "Zamzummim"—*enterprising people*ᵍ—being, by the account above quoted, only a distinctive epithet applied to them by the descendants of Lot.

It has always been taken for granted, from this passage, that the Rephaim were *destroyed* as well as *replaced* by the children of Ammon. But there is no direct statement to that effect in the Bible. The only intimation it affords of that people's fate, is the above summary reference of Moses. "THE LORD"— certain dispensations of Providence in which the Ammonites are not even named as instruments—"destroyed the Rephaim from before them," and reduced this once "numerous, great, and haughty people" to the stricken and dismembered remnant we find them under Moses; while the Ammonite colony increased and flourished on their border, extended itself over a considerable portion of their lands, identified itself and its political interests with their's, and finally took their place in history. The traditional and monumental annals of Egypt will now explain how this mighty nation were brought so low as to fall an easy prey to the first resolute invader who openly attacked them ;— how the ancient lords of the soil were swept off to make way for the troops of unsettled Canaanites who supplanted them, and

---

f רָם. Commonly translated *tall;* but another expression is generally used to denote expressly, bodily stature: אַנְשֵׁי מִדּוֹת *men of dimensions.* רָם in usage, rather implies elevation of mind or position—or the assumption of it. *Haughty* renders both the root, and the particular sense of its application here. Comp. 2 Sam. xxii. 28; Job xxi. 22; Isa. ii. 12, &c.

g From זָמַם to devise, purpose, undertake.

established themselves in the depopulated cities of Bashan and Argob.

CHAPTER VI.
Wars of the Hyksos and Thebans.

The distinction between the two Hamite races who colonized the valley of the Nile, suggested by the fusion of their religious systems, is equally discernible in the nature of their monumental remains. The aboriginal Mizraim were a tomb-building, and the intrusive Cushites a temple-building race. The ruling spirit of the Mizraim was attachment to their land, their ancestral institutions, the memory of their illustrious dead. This was manifested in the territorial character of their gods, the patriarchal and sacerdotal character of their government, and the grandeur of their sepulchral piles. The ruling spirit of the rival Southern race, on the contrary, was a grasping ambition. Conquest was its aim, dominion its end; and the king was honoured in proportion to his success in augmenting the national glory by his personal valour. The chieftains of this race raised the Egyptian empire on the foundation of pre-existing national institutions; but they did not maintain without a struggle the vast monarchy they had founded. Five generations had scarcely passed, ere the supremacy reverted to the aboriginal Mizraimite race. This was the era of the Pyramid-builders, during which the Thinite successors of Menes occupy the subordinate position of local rulers. But when their Theban descendants recovered the ascendancy, the era of Palace-temples began. The walls of these national edifices were blazoned with pictorial representations of the triumphs achieved by their royal builders for the glory of their country, which was thus committed to the safe-keeping of the gods. And it is a very remarkable fact, which the reader will have every opportunity given him, of verifying for himself, that, (with the exception of another aboriginal revolted race, the blacks of Ethiopia) the members of the three Rapha nations, and their tributaries, form *exclusively* the subjects of these historical sculptures. They are the only people upon whom Egypt has conferred the special and ignominious distinction of holding up to the contemptuous gaze of posterity the representation of their multitudes, in the very act of falling under the irresistible might of the conqueror's arm.

The earliest record of open hostilities between the Rapha branch of the Mizraimite race, and Egypt, is contained in the fragments of early Egyptian history quoted by Josephus from

Manetho. The substance of this account is that a people who called themselves Hyksos (or Royal Shepherds) invaded Egypt, and took possession of the country in a most unaccountable manner, without fighting; established the seat of their government at Memphis, and cruelly oppressed and ill-treated the Egyptians, as though they were bent on rooting out the race. They set up one of their chiefs as king, who, with his five successors, make the XVth dynasty of "*six foreign Phœnician kings who took Memphis*" of Manetho's lists. Their names and reigns are as follows :—

Manetho, as quoted by

I. Africanus.	II. Josephus.	
Reigned.		Reigned. Monumental Royal Titles.
1. Saïtes . . . 19y.	1. Salatis . . . 19y.	Ra·nefru·ka.
2. Bnon . . . 44	2. Beôn 44	Ra·s·nefru P·Anchi.
3. Pachnan . 61	3. Apachnas . 36y 7m.	Ra·shu Ab . . .
4. Staan . . . 50	5. Ianias . . . 50y. 1m.	Aân.
5. Archles. . 49	6. Assis . . . . 49y. 2m.	Ra·tet·ka Assa.
6. Apophis . 61	4. Apophis . . 61	. . . . *(unknown).*

The chronological place of these kings is most probably coeval with the successors of the great Sesertasen, the Sesostris of Manetho and chief of the XIIth dynasty, "who conquered all Asia in nine years."[h] How far the ambitious Theban's exploits may have contributed to generate a hostile feeling between the two races, leading the Mizraimite tribes of the lower country to invite the help and favour the establishment of their Rapha kindred, can only be surmised. But the issue is recorded, that the invaders were successful, that they seized on the capital of Middle Egypt, Memphis, from whence they brought the lower and upper countries so completely under subjection, that the latter Theban kings of the XIIth dynasty were reduced to share the empire with their spoilers, retaining only the government of Upper Egypt. At the close of this double dy-

---

[h] Since the above was written, the publication of Mr. R. S. Poole's researches into the chronology of Manetho's seventeen earlier dynasties enables us to consider this supposition well established on monumental evidence. The names of Sesertasen's successors, and those corresponding to the "foreign Phœnician Shepherd-kings" have been found together on inscriptions. By this, it appears that the 11th Theban and 6th Memphite dynasties were coeval, the latter closing after the beginning of the 12th Theban, with the seizure of Memphis by the 15th.

Moreover, by his valuable discovery of the identity of the kings of the two Thinite dynasties with those of the Tablet of Abydos who precede the 11th and 12th Thebans, Mr. Poole has further demonstrated a point which I had ventured to assume on grounds of historical induction—namely, that the Theban line of Egyptian conquerors were the lineal descendants of Menes, founder of the Egyptian monarchy which they strove to restore.

nasty, a period of confusion arises, and the thread of Egyptian
history is completely broken. The shepherds appear to have
fully established their power in the south, and reduced the
Theban kingdom to the degraded position of a tributary province.

The lapse of time covered by this state of things is unknown,
but has doubtless been greatly over-estimated by some recent
chronologists. At last, an effort was made to shake off the
foreign yoke. The king of Thebes, and the other kings of the
Thebaid who were not yet subjected, combined against the
usurping race; a long and fierce war ensued, which ended in the
complete reduction of the shepherds. The remnant of their army
was driven to a frontier-city of the Delta, called *Avaris*, where
they fortified themselves so effectually, that after besieging them
a long while in vain, though with an army of 48,000 men, the
Theban leader Tethmosis (or Amôsis) despaired of taking the
place, and capitulated with them, on condition that they would
leave the country. They accordingly marched out in a body of
24,000 men, with their cattle and goods, and settled themselves,
concludes Manetho, "in the country now called Judea, where
they built a city large enough to contain so great a multitude,
and called it Jerusalem."[i] Thus began the XVIIIth dynasty
of Theban kings in Egypt, when the monarchy founded by
Menes was restored entire in the line of his descendants.

At this period, a series of illustrated monumental records
commences; and the conspicuous part borne in them by a
people called the sʜᴀꜱ·ᴜ leaves no doubt that they are the Σως
or Shepherds of the foregoing accounts. Their geographical
identification with the Rephaim of the northern division—the
Zuzim of Scripture—does not rest on the verbal similarity of
the name, alone, but on a great number of collateral details
which will be fully developed in the sequel. These, however,
are so intimately interwoven with the monumental records relating to the cognate tribes of Sheth and Anak, that they could
not be separated without losing much of their force. In consequence, I shall not be able to avoid anticipating a little
the history of those tribes, in the present section, in order to
exhibit such among those details as are indispensable to prove
the point I now appear to assume, and on which so many historical and chronological conclusions depend.

It appears from a tablet quoted by Mr. Birch from Champollion,[j] that the Delta was the seat of war between the two

i *Josephus* c. *Apionem*, l. 1, c. 14—16.
j Birch on *Statistical Tablet of Karnak; Trans. Royal S. of Literature*, 2nd
Series, vol. ii.; Champollion, *Egypte Ancienne*, p. 300.

races of Upper and Lower Egypt until the sixth year of Amôsis. Thus his first year is dated from the recovery of Memphis. The earliest campaigns against the SHAS·U in their own territory, are recorded under Thothmes II., and continue to be noticed under the chief conquerors who succeeded him, during the ensuing century. The notices of these wars cease with the latter part of the XVIIIth dynasty. At this time, the power of the Theban kings was greatly curtailed by another foreign invasion from the south. The names of these foreign aggressors, and representations of them worshipping the sun, are found on sculptures coeval with the reign of Thothmes IV. and his immediate successors, Horus, Amenoph III., and Rameses I.

The illustrious son of the latter king opens a new dynasty. His name is variously read, but SETI-MENEPHTAH seems the most authentic reading.[k] By his valour, he completely re-established the power of Egypt; and the sculptured records of his numerous triumphs over the great enemies of his nation in Palestine, cover the walls of his palace at Karnak.[l]

It appears by these memorials that, during the period of the above-mentioned foreign intruders, the SHAS·U had taken advantage of the weakened state of Upper Egypt to regain a footing in the Delta; for the opening event in the series, dated in the first year of the king's reign, is the overthrow of the SHAS·U, and the capture of a city by the sea, called "the fort of PAIROU (Pelusium[m]), which is towards the land of KANA·NA." The seat of the war is called the land of AÂN·T.[n] After routing

---

[k] This king's proper name SETI was written ideagraphically with the figure of the god SETH; but as this god became odious to the Egyptians, the figure was erased from inscriptions and that of OSIRI substituted; accordingly, Sir Gardner Wilkinson gives the name Osirei. (*Anc. Egyptians*, vol. i.) Mr. Sharpe (*History of Egypt*, ch. i., p. 41) takes the figure for a phonetic of *a* or *o*, and thus reads the name O-i Menephtah. Manetho's calling this king *Sethos* seems to countenance the reading which, on that account, I have preferred as the best authenticated.

[l] *Vide* the plates 48 to 57 inclusive, Rosellini, *Monumenti Reali.*

[m] Some read the name PAI-ROU ideagraphically, taking the sign *pai* for the article, and the lion (R) for the proper name. The article before a name written ideagraphically is unusual; and the phonetic reading adopted by Mr. Birch is supported by its agreement with the Coptic name Pheremoun, preserved in the modern Arabic name of the ruins, Farama, and which Champollion interprets to mean a place in a miry soil; so that its Greek form, Pelusium, derived from πηλος, mud or clay, is a translation of the Egyptian name, Phere-moun or Phero-mi, of Champollion. (*L'Egypt sous les Pharaons.*)

[n] It may be worthy of remark that the western arm of the Arabian Gulf, called the Gulf of Heroopolis by the Greeks, is said by Pliny to be called the Gulf of *Æant.* (*Geog.*, l. vi., c. 29.) This suggests that both synonyms of the Gulf were taken from the land it bathed. AÂN·T would thus denote the land east of the Delta—Arabian Egypt—the Scriptural Goshen, of which the southern part is the Heliopolitan nome, called in Gen. xlvii. 6, "the land of Rameses, the best of the land,"

the SHAS'U, Seti-Menephtah marched into Palestine and pursued them in their own quarters, cutting up on his way the kindred tribes who opposed his progress. The leading incidents of this campaign, delineated in the Karnak sculptures, are:— the rout of a party of AMĂR herdsmen, and capture of the fortress of ATESH; a terrible battle with the SHET'TA. The submission of the SHĂR, who offer him tribute or presents; that of the lower LET'N, and RMN'N, whom he employs as hewers of wood in his service, as equivalent to tribute; (comp. Josh. x. 21—27.) A fierce engagement with the upper LET'N, who resisted his passage; and another with the TAHI, of the MNA'N nation. The conqueror led the chiefs of these nations captive to Thebes; and the final tableau exhibits him presenting his captives, with the spoils of the conquered, and the names of all his foreign tributary lands and cities, in triumph before the local gods of Thebes, AMUN, MUT, and KHONS. It is remarkable that PI'BASH (Bubastis) occurs among these. It proves that the Theban kings looked upon Lower Egypt as a different people and a tributary state. According to Manetho, as quoted by Josephus, the title of Αἴγυπτος was first borne by Sesostris-Rameses II. The annotations to other copies of Manetho's dynastic lists say that it was Sethos himself who was so called. At all events, the circumstance that the territorial name *Ai-kupt* "the land of Copt" (= Caphtor) was first assumed by the kings of the XIXth dynasty who permanently annexed the Delta to their dominions, is too remarkable to be passed over without notice.

The national foes of Egypt were thus brought under subjection by Seti-Menephtah I. Nevertheless, the war broke out again under his illustrious successor, Rameses II. But the power of the SHAS'U, the leading tribe, had been too severely shaken by their disasters in the late contest, to risk the chances of another campaign. When the conqueror, in the fifth year of his reign, marched into Palestine with an immense army, preparing to march against the SHET'TA (Emim) who on this occasion took the lead in raising the standard of rebellion, the SHAS'U are said to have been so struck with terror at the vastness of the armament, and at the might of the Egyptian archers, that they sent ambassadors to the king, tendering their alle-

---

the part in which the Hebrew colony first settled, near Heliopolis (Rameses) and Scenæ Veteranorum (Succoth).—(Sharpe, *Hist. of Egypt,* p. 31.) It is not unlikely that AAN'T is only the Egyptian (feminine) form of Aôn, אן, the ancient name of Heliopolis, the most noted city of that region, enlarged by the Thebans, and by them named Rameses "the sun-bearing."

giance and offering him the custody of their lands in the name
of the nation.[o]   There are no monumental records relating to
the SHAS'U under the weak and superstitious PTAH-MEN or
MENEPHTAH, (Amenophis), the son and successor of the great
Rameses.   But Manetho relates a revolt of the oppressed captive race in Lower Egypt, who called in the aid of their kindred
in Palestine, the Shepherds of Jerusalem expelled by Amosis.
Menephtah fled from before these invaders, and retired into
Ethiopia for thirteen years, during which they tyrannized over
all Egypt.   His son, Sethos, (who is also called Rameses) expelled
them, and pursued them to the frontier of Syria.   Josephus
quotes in full Manetho's narrative of this event; and is rather
severe in his strictures on the mis-representations and anachron-
isms he charges upon the Egyptian priest.   The fault, however,
lies at the door of the Jewish historian, who has evidently mis-
understood the tenor of the story, by applying it to his Hebrew
forefathers, from the circumstance that, like them, the remnant
of Hyksos population in Goshen had been subjected, as conquered captives, to the most oppressive bondage,—a bondage in
which the Hebrews, from motives of state policy, were ultimately made their fellow sufferers.   The sculptures of Rameses
III., at Medinet-Abou, relate the close of this eventful history,
which sealed the fate of the Rephaim.   The pictures are most
important, and the inscriptions copious.   Two memorable campaigns are specially recorded, subsequent to the expulsion of
the last Shepherd invaders.[p]   This time, the Rephaim of Judea
take the lead—the formidable children of Anak.   The other
tribes appear only as auxiliaries;—nay, in the first of these two
expeditions, dated in the fifth year of the king's reign, the
PULSA'TA (Philistines), are represented as having submitted
to the conqueror, like the SHAS'U to Rameses II.; and the
TAKKAR'U (Ekronites) are actually employed as mercenaries or
as allies of Egypt against their neighbours and kindred of RBO
(Arbâ) in the chief commemorative battle-scene of this war.
The capture of SHALÂM (Shalem) is also recorded on this occasion.   These details suggest that the SHAS'U, or Rephaim of
Bashan probably were not the leaders in the last irruption of
the Shepherds, but those of Judea.

However, the whole body of the nation again collected their
forces, in a final effort to shake off the yoke of Egypt.   We
learn that all the Rapha tribes took part against Rameses in

    [o] Rosellini, *Mon. Reali*, pl. lxxxvii.   The details of this campaign belong to
the history of another nation,—the Emim.
    [p] *Ibid.*, plates 136 *et sqq.*   The particulars of this war belong to the history of
the Anakim.

this last campaign, which occurred in the twelfth year of his reign, from the curious and invaluable series of portraits of their chiefs, selected from the most illustrious among the captives he brought in triumph to Thebes, and which are sculptured round the wall of a chamber, known as his harem, at Medinet-Abou.[q] For among them are found the chief of a land called SHAIRTA‘NA, whose costume is the same as the people who are united with the PULSA‘TA (Philistines), and TAKKAR‘U (Ekronites), against the Egyptians in the great picture of a naval engagement, forming the leading event of this campaign, and who are also identical in every respect with the SHAS.U warriors represented as tendering their submission to Rameses II., in the great historical tableau of his celebrated expedition against the SHET‘TA. The helmet of these people has for a crest, the emblem of ÂSTRTA, "the two-horned Ashtaroth, tutelar goddess of the metropolis of Bashan, and of all the Rapha nations,—consisting of a pair of cow's horns surmounted by a globe; this would have sufficed to indicate their land, even if we had not found the city of SHAIRTA‘NA (Zarthan) within the domains of Bashan. Another chief, whose legend SHA.... is mutilated, is nevertheless recognizable by his strong likeness to the former, and the shape of his crown, as one of the SHAS‘U, which is probably the restoration of his name. The chief of SHET‘TA also is there; a sly, ignoble, bloated, and singularly repulsive countenance! Among them, too, is the great chief of RBO, the 'father of Arbâ himself, and another chief, who might be cousin-german of the latter, by the strong family-likeness of their features, only that he is a rather longer-faced man; wearing also the small peaked beard and the long curl or braid hanging down the side of the smoothly-shaved cheek and temple, which are characteristic points in the costume of the Anakim, and stamp him as one of that race, although the name of his district or city, MASHUASH, is not to be found among the biblical notices. We have also the chief of TAKURI, the Ekronite Philistines, and of the AMÂR, their Amorite dependants. In the inscriptions of Medinet-Abou, the land of AMÂR is called "a land of the TAKKAR‘U;" and in the biblical notices, we find that Ekron was one of the Philistine principalities in the land "accounted to the Canaanite."

All these captive figures are represented kneeling, stripped of their upper robe or mantle of distinction, with their hands bound behind them, and a rope round their necks. Notwithstanding the strong cast of individuality in features and expres-

---

q Rosellini, *Mon. Reali*, pl. 111—113.

sion that characterizes each separate profile, there is a common type by which all the countenances belonging to the Rephaim can be distinguished from the rest; it is impossible to doubt that they were all literally copied from nature. There is nothing conventional about them. The characteristic Rapha type is its *angular* profile. The nose, though arched, is not prominent; but, like the Egyptian nose, was rather flattened about the nostril; nevertheless, the profile has a sort of prominence, caused by the retiring line of the forehead above, and of the underlip and chin below. In this respect, the countenance of this race forms a striking contrast to the Hebrew profile, which, exclusive of the prominent Shemitic nose, presents a nearly perpendicular outline, from the fulness of the forehead and the frequent tendency of the underlip and chin to advance. The eyes of the Rapha face are long, flat, and rather slanting upwards at the corners, like the Egyptian; whereas the eyes of the Hebrew are full, rather round, and set on a horizontal line. The lips are somewhat flat and broad, like the Egyptian; those of the Hebrew are generally either thin or full, but never, in the genuine type, present that peculiar flattened character rendered so familiar to our eyes by the Egyptian statues.

Thus do we gather from the boastful memorials of the last great Theban conqueror's prowess, not only the fate of this doomed race, but those minute particulars of their physical characteristics from which we might venture to assign their ethnological position, as members of that prolonged line of primeval civilization that extended from the foot of Mount Hermon to the extreme borders of the Thebaid.

After the conquests of Rameses III., none of these people are ever mentioned again as enemies of Egypt, in the national records. Their civil polity was finally broken up, their remnant dispersed; their fortresses were razed to the ground, their cities depopulated. From that time they cease to be reckoned among the nations. "The land that had been left of them" retained for a brief season the name of that once "great, numerous and haughty people," as the popular type of all that had been terrible to the nations around; and from the dim traditions of departed greatness associated with its memory, that name was only lost from among the living, to pass over into the language of the country as a poetic synonym for the mighty dead.

Under this sense we meet with the closing allusion to the Rephaim, in the sublime prophetic denunciations of Isaiah. Many centuries have past away since their race was rooted out of the land. Meanwhile, the power of their ancient rival and foe, Shinar, has reached its summit, surpassing even their own.

All Asia groans within its iron grasp. Yet the prophet foretels the dissolution of this mighty empire. In a strain of the most exalted poetical imagery, he introduces the fallen power of Babylon under the figure of a man slain by the sword, and cast into an untimely, dishonoured grave, from whence his ancient adversaries are evoked, to taunt him :—

" Hades below is thrilled, to greet thy coming,
Stirring up against thee the Rephaim, all the chiefs of the earth ;
He hath raised from their seats all the kings of the nations ;
    They address thee, saying unto thee :

" ' Art thou, too, enfeebled as we ? art thou become like ourselves—
Thy pomp, the tumult of thy viols, brought down to the grave—
The conch beneath thee, worms,—the grub, thy covering !
    How art thou fallen from the skies, Lucifer, son of the dawn '
    How art thou cut down to the ground, waster of nations !' "—

Isaiah xiv. 9—12.

CHAPTER VII.

Geographical Identity of the Zuzim and SHAS'U.

The biblical student will perceive that this rapid sketch of the great Egyptian revolutions involves an important chronological problem. If the SHAS'U, the MNA'T'U'N ... (ANKA ?) and the SHET'TA of the events described in the Egyptian historical series, can be proved to be identical with the three Rapha nations known as the Zuzim, Anakim, and Emim of the biblical series, it will necessarily follow that the overthrow of these nations by the Theban kings of the nineteenth and twentieth dynasties must have preceded the Hebrew conquest of Palestine. For the Egyptian monuments that record the deeds of these people,—that bear their names, with the names of the kings who contended with them, and the dates of the respective expeditions, accompanied by references to the geography, history, and worship of the inimical race which will enable us to place their identity beyond the reach of a reasonable doubt,—these very monuments expressly represent them as sufficiently powerful and daring to withstand the power of Egypt, and even to invade the country, under the two most renowned kings of the nineteenth dynasty Seti-Menephtah I. and Rameses II. Yet Moses distinctly affirms that, in his time, the political existence of the Rephaim was at an end, and that other races had the dominion over their lands. Accordingly, under any system of *relative* chronology which attempts to connect Egyptian and Hebrew

history by placing the Exodus and conquest under the eighteenth
dynasty, it is necessary to suppose that in the reigns of Seti-
Menephtah and Rameses II., who recorded their triumphs over
the SHAS'U, SHET'TA, and MNA'T'U'N (ANKA?) the lands of the
Zuzim had, for more than a century, been occupied by the Manassites and Ammonites; those of the Emim, by the Renbenites,
Gadites, and Moabites; and those of the Anakim, by the children
of Judah, Benjamin, and Ephraim;—which is as much as to
say, the seat of those wars could not have been Palestine, and
those inimical nations could not have been these tribes of the
Rephaim.

And as to the *absolute* place in time of the corresponding
events :—the reign of Rameses II. is fixed by the astronomical
sculptures of the Ramesseum, to within a very limited range,
either way, from the beginning of the Canicular cycle, 1325 B.C.
Accordingly, if I can substantiate the identity of the Rephaim
with the great enemies of Egypt, it must inevitably follow that
the most generally received chronology of the Bible history,
which places the Exodus 1491 B.C., is nearly two centuries out
of time; as that event ought to fall somewhere between the years
1325 and 1300 B.C., that the conquest of Palestine by the Israelites may follow, after a sufficient interval, the last expeditions
by which Rameses III., in the twelfth year of his reign, struck
the death-blow at the political existence of all those nations
above mentioned.[r]

A fuller discussion of this chronological point, and a more
definite adjustment of its dates, belong to a different section of
a comprehensive history of the Mosaic Period, which our present
subject is only intended to introduce. Nevertheless, this short
digression could not be avoided; for, as we draw nearer to that
period, we cannot follow up the destinies of the Rephaim, without encountering events which would have compelled me to assume this chronological position, at the risk of drawing the
reluctant reader along a track he regarded as undermined by an
inherent anachronism. It is better, therefore, to look the difficulty full in the face, and let the issue depend on the evidences
I will now bring to bear on my side of the question. If they
be insufficient to establish the fundamental point of identity,
neither history nor chronology will have received any fresh illus-

[r] The reader is here referred to some most interesting and valuable remarks,
by the Duke of Northumberland, inserted by Sir Gardner Wilkinson in vol. i. of
Ancient Egyptians, pp. 76—81. Those remarks trace a series of etymological coincidences, well worthy of the historian's attention, as pointing to the very same
chronological connexion as that suggested by Manetho, and illustrated by this history—whereby the Exodus falls within the reign of Amenophis or MENEPHTAH.

tration. But if they prove satisfactory to the enquirer, the chronological consequences they entail cannot be avoided.

The resemblance between the Egyptian and Hebrew transcripts of a name may be accidental. The chances of uncertainty are increased by the fact that a few sounds rendered in Hebrew by two letters, namely, *l* and *r*, *d* and *t*, *g* and *k*, *sh* and *ch*, are both represented by one Egyptian character. This ambiguity, added to the frequent omission of vowels, often leaves the identity of a name uncertain, unless we can find some more decisive criterion to confirm it. The verbal coincidence of the name and title of the זוזים ZUZIM or SHAS'U of *gHoug*, with the Huk-Sôs of Manetho,—of the Scriptural שטים SHT'IM with the Egyptian local name SHT'TA'N or *Land* of *Shet* ; of the Scriptural ארבע Arbâ with the Egyptian RBO, would have *suggested*, but would not have sufficed to *establish* a case of identity to my satisfaction, if I had not also been able to ascertain that the cities monumentally referred to these several nations, were to be found in the lands of the corresponding nations, the Zuzim, Emim, and Anakim of Scripture.

But there is an Egyptian document which enables me to bring the question at once to a test as decisive as the most cautious theorist could require. This document is referred to by Mr. Birch in his invaluable translation of the statistical tablet of Karnak,[s] which enumerates the campaigns of Thothmes III., the people he conquered, and the amount and nature of the tribute he levied upon them. Among other fragments of illustrative matter relating to these nations, and especially that called the SHET'TA, quoted by Mr. Birch from a variety of monumental sources, he gives an extract from the *Sallier* Papyrus, which professes to describe, in a semi-poetic form, "a journey to the land of the SHET'TA ;" giving the names of the principal places which occur on the road, and of some which are situated above it, or which are visible from it. From several of the names, which he recognized, Mr. Birch remarks that this route partly lay through Palestine. By carefully searching for the biblical correspondents of the rest, I found that they were all recoverable, in positions exactly corresponding to those indicated by the ancient Egyptian itinerary ; and that the route thus traced led to the very land I had previously identified by name as that of the SHET'TA. As the traveller is directed to pass through the land of the SHAS'U on his way, the proof that confirms the geographical identity of the former, equally confirms that of the latter. On this account, although it may be anticipating the subject of a future section of our history, it will be more expedient to

---

introduce in the present one a complete analysis of this route, than to dismiss our account of the Zuzim with the question of their identity in any degree unsettled.

The wars of Rameses II. against the SHETTA form the subject of the papyrus from which this fragment is taken; and the document is not less curious from its remote antiquity, than from the interesting comparison it enables us to institute between the geography of the Bible and that of the ancient Egyptians.

"Thy journey lies to the land of the KHITA.[t] AUBA and SHATU·MA appear to you. In the same manner I tell you of CAFIRI, it is that which is the *Baita* of Ramessu, the fortress of the CHIRUBU; in its waters...... its course resembles that which you make in going to the ATI and TUBASHI. You go to the bow-bearing SHASU, crossing the road at MAKARU......the heaven is...with light; it is planted with clumps of (cedars?) and acacias. You disturb the wild animals and deer, and the camels ridden by the SHASU on its road; it leads thee up to the hill of the land of SHAVA...... I subsequently tell you of the fortresses which are above these, as thou goest to the land of TACHISA. CAFIR-MARUCHANA, TAMNEH, ATI, TAPURU, ATAI, HARUNEMA. You look at KARTA-ANBU, BATA-TUBAR;—you know ARUTUMA, TITPUTA, in the same manner. I tell you the name of CHAN-RUTA, which is the land of AUBA, the bull of the frontiers in its place"...... *Pap. Sallier.*, pl. lii., p. 18, lines 7, 8.

"The writer also mentions BAITA-SHA(N), the TARUKA ARU, and the passage of the IURTANA."

ANALYSIS.

"Thy journey lies to the land of the SHET·TA. AUBA and SHATU·MA appear to you."

A traveller who enters Palestine from Egypt by the usual route from the Sinaitic desert to Hebron—"the way of the spies" (Nu. xiv., xxi. 1) will have the land of Canaan before him on his left; and the Dead Sea, with the contiguous lands, on his right, as he first comes out of the desert upon the cultivated lands near *Tel Arad.* By the analysis of the concluding passage of our extract, we shall see that AUBA must have been the local name of the land of Canaan, known in Scripture only by its patronymic.

SHAT·U is the Egyptian plural form of the radical SHET; consequently, the equivalent of the Hebrew שֵׁט, the name of the land which the Israelites conquered from the Amorites. Its monumental form is SHT·TA·N, referring to the land; and SHT·TA·U·N,

---

[t] In this quotation I copy Mr. Birch's orthography of the names: the variation in his reading of KHITA=SHETTA arises only from the ambiguous power of the initial letter (the *sieve*=ש or ח), so that in such cases it is really necessary to have identified the names correctly, before you can be sure of the right reading. The original Egyptian text has no vowel; when this is the case, an *e* is supplied.

or SHT'TA, referring to the people. SHAT'U'MA is equivalent to the latter, substituting the formative of locality MA, *a place*, for the ordinary terminal N. The name is thus, "the place of the SHAT'U;" *i.e.*, the land of the children of Sheth. In another passage of the papyrus, it is called the land of SHET.

By this opening of the Egyptian description, it is obvious that some part of the land of the SHET'TA was visible to the traveller, though from a distance, on his first emerging from the desert and coming upon the high lands of the wilderness of Judea; and consequently, that the SHET'TA were very near neighbours of the Egyptians. The next station defines this land, and identifies it, still more clearly.

"In the same manner I tell you of CAFIRI; it is that which is the House of Ramessu, the fortress of the CHERB'U."

Thus, CAFIRI is the next place that appears to the traveller "in the same manner." By continuing to advance northwards, we soon come upon a site called, in ancient times, Caphar-barucha. It stands on a height commanding the desert of Judea on the right; while on the left, it covers the entrance to the vale of Hebron, from which it is distant scarcely three miles. The name כפר means "a cover," a house of defence. From its being here called the *Baita* or House of Ramessu, the conqueror evidently had obtained possession of this important frontier stronghold, the fortress of the CHERB'U.

Since SHAT'U'MA "appears to you" even before reaching CAFIRI, it is clear that the southern part of the land of the Emim is the country thus described, the mountainous part which becomes visible behind the Dead Sea to a traveller in the position indicated above. Thus the local name Shittim of the Bible was not limited to the plains of Heshbon, but included all the land of the Emim. The Egyptian forms SHET'TA'N and SHAT'U'MA correspond equally to the Hebrew שדים Shiddim, by which name the Royal valley of the Pentapolis is designated.

When we thus come upon CAFIRI or Caphar-barucha so near Hebron, and find it called the fortress of the CHERB'U, we cannot doubt that CHERB'U is HEBR'ON. The transposition of the two last radicals does not occur in the same name at Medinet-Abou. But the identity is substantiated by the fact that, in the monuments, the two names CHERB'U and RBO denote the *same people;* and in Scripture, the two corresponding names of חברון Hebron, and קרית ארבע Kiriath-ARBA, (the city of Arba,) denote the *same city*. The Septuagint retain the primitive value of the Hebrew letters in their transcript, πολις Ἀρβοκ, which, accordingly, much more closely resembles the Egyptian form

B

—RBO—than the pointed text *Arba.*ᵘ (The final κ is an attempt to indicate the rough articulation of the guttural Hebrew vowel ע.) The numerous historical and geographical references which further confirm this identity must be deferred to the future section treating of their history of this formidable race, the terror and scourge of KHAM; who proved themselves to the last true to their friends—and terrible to their foes.

" Its course (*i.e.*, the road to the land of the SHET·TA,) resembles that which you make in going to the ATI and·TUBASHI. You go to the bow-bearing SHAS·U, crossing the road at MAKARU."

"TUBASHI verbally corresponds to Thebez צבץ, and still more closely to the modern name of the site, *Tubas*. It is the city Abimelech the son of Gideon was besieging, when he met his death (Jud. ix. 50—54). It lay a little to the north of Shechem. The line of road must therefore take in Aiath, עיה, the ATI of our text.

The traveller is evidently told to follow the road that would lead from CAFIRI to those places, but he is not told to go to them; he is to make for the land of the SHAS·U, by crossing some remarkable road or pass at a place called MAKARU. There is precisely such a pass to be crossed at מגרון Migro·n. It is particularly described in 1 Sam. xiv. 2, 4, 5, "The garrison of the Philistines went out to the passage of Michmash . . . and Saul was tarrying at the extremity of Gibeah, beneath the pomegranate tree in Migron . . . and between the passages by which Jonathan sought to cross over to the garrison of the Philistines, there was a steep rock on one side, and another steep rock on the other side. . . The steep of one rock was situated northward, facing Michmash, and the other, southward, facing Gibeah." This description shews that the passage bore east and west, and accordingly intersected the northern Thebez road, which, up to that point, had been the traveller's course. Another reference to this road or passage—for it is the bed of a small winter-torrent—occurs in Isaiah x. 28, in conjunction with Aiath or ATI. The prophet is describing the sudden march of the Assyrian invader upon Jerusalem, supposing him to have crossed the Jordan at the *Shibboleth* ford, near the Wady Zurka.ᵛ "He is come to Aiath, he has passed by Migron, at Michmash he hath laid up his baggage; they have crossed the passage—they have taken up their lodging at Geba; Ramah trembleth—Gibeah of Saul hath fled."

ᵘ In this important name we must again set aside the Hebrew vowel-points, to obtain the true pronunciation of the original radicals.

ᵛ *Vide* Judges xii. 5, 6.

As no more places are mentioned between MAKARU and the land of the SHAS·U, the distance between the two cannot have been great. If the SHAS·U be the Rephaim of Gilead, as I infer from their name, the traveller is in their land as soon as he has crossed the Shibboleth ford, which is found a few miles below the confluence of the Jordan and the Wady Zurka. The journey thither, from the point where the great northern or Thebez road is intersected by the passage of MAKARU, may be accomplished in a few hours, by cutting across the naked desert which, in that part, separates Judea from the valley of the Jordan.

The direction to cross the river is not given in its place; but this poetical fragment is not a regular geographical itinerary; nevertheless, a subsequent reference to the PASSAGE of the IUR-TANA in conjunction with the TARUKA ARU leaves no doubt on the reader's mind that the Shibboleth ford was a well known point of the route, and the one here alluded to. For although the Israelites gave the name of Jabbok to the river which runs into the Jordan near this ford, in memory of their ancestor Jacob's contest with the celestial messenger[10]—and although that river is always called the Jabbok in the Hebrew history—we find, by the Egyptian form TARUKA ARU (or river), that the Wady *Zurka* still bears its primitive name, and that the " Passage of the Jordan" alluded to, must have been the celebrated ford in its vicinity. Thus the Egyptian route is precisely that taken by Sennacherib's army—only reversing the direction.

Having landed his traveller in the country of the SHAS·U, the Egyptian poet indulges in a short description of its leading physical features—which gives an interesting test of its identity.

"The heaven is . . . with light. It is planted with clumps of (cedars ?) and acacias. You disturb the wild animals and deer, and the camels ridden by the SHAS·U on its road; it leads thee up to the hill of the land of SHAVA."

It is impossible to give in fewer words a more lively representation of a thickly-wooded country. It is not a description, but a living picture. For the accuracy of the likeness, I need only refer to the Rev. Eli Smith's account already quoted (vide ante, chap. v.), and also to the forests of thick oak in the hilly regions of Bashan and Gilead, mentioned by Burckhardt, especially one near Ammân.[z] Lord Lindsay describes these forests, like Mr. E. Smith, as consisting chiefly of evergreen oak.

---

[10] צבה akin to צבא to collide, contend. Hence the Jabbok is "the river of *the contest.*"

[z] Burckhardt, *Travels in Syria*, pp. 265, 348, 356.

The word Mr. Birch translates "cedars" is marked (?) as doubtful. It should probably be oaks.

And that this land was a thoroughfare for caravans with camels, is shewn by Gen. xxxvii. 25 : "Behold, a company of Ishmaelites came from Gilead, with their camels, bearing spicery and balm and myrrh, going to carry it down to Egypt."

As the entrance to the land of SHAS·U is placed at the ford, the hill of the land of SHAVA must be the Jebel Jelâd or Es Salt. This mountain marked the boundary of the Zuzim and Emim.[y] Immediately to the south is the scriptural Shittim. Here the description ends—the traveller has reached the goal—he is in the land of the Children of Sheth.

The name SHAVA, which here denotes that land, was in fact its local name. The Hebrew form, Shittim, is only a synonym, derived from the patronymic SHETH, guardian divinity of the land. As early as Gen. xiv., we find (ver. 5) one of the cities of the people whom the Moabites called Emim, bearing the name of Shaveh-kiriathaim, *the double city of Shaveh;* and in ver. 17, the Metropolitan vale of Shiddim is also called "the valley of Shaveh, the royal valley." By finding this name under the form SHAVA, referable to the northern boundary of the land of SHET;—again in Gen. xiv., to a city in its central province, afterwards given to the Reubenites,—and again to a district in the southern extremity of the land, precisely where SHAT·U·MA "appears to you,"—we have thus a clear proof that SHAVA or SHAVEH, שׁוה, was not a mere province, but that this name included the whole country of the Emim.

We shall pass very lightly over the places mentioned in the second part of our extract; it is interesting to find them all equally referable to cities of note in Palestine,—and all fulfilling the only condition required by the Egyptian description—that of being situated above (or beyond) those passed on the route, and consequently more or less out of the way of a traveller bound for the land of the SHET·TA. A list of the names, with their Hebrew correspondents, will suffice to shew their identity.

"I subsequently tell you of the fortresses which are situated above these as thou goest to the land of TACHISA."

---

[y] At the foot of this hill lay Jâzer. In Numb. xxi. 24, we read : "for the border of the children of Ammon was strong." כִּי עַז גְּבוּל בְּנֵי עַמּוֹן but the Septuagint have ὅτι Ἰαζὴρ ὅρια υἱῶν Ἀμμῶν ἐστι—having read כִּי יַעְזֵר " For Jâzer is the border of the children of Ammon;" probably the true reading, as it gives a geographical limit required by the context, whereas the Hebrew reading has no obvious connexion with it. Jâzer was at the foot of Jebel Jelâd. Moses sent to "spy out Jâzer"—intending to cross the ford, had not the Amorites interfered with his movements and compelled him to give them battle.

CAFIR-MARUCHA-NA, כְּפִירָה, "Chephirah of the royal abode," a
fortress a little to the north of Shalem (Josh. ix. 17).

TAMNEH, תִּמְנָה, Timnath-Serah or Timnath-Heres, city of Joshua
in Mount Ephraim (Josh. xix. 50; Jud. ii. 9).

ATI, עַיָּה, Aiath, generally supposed to be the same as Ai, a little
eastward of Beth-El.

TAPURU, תָּבוֹר, Tabor, a Levitical city (Josh. xix. 22; 1 Chr. vi. 77).

ATAI, עִתָּה קָצִין, (ÂTAH). Probably Ittah-kazin or Ittah *"the chief"*
(Josh. xix. 13).

HARUNE-MA, בֵּית חֹרוֹן, Beth-Horon. The place, or House of Hor.
A noted fortress on the Benjamite border (Josh. x. 10),
and a Levitical city (Josh. xxi. 22). Site extant:
Beit-Ur.

"You look at KARTA-ANBU, BATA-TUBAR; you know ARUTU-MA,
TITPU-TA, in the same manner."

This means that these places are visible to the traveller from
the road, either from their proximity, or their conspicuous situa-
tions. Such is the case with the following places, to which
they correspond by name:—

KARTA-ANBU, עֲנָב, Anab, a city of the Anakim. In the Bible,
the prefix קִרְיַת, *a walled city*, characteristic of the chief
cities of the Rephaim, is wanting; the Egyptian text
supplies it (Josh. xi. 21). Site extant: *Anab.*

BATA-TUBAR, דְּבִיר, Debir, otherwise Kiriath-Sepher. From being
here classed among cities *visible* from the road above
particularized, it must have been on the eastern side
of the mountains: but the site has perished. The
occurrence of the name Debir, like that of Hebron,
is remarkable: for it proves the antiquity of these two
local names (Josh. xv. 15—19; xi. 21.)

ARUTU-MA, עֲרָד, Arad. A city of the Amorites in southern
Canaan (Numb. xxi. 1). Site extant: *Tel Arad.*

TITPU-TA, בֵּית הַתַּפּוּחַ, Beth-Tappuah,[c] on a height of the mountain
pass, overlooking the vale of Eshcol (Josh. xii. 17).
Site extant: *Teffúh.*

"I tell you the name of CHANRU'TA, which is the land of AUBA,
the bull (chief or principal place) of the frontier in its place."

Since the land of AUBA begins as you enter Palestine from
the south, and the city of Chinneroth, כִּנְּרֹת, on the border of
the lake to which it gave its name, is still "the land of AUBA,"

---

[c] In the Hebrew form, the letter ה coming awkwardly before פ at the end of a
syllable, is struck out, and supplied by doubling the פ.

it is clear that the Egyptians must have understood all Canaan by that name; it was probably derived from אוב, Aub, (producing,) name of a Canaanite god, often alluded to in Scripture, but usually mistranslated by *a familiar spirit.* The priests and priestesses of this god pretended to possess oracular powers; hence the Israelites are repeatedly warned not to be ensnared by their juggleries; and having recourse to the אבות Auboth, and ידענים Iddônim, "*knowing ones*," was made a capital offence. Saul went to consult a priestess of Aub, בעלת־אוב, (lit. *mistress of Aub,*) at Ain-Dor, when the oracle of the Lord had refused to answer him (1 Sam. xxviii. 6, 7). The region of Dor was contiguous to Chinneroth, which is "the land of Auba" (Josh. xi. 2).

It is particularly worthy of notice that the Egyptian author of this geographical fragment, by calling CHANRU'TA "the chief place" (bull) of the frontier of AUBA, corroborates in a remarkable manner the ethnographical division of Palestine laid down by Moses, who, as we have already seen, assigns the lake of Chinneroth as the eastern limit of the Canaanite.

CHAPTER VIII.

Cities and Dependencies of the Zuzim.

Our chance of identifying whatever cities of the Zuzim are mentioned separately on monumental inscriptions, are but slender. Of the three-score they boasted, very few are alluded to in the passing references to this land, in the Bible. Among these, two very important frontier-cities can be traced with certainty to well-known monumental names, viz.: Zarthan and Pethor. The lists of Rameses III. at Medinet-Abou give, among other names, GAL'NA and ADAR, which correspond so exactly with גולן, GOL'AN, *(Jaulan,)* and אדרעי, ADRÂI (Edrei, now *Adra* or *Drâa)* as to render their identity more than probable, notwithstanding the double power of their radicals.

Zarthan, צרתן (also Zartanah,) SHAIRTA'NA, is mentioned three times in the Bible, so as to define its geographical position very satisfactorily, although the site is not extant. From Josh. iii. 16, it appears to have been a remarkable place, well known to the Hebrews:—

"The waters which were coming down from above, stopped; they rose in an accumulation* very far beyond Adam, the city which is by the

---

* נד literally *a removal* or transposition, indicating that the waters were transferred from their usual course or place. There is no English word to convey this idea with precision, but *heap* does not: it gives a false idea of the physical aspect

side of Zarthan; and those which were coming down towards the Sea of Arabah, the Salt Sea, failed, were cut off, and the people passed over, opposite Jericho."

The site of Adam is unknown; but from 1 Kings iv. 12, we gather that Zarthan itself was very far up the Jordan; as Beth-Shân is there placed—צ‍ר—on the opposite side of Zartanah. Finally, in 1 Kings vii. 46, we find that Solomon cast the brazen vessels for the temple, in the valley of the Jordan, in the clay-ground between Succoth and Zarthan; whence we infer it must have been on the opposite bank of the river, for the foundries in the cavity of the watercourse (כּכּר) to have Succoth on one side, and Zarthan on the other.

The inscription facing the Zarthanian captive " sha ïrta'na n pai iuma," "Zarthan by the sea," may be urged as an objection to my referring this name to an inland city. However, it only proves that the ancient Egyptian *iuma* was a term as comprehensive as its Hebrew correspondent *iam* ים, and the modern Arabic equivalent *bahr*, which at the present day—both in Egypt and in Palestine—stands indifferently for any considerable body of water, whether a sea or a lake, a river, or even only a canal. Nahum (chap. viii. 3) compares Nineveh to No-Amun, "whose rampart was the sea, and her wall from the sea;" meaning the Nile. Dr. Robinson's Arab guide, who spoke English, always translated his native term *bahr* by *the sea.* And Jeremiah (chap. xlviii. 32) calls the Jordan "the sea of Jâzer," because that city was near it, opposite the Shibboleth ford. The ford of Beth-Shan *(Beisan)* is the next place where the Jordan is passable. Zarthan overlooked and guarded this critical spot. Some ruins not far from Jabesh-Gilead *(Yabes)*, nearly opposite Succoth *(Sukhot)*, probably mark the site of Zarthan.

Petur is mentioned as early as in the reign of Thothmes III., in the statistical tablet of Karnak, and again in the inscriptions of Rameses III. The identity of this name with the Pethor of the Pentateuch has never been doubted, from its collocation with naharí'na, which is universally and indisputably referred to the Aram-Naharaim of the Bible. But most Biblical and Egyptian scholars will be somewhat startled at finding Pethor ranked among the domains of Bashan, having been accustomed to the prevalent opinion that it was in Mesopotamia beyond the Euphrates.

---

presented by the phenomenon, both in this place and in Exod. xv. 8. *Vide* Isa. xvii. 11, where the translation is judiciously corrected in the margin, to "the harvest shall be *removed*." In Ps. xxxiii. 7, *heap* also very inadequately expresses the gathering together of the waters to form the natural ocean.

This city is first mentioned as the residence of Balaam, (Nu. xxii. 5.) "Pethor, which is near the river of the children of עַמּוֹ, *his people*," is the reading of the printed Hebrew text; whereupon Kennicott justly observes that although this passage was evidently intended to convey a definition of Balaam's abode, it is really very indefinite, as the form of expression describes no particular land or river. But the Samaritan Pentateuch clears up the obscurity by supplying the terminal ן, accidentally lost out of the Hebrew עמו, and thus gives the description: "Pethor which is near the river of the children of Ammon;" and as this reading is supported by the Syriac and Vulgate versions, and fourteen ancient Hebrew MSS. of high authority, twelve of which were examined by Kennicott, no stronger evidence can be desired to settle its authenticity; whereby the site of Pethor is transferred from the neighbourhood of the Euphrates to that of the Jordan.

The Eberite prophet's own allusion to his birth-place :

> "From ARAM hath Balak, king of Moab, led me ;
> From the mountains of the East."

suggests that Pethor was situated among the mountains out of which the river in question takes its rise, though we cannot be certain whether this was the Wady Zurka or the Moiet-Ammân. It also implies a very important geographical fact: that in the primeval distribution of races, these mountains were part of the Aramite settlements.

All the country included between the land of the Rephaim and the great Syrian desert, seems to have been known as "the East country" by the people of Palestine, although its patronymic was "the land of Uz," derived from the elder branch of the Aramite family, its earliest settlers. The vale of Damascus, its northern limit, still retains the old name חוץ *Hûtz* in the modern form "El Ghuta;" and we learn from Lam. iv. 21, that it also extended southward so as to include Edom ; whence, the Edomite Job, who dwelt in the land of Uz, is called "the greatest of the children of the East." The statement of Balaam, that the land on the eastern Ammonite frontier was Aram, is thus well supported by other Scriptural references. The land actually occupied by the Ammonites, as we have already seen, was that which was formerly the land of the Rephaim.

From Deut. xxiii. 4, we further gather that Pethor was geographically referable to that part of the Aramean settlements known as Aram-Naharaim. Here, as in many other places, the Septuagint has taken upon themselves to paraphrase the Hebrew name by Μεσοποταμια, a "land *between rivers*," in-

stead of simply transcribing it, and leaving it to expound itself,
a land of two rivers נַהֲרַיִם. This led to the inference that
the two rivers understood must be the Euphrates and Tigris,
although in no part of Scripture is there any authority for thus
transporting the Aramites beyond the Euphrates into the land
of the Chasdim. It is much to be regretted that by copying
the Septuagint form of the name, instead of the Hebrew, our
old English translators have unfortunately contributed to disse-
minate this mistake so far and wide, that we are completely
thrown off our guard by its very universality; and every one
has accepted the proposition that Aram-Naharaim is Mesopotamia beyond the Euphrates and Tigris, without stopping to
examine the foundation upon which it is propounded. Rosen-
müller even makes it an objection to our receiving the corrected
reading, "the river of the children of Ammon,"—that the Ammonite settlements never extended so far!

Dr. Beke was the first to notice this grave misapprehension;[b]
and ingeniously suggests that Aram of Damascus may have been
the land known descriptively, in early times, as Aram of the
two rivers, these being, in his opinion, "Pharpar and Abana,
the rivers of Damascus." (2 Kings v. 12.) He further remarks
that the fact of Abraham's relative, born in his house, being
called "Eliezer of Damascus," implies that the residence of his
family must have been near that city. But another reason
added to these by Dr. Beke, appears to me even more conclusive
against the site generally chosen for Padan-Aram, than against
that of Aram-Naharaim; for these two different localities are
usually confounded, as though they were the same place under
another name, which is not altogether true. It is expressly
stated, in Gen. xxxi. 26, that Laban overtook Jacob in the
mountains of Gilead, on the seventh day after his departure
from Padan-Aram. Now between the central summit of the
Gileadite mountains (north of the *Jebel-Kafkafa—)* and Charræ
of Mesopotamia beyond the Euphrates, so commonly supposed
to be the Scriptural Haran and city of Nahor,—the distance is
upwards of three hundred geographical miles. It would take,
not a week—but a month—to accomplish this journey on foot,
considering also the difficulties of a route partly across the desert, and the additional circumstance, pleaded by Jacob as an
excuse for journeying more slowly than his brother—that it was
the breeding-season of the flocks, and it would be unsafe to
urge them on the road. (Gen. xxxiii. 13, 14.) This incident
involves a fact absolutely fatal to the assumption that Padan-
Aram lay beyond the Euphrates.

[b] *Origines Biblicæ,* pp. 122—132.

But if we refer the Scriptural Padan-Aram, "Aram of the fields" (or plains), to those extensive plains of well-watered and luxuriant pastures which are now well ascertained to extend for more than three days' journey eastward beyond the Jebel Hauran, the distances, and all other circumstances relating to this land in the course of the Patriarchal history, will be found to agree perfectly with this supposition. For—firstly : we have already shewn satisfactory Scriptural authority for fixing the "land of Uz" and chief Aramite settlement, along a line of which the Hauran mountains form the nucleus; and to which these very plains belong;—secondly : the name of Nahor's settlement, Haran, is actually found unchanged in the present name of those mountains, known to Patriarchal antiquity as "the mountains of the East;" (comp. Gen. xxviii. 2; xxix. 1;) and the central rocky region, Kelb-Hauran, abounds in remains of deserted villages, frequented only by the wandering Arabs who pasture their flocks on the plains beyond. Thirdly : it is from the southern prolongation of those mountains, that the river Zurka descends— and beyond that, its tributary the Moiet-Ammân, either of which may be taken for "the river of the children of Ammon." Lastly, all this region,—the plains and the mountains,—as part of the "Land of Uz" or "East country," was reckoned in the domains of the chief Aramite tribe, whose seat was Damascus; and would thus be politically referable to Aram-Naharaim as the head of the nation. In this sense only can Pethor be alluded to in Deut. xxiii. 4, as "Pethor of Aram-Naharaim;" not as situated in the part of the land strictly so called, but as included in the range of its dominion;—just as a city in Wales might be spoken of as an English city, in a general historical statement, by a foreign writer, without entailing upon him a charge of geographical inaccuracy.

In thus adopting without hesitation Dr. Beke's valuable suggestion as to the true position of the scriptural Aram-Naharaim, which seems fully borne out by a long series of biblical references, I nevertheless find it necessary to make its application "with a difference;" as there are strong reasons for believing that this name, in its geographical acceptation, should no more be limited to the limits of the present vale of El-Ghuta, than that vale, which represents in *name* the ancient land of Uz, should be taken to represent in *fact* the whole of that land. It is even more than doubtful whether the present site of *Esh-Shum* or Damascus be that occupied in primeval antiquity by the "Head of Aram." It is a very remarkable fact, that, in a land singularly tenacious of primitive local names, a city should be found as far down as the south-western extremity of Jebel-

Hauran, bearing to this day the significant name of *Esky-Sham*, Old Damascus—or rather "Old Shem," patronymic of the Aramite race; though in scriptural and classical antiquity it bears another name, Boshtrah or Bostra;—that it should be historically included in the domains of the king of Bashan, and as such, pass over to the Israelites by right of conquest;—and yet form, geographically and ethnographically, no part of his land; for the modern province *Ard-el-Bathanyeh* ceases a little beyond the sources of the river Mandhur—near Mezareib, the site of its ancient metropolis, Ashtaroth-Karnaim; and Boshtrah or Esky-Sham itself is in the province En-Nukrah, the fertile agricultural region of the Western Hauran. Salchah or *Salkhad*,—Boshtrah, which, from being a place of consequence, was made a Levitical city;—and Kenath, to which Nobah the Manassite gave his own name, and which bears that name in Scripture, (comp. Numb. xxxii. 42; Jud. viii. 11,) although it still retains its primitive name Kunawath, and was always known to the ancients as *Κavaθa*;—all these cities of note were in the Hauran; not in Bashan proper. They are found under the rule of the Rephaim; as such, are acquired by the Israelite conquerors. But the geographical and historical notices of yet earlier scriptural ages all demonstrate that they must be "counted to the Aramite," in like manner with Pethor itself.

The inference so manifestly deducible from the transfer of those cities—that the Aramites were subject to the Rephaim— is confirmed by a direct admission of the fact that the lands of two genuine Aramite tribes were in the same manner obtained by the Israelites, by right of conquest, namely: the Getherites, whose province, north of Bashan proper or *Bathanyeh*, is called *El-Jeidur* to this day;—and the Maachathites: "Gilead, and the border of the Geshurites and Maachathites, and all Mount Hermon, and all Bashan, unto Salchah; all the kingdom of ⁰Houg (Og) in Bashan, who reigned in Ashtaroth and in Edrei, —he who was left of the remnant of the Rephaim: for these did Moses smite, and cast out. Nevertheless, the children of Israel expelled not the Geshurites and the Maachathites; the Geshurites and Maachathites dwell among the Israelites to this day." (Josh. xiii. 11—13.)

This casts the much-desired gleam of light over the political relation of the Shemite race of Aram to the Hamite Rephaim, dimly shadowed forth by the indications deducible from the monumental history of Egyptian conquest. There, the name of NAHARI'NA, is usually connected with the SHAS'U, or with names referable to their domains. In the notices of wars with the SHET'TA, we also encounter NAHARI'NA among the allies or

subsidies of that nation. Mr. Birch quotes from an ancient
Papyrus in the British Museum[c] an enumeration of troops sent
to aid the SHET·TA: 1205 of Naharina, 270 Shairtana, etc., etc.
We shall moreover find the names of NAHARI·NA and PADI together, in the expedition of Rameses II. against the SHET·TA,
among the lands "stricken in the war." This collocation proves
the identity of PADI with the scriptural פדן or *Plain*-Aram.[d]

From these indications, the political status of the Aramites
among the Rephaim is made clear. Like the Canaanites under
the Hebrew invasion, they appear, in course of time, to have
yielded with a good grace to the dominion of a more powerful
people, whom they found they were not strong enough to withstand. By thus timely consenting to join the great political
body of the Stranger race, they secured the advantages of its
protection; and, at the expense of a nominal national independence, they preserved their national existence, so as to survive
even the destruction of their subjugators, and recover the dominion of their own territories.

During the last century of their political existence, when
the ranks of the Rephaim had been decimated by the war of
extermination waged against them by Egypt, and their cities
were left defenceless by the destruction of their fortresses and
the wholesale deportation of the population as captives into
Egypt—the Canaanites began their inroads into the land. The
Girgashites spread their habitations southward of Lake Chinneroth into Bashan. The Amorites of Southern Canaan, originally co-residents with the Anakim, began also to establish themselves in the southern provinces beyond Jordan, from whence
they ultimately extended their settlements to the banks of the
Zurka. Thus, in the time of Moses, half the people who lived
under the sway of the ancient sovereigns of Bashan may have
consisted of these encroaching settlers. On this account, the
last king of the native race, and the usurping Amorite chief
who had seized the metropolitan province of the neighbouring
nation, are both referred to in the general terms of the narrative
as "the two kings of the Amorites;" from which it has been
rather hastily inferred that the king of Bashan also was an
Amorite, and the Rephaim themselves, in consequence, a tribe

---

[c] *Select Papyri*, published from the British Museum: *Papyrus Anastasi*, i.,
p. 13.

[d] It further confirms the distinction I have already insisted on above, to be made
between the two regions of the land of the Uz or east country: Aram of the two
rivers—Naharaim—west of the Jebel Hauran; and Aram of the plain—Padan—east
of it. The Wady Burada and the Wady-el-Liwa, both running into the Bahr-el-
Merj from opposite directions, may be the two rivers marking the nucleus of the
country understood by Aram Naharaim.

of Canaanites. Independently of the reasons I have already given, which exclude the Canaanites as original claimants of any part of the lands beyond Jordan,—it is easy to shew this inference to be grounded on a mistake. A sovereign of one race may rule over a nation of another. The bulk of the people with whom the Israelites were brought into collision, were the Amorites who resided within the realms of Bashan, on the river Zurka; they had not, like their southern brethren, gone the length of setting up a king of their own race, but apparently yielded a partial obedience to the native sovereign of the land. Thus, when the last *Houg* of Bashan had become the nominal leader of a considerable body of Amorite people, and the ally by necessity of a genuine Amorite chief established in a neighbouring province, it is no great lapse of ethnographical accuracy on the part of the sacred historian, to designate him and this chief together as "the two kings of the Amorites;" a form of speech that in no wise justifies our classing the king of the Rephaim himself and his almost extinct race, among the Canaanites who were only interlopers among them. The Amorites of Sihon—themselves usurpers—evidently regarded the Israelite newcomers with suspicion; the king of the Rephaim likewise. He was therefore willing to join the Amorites, in the hope of preserving the small domain over which he yet retained a nominal rule, when the Israelites, by requesting a passage through their territories, alarmed him for the safety of his own, and he thus became impelled to his doom by courting the hostile demonstration he so greatly feared.

As the Moiet-Ammân formed the western limit of the Ammonite settlements on the south side of the upper Jabbok, the country between it and the Jordan, acquired by the Israelites after the defeat of Sihon, formed no part of the lawful Ammonite territory, but only of so much of their predecessors, the Zuzim, as had been taken by the Amorites. The injunction of Moses, to respect the lands originally allotted to the tribe of Ammon by the Rephaim, and in no wise to molest them, was scrupulously fulfilled. "Thou didst not approach the land of the children of Ammon, neither the bank of the river Jabbok, nor the cities of the mountain-tract; nor any place which the Lord our God had prohibited." (Deut. ii. 37.)

The Israelites paid the same regard to the lawful territorial claims of the Aramean sub-tribes of Geshur and Maachah, who remained in the land. The elder branch had probably removed its seat of government farther to the north. The fact that its former lands in the Western Hauran were appropriated by Israel, sufficiently accounts for the aggressive course taken by the king of Aram-Naharaim, soon after the death of Joshua.

We must not suppose that the residue of the Rephaim in
Bashan were utterly extirpated, because the army of Israel had
routed the mixed Amorite and native forces, and slain their
king, who marched upon the frontier to oppose its passage. It
is said in Joshua xiii. 12, that Moses *smote and cast out* the
remnant of the Rephaim. They were so weakened, that a single
defeat sufficed to crush their power of resistance. They fled
before the victorious Israelites. They knew that the land of the
children of Ammon would be respected by Israel. The Ammonite tribe had long considered itself a member, by adoption, of
that ancient nation under whose civil jurisdiction it had been
allowed to settle. Among the children of Ammon, the scattered
and broken remnant of that nation found protection in its ad-
versity. The Ammonites gratefully requited the hospitality
granted to their forefathers, and continued loyal to the chieftains whose ancestors, in the days of their power, had received
and befriended their infant colony. The ancient race and its
name thus became lost among the Ammonites. Under their
influence, these learnt to consider themselves aggrieved by
Israel's occupation of the land from which their legitimate
sovereign had been driven. From that time, they shewed themselves ever ready to join in hostility against the Israelites with
the kindred border nations, the Midianites, Moabites, Amalekites, Aramites of the north, and Children of the East. At
last, in the reign of David, their turbulence was finally checked.
Their chief city Rabbah was captured, and reduced to servitude.
The royal couch or throne of the ancient line of chiefs, preserved in this city, bears witness to the fact that the children
of Ammon regarded these chiefs and their dispossessed successors as the head of the nation, and themselves, as one of its
members; and the territorial pretensions which they grounded
on this fact sufficiently explains their subsequent enmity towards
their Eberite kindred, Israel.					F. C.

P.S. At the end of the tabular list of local names, will be found three
which cannot be referred with certainty to their proper ethnographical
group, because their exact sites are unknown. One of these is TUIRSHA
by the sea, the legend of a captive chief of Medinet-Abou, placed immediately behind those of SHAIRTA·NA and SHA(SU), whom he closely resembles. TUIRSHA is obviously the strong fortress of Tarichæa on Lake
Tiberias. (Jos. *Bell. Jud.*, b. 2, ch. xxi. ; b. 3, ch. x.) But it is uncertain
whether this place was on the Canaanite or on the Golanite side of the
lake. On the other hand, the characteristic points in the costume of the
figure, especially the beard—from which we might have learnt whether he
was of the Rapha or Canaanite race—are unfortunately destroyed.

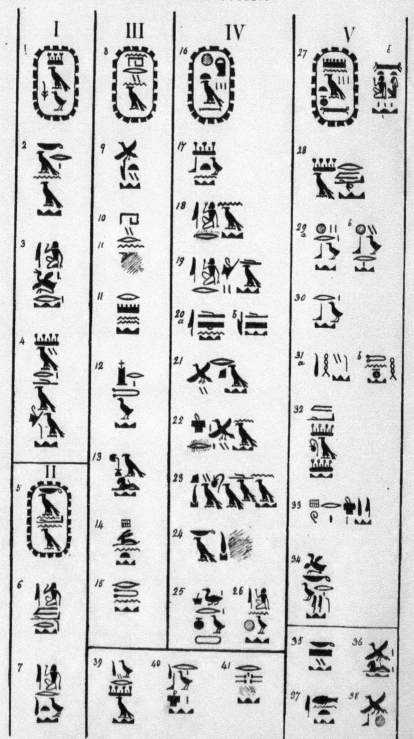

GROUP I.
Rephaim (of Bashan.)

1. R. pl. LXI. SHAS·U — ZUZIM — Σως. M. — זוזים — Zuzim

2. Ch. CCIV. GAL·NA — GOL·N — Γαυλων — גולן — Golan / Jaulan

3. Ibid. ADAR — ADR-AI — Ἐδραιμ — ארדעי — Ἀδραμα. P. — Edrei / Adra

4. R. CXLIII. SHAIRTA·NA — ZRTh·N — Σεσυρθαν — צרתן — Zarthan — ·········

GROUP II.
Canaanites.

5. R. XLVIII. CANA·NA — CNA·N — Χαναυν — כנען — Canaan

6. R. CXLII. AMAR — AMOR — ὁ Ἀμορραιος — אמור — Amor

7. L. ARD·TU — ARD — Ἀραδ — צרד — Ἐλανα... — Arad / Tel Arad

GROUP III.
Aramites.

8. L. NHRI·NA — ARM-NHRIM — אדם נהרים — Aram Naharaim

9. R. c. PADI — PDN-ARM — פדן ארם — Padan Aram

10. Ch. CCIV. HAHR·N... — HR·N — Χαρρων — חרן — Haran / Jebel Hauran

11. R. XLVI. RMN·N — HRM-ON — Ἑρμων — חרמין — Hermon

12. L. PTUR — PTHOR — Φαθουρα — פתור — Pethor

13. R. LXV. SHAR — SHAIR — Σηειρ — שעיר — Seir / Esh Sherah

14. R. LXI. PUN·T — PUN·N — Φινω — פונן — Punon

15. Ibid. LT·N — ELTH — Αιλαθ — אילה — Ἐλανα. P. — Elath

GROUP IV.
Emim.

16. R. LXI. SHT·TA·N — SHT·M — Σαττειν — שטים — Shittim

17. R. CI. SHPT·UN — HSHB·ON — Ἐσεβων — השבון — Εσβουτα. P. — Heshbon / Hesban

18. R. CXVI. AR·NA — AR — שבדעיר — Dwelling of Ar.

19. Ibid. ARNA·TA — ARN·ON — Ὀρωνας. J. — ארנון

20. R. XCI. ATSH·N

21. R. CXVI. PILKA. — Kalat Belka

22. Ibid. SAR·PA·NA — BAN — Βαιαν — בין

23. Ibid. KAITAVATA·NA — KHZV·TH — קרית הצות — Kiriath Huzoth

24. Ibid. KADA.... — KDM-OTH — Κεδαμωθ — קדמות — Kedemoth

25. R. LXI. BAR-NU·MA — BR-NO — Καδης Βαρνη. — ברנע — Kadesh Barnea

26. Ibid. ANSHU — Ἰηνυσος. H. — ·········

GROUP V.
Anakim.

27. R. LXI. CXXXIX. MNA·T·UN — ANKA — Ποιμενες Φοινικες. M.

28. R. CXL. SHALAM·U — SHLM — Σαλην — שלם — Shalem / Jerusalem / El-Kuds

29. R. c. Ch. CCIV. CHEBRU — HBRO·N — Χεβρων — חברון — Hebron / El Khalil

30. R. CXLII. RBO — ARBO — πολις Ἀρβοκ — קרית ארבע — Kiriath Arba

31. R. LV. R. TAHI TH·N·NU — ITAH — Ιταν, Ταυυ — יטה — Iuttah / Yuttah

32. R. CXLIII. MASHUASH — Μααχως ? — ·········

33. R. CXL. PULSA·TA — PLSH·TH — Φυλιστιειμ — פלשת — Pelesheth

34. R. CXLIII. TAKURI — AKRON — Ἀκκαρων — עקרון — Ekron / Akir

---

R. CXLIII. **39.** TUIRSHA . . . . Ταριχαια. J.

Ch. CCIV. **40.** TARBUSA . . . . Θαραβασα. J.

Ibid. **41.** LUSS··· . . . . Λυσσα. J.

APPENDIX. *Delta.*

R. LXV. **35.** GSHI — Goshen ?

R. XLVIII. **36.** PAIRU — Pelusium.

Ibid. **37.** AANT - — On ?

R. XCI. **38.** PAI-BASH. — Bubastis

As the Egyptian forms of proper names will often recur in the course of these papers, it is desirable that the student should be able to verify the readings, by a reference to the original orthography. I have accordingly drawn up a classified list of these names, selecting, from the numerous monumental sculptures which yield them, the fullest and most accurate forms, when they happen to vary.

The Egyptian names are rendered, *letter for letter*, from the hieroglyphics, in upright capitals, with the corresponding Hebrew form beside each, in slanting capitals. In both, the root or *true name*, is separated from the grammatical affixes by a point.

The student will find the following remarks on the latter, useful in facilitating his comparison of these and similar names.

The Egyptian formatives are always suffixed in the same order, though all are not often combined in the same name, viz. :

1. The sign of gender, when *fem.* or *neut.*, next to the root; T, TH, or, written full, TA. It corresponds to the Hebrew ת and ת.

2. The sign of number, *pl.*, U, dual, UI; corresponding to the Hebrew ים and dual ים.

3. The terminal formative of a proper name, N, or NA, sometimes UN or NU, corresponding to, and resembling the Hebrew ן, or ן Occasionally, the formative of locality MA, "a place," is suffixed. This is rare in hieroglyphics. Vowels that are not radical, are often written *after* the name or syllable. The reader will find that in the Egyptian form of a name, the gender has sometimes been changed, or that the finals differ; but with these simple rules to guide him, he will not be perplexed in discovering the identity of any two names which agree in the radical letters.

A few of the names in this list have already been satisfactorily identified. Since the days of Champollion, 5, 8, and 12, CANANA, NAHARINA and PETHOR, have become universal property. Mr. Birch's opinion that 33 is the Philistines, has never been questioned; and I am indebted to his suggestions for the identity of 28 with Jerusalem or Salem, and follow him in reading 36, Pelusium. Mr. Osburn, in his *Ancient Egypt*, has also indicated the correspondence of certain groups to several biblical names, which I cannot but assent to, though differing materially from him as to the nations they represent. His referring 6 and 34 to the Amorites and Ekronites, is quite satisfactory. I have little doubt that his suggestion that 38 and 25 are Bubastis and Kadesh Barnea, is correct, though the final M of the latter never was part of the Hebrew name, being only an Egyptian formative. He also refers 14, 11, and 1 to Punon, Hermon, and the Zuzim, but appropriates those names and places to the Arvadites and Jebusites, to whom we have no Scriptural authority for assigning any territories beyond the Jordan. The geographical position of the two former localities clearly brings them within the Aramean group, to which their costume corresponds; and my reasons for setting aside the supposed connexion of the Zuzim with any Canaanite family, have been fully explained.

ABBREVIATIONS.

R., Ch., L., denote respectively a reference to the monumental illustrations of Rosellini (*Mon. Storici*), Champollion, and Lepsius: H., Herodotus: M., Manetho: J., Josephus: P., Ptolemy. Greek forms without initials, are those of the Septuagint. Recent names of sites are put in italics.

THE REPHAIM, AND THEIR CONNEXION WITH EGYPTIAN HISTORY.[a]

CHAPTER IX.

The Emim.

The Emim—"the terrible people!" Such is the name by which the descendants of Lot designated the powerful, hospitable, and brave, but fearfully depraved nation, in whose land their father had taken up his abode. But they called themselves "the children of Sheth," or, according to the Hebrew form that designates their land, Shittim; and from the perfect correspondence of this form with the SHETTA of Egyptian monuments, I was led to infer what subsequent research has developed with abundant proof,—the identity of that formidable race with the tribe of Rephaim known in Scripture as the Emim.

The territories of the Emim were to the full as extensive as those of the Zuzim. The hill of *Jelád* was their northern boundary; the mountains of Aram, and plains of Padan-Aram, and the Horite valley, their eastern. The Jordan and Dead sea separated them from the Canaanites westward; while the great Wady Arabah, commanded by their ancient metropolis, Sodom, connected the domains of the chief tribe that dwelt in the region of the Arnon, with its junior branches and kindred dependencies —Ken in the mountains of Seir, and Amalek in the desert of Paran.

At the time this people are first introduced to our notice, all the southern bay of the Dead Sea was a fertile valley, "well watered everywhere like the garden of the Lord, like the land of Egypt, before the Lord overthrew Sodom and Gomorrah." (Gen. xiii. 10.) This was the vale of Shaveh, the Royal Valley, otherwise called "the vale of Shiddim," from the people to whom it belonged. Of the five cities it contained, the sites of only two are known,—Bela, called Zoar by the Moabites, and which retains that name in Scripture; and Sodom, the chief city, which must have occupied the southern extremity of the valley, not far from the salt-hill *Usdum.* But not a vestige of the city itself, nor of Gomorrah, Admah, and Zeboim, has ever been found.

It had long been supposed that the eruption, by which the four cities were destroyed, had produced the chasm of the Dead

---

[a] Continued from the January Number of the *J. S. L.*

Æ

Sea. Dr. Robinson's researches in that region cast great doubts
on this hypothesis; and the results of a more methodical survey,
under Lieut. Lynch, have brought out facts which disprove it
altogether. The soundings gave an average depth of between
150 and 200 feet along the central line of the sea, till the pro-
montory in front of Zoar. In this part, the lake is usually ford-
able; and the whole of its southern end is so shallow, that such
a volcanic explosion and conflagration as the narrative of Gen.
xix. 25 seems to imply, if followed by the not unusually associated
phenomenon of subsidence, to the amount of 12 or 15 feet,
would suffice to submerge to its present depth a cultivated low
tract occupying that site, without sensibly increasing the area
of the sea in other parts.

But the rest of the country belonging to the Emim remained
unaffected by this catastrophe; and the royal seat appears to
have been transferred to Heshbon, in the centre of the chief
province, and a remarkably fertile and beautiful tract, abound-
ing in ruins of deserted cities and villages.

After the catastrophe of the cities, Lot and his family dwelt
apart in the mountainous region behind Zoar. The first fixed
settlement of his descendants is traced to the contiguous city,
Rabbah (*the great* or chief city), occasionally alluded to in
Scripture by its local name Ar. Its site is well known. The
children of Lot grew into a considerable tribe, which separated
under two heads; the junior branch, as we have seen before,
establishing itself, in like manner, in the mountainous back
settlements of the Zuzim.

The hilly tract occupied by the Moabites is called in the
itinerary of Moses, "the mounds" or low hills of the Abarim,
שֵׁי הָעֲבָרִים; and the Moabite mountains beyond them, "the mountains of the Abarim." (Nu. xxxiii. 44, 47.) These may be considered as a prolongation of the "mountains of Aram," or of
"the East." They doubtless received that name from the native
race, because they were the settlement of the Eberite family of
Lot; as Abram also, in Gen. xiv. 13, is called "Abram the
Eberite." In Balaam's prophecy, the whole race descended
from these two patriarchs is included under the patronymic
Eber. *Abarim* עֲבָרִים is the same word as *Ibrim* (Hebrews) עִבְרִים,
save that its etymological import has been disguised, through
the alteration in the pronunciation caused by the vowel-points.

The original tribe-name of the Emim—"the Shittim"—the
name by which they were known among themselves, is not directly recorded, like that of the Zuzim, in the earliest notice of
them, Gen. xiv. 5. Nevertheless, we may obtain it by collating
several passages in other parts of their history.

When the Israelites had conquered and expelled the Amorite usurpers of the metropolitan province, we learn from the itinerary of Nu. xxxiii. 49, that they encamped in the plains of Moab, by the Jordan of Jericho, from Beth-Jeshimoth (בית הישמת the house of Jeshimoth) to Abel-Shittim (אבל השטים Abel of Shittim.) The historian's meaning, here, is evidently to assign the extreme limits of an encampment along the valley of the Jordan, too extensive to be descriptively referable to one particular city. By a reference to Nu. xxv. 1, we further learn that Israel was abiding in Shittim, when, at the instigation of Balaam, an attempt was made to corrupt their religion, which brought on the war against the Midianites. As Israel was still abiding in Shittim, when Joshua sent out the spies into Canaan, and as they only removed from thence to cross the Jordan, the term of their sojourn in the region so called, cannot have fallen much short of two years.

It is obvious from this, that "Shittim" cannot be meant to designate a city. Neither among the lists of Moabite cities in the later historical or prophetical books, nor in Josephus, nor in the ancient classic geographers, is any such name to be found. Yet any single city sufficiently large to contain all the victorious host, their wives, children, cattle and goods, for two years, must have been too considerable to escape subsequent notice, had such a city existed. These considerations go far to shew that the name Shittim, by which the Hebrews designate this locality, was not applied to a mere city, but to a very considerable extent of country.

This will be made still more evident by another circumstance to be taken into consideration. Nu. xxi. 24—32, relates the conquest and first establishment of the Israelites in the plains of Moab, which excited the jealousy of the Moabites, and led them to plan the destruction of Israel through the denunciations of Balaam, as related in the succeeding chapters, xxii—xxiv. Between this incident, and the cause of the Midianite war narrated in ch. xxv., there is an interval of more than a year, since this war was the closing event of the forty years' probation in the wilderness, whereas the conquest of the Transjordanic provinces occurred at the beginning of the thirty-ninth. This narrative follows close upon the preceding chapters, not because it follows them in order of time, but because it relates the continuation of the same series of political machinations. Having thus brought up the history to the eve of the Midianite war, the historian breaks off to relate the occurrences which fill up this intermediate period; after which he resumes the history of the war itself, the last event of his life.

Among these parenthetical chapters, we learn (ch. xxxii. 1—32) that after the destruction of the Amorites, and expulsion of the Rephaim, the tribes of Reuben, Gad, and Manasseh besought Moses to bestow upon them the conquered territory. The request was granted, and these tribes established themselves in their possession; the rest of the nation, having as yet no lands, continuing to occupy the encampment along the Jordan, described in Nu. xxxiii., as extending from the house of Jeshimoth to Abel of Shittim." To suppose that this allotment is related in order of time, and consequently as having taken place *after* the seduction of Israel, involves the very improbable supposition that the Israelites, after acquiring by force of arms the mastery over a country stretching across more than a hundred geographical miles, neglected to take possession of their conquest, left all the cities and lands they had acquired, unguarded, unoccupied and deserted for nearly two years, to encamp on the arid bank of the Jordan—and that, too, without any apparent fear or chance of molestation on the part of the nations they had deprived of those lands; while the partisans of those very nations were actively engaged in plotting the destruction of their new conquerors! Such a proceeding would have been so senseless, that its absurdity need only be pointed out, to dismiss the supposition altogether. The allotment of the first-fruits of conquest to the three elder tribes of Reuben, Gad and Manasseh,[b] must be allowed to follow close upon the conquest itself; garrisons being placed in the chief cities, both to watch over the newly-acquired possession, and to protect the flocks and goods of the conquerors. These likewise watched over the welfare of their brethren, who had pitched their tents in the plains of the Jordan; supplying them with necessaries till their turn to take possession of their own inheritance should arrive. The Reubenites, Gadites, and Manassites certainly did not neglect their possessions, since we are told that before the death of Moses they had repaired the cities which had been devastated in the war. Their departure from the common encampment, though not mentioned in the narrative, must be understood by the subsequent events.

As the line of this encampment is described as extending from the mouth of the Jordan to a place called Abel on the

---

[b] Reuben and Joseph were firstborn sons of Jacob's lawful wives; and Gad, of his concubine Zilpah, handmaid of the senior wife. Dan, the fourth firstborn son in rank, was born (like Ishmael) of Rachel's handmaid, substituted for her childless mistress; consequently, the subsequent birth of Joseph, of the lawful wife, displaced him from the privileges he would otherwise have enjoyed as son of Rachel by adoption, placing him fourth only in rank, instead of second. Had there been a fourth apportionable province, it would doubtless have been given to him.

northern frontier of Shittim, it seems that the Hebrews must
have understood by "Shittim" generally, the whole country of
which the "plains of Moab," where the tents were pitched,
formed only a part; the part extending along the eastern bank
of the Jordan, in front of Jericho. As in the case of Canaan,
they put the patronymic of the *tribe* for the name of the *land*
that tribe occupied; for the people called themselves the Shittim, but the local name of their land, as we have already seen
in a former chapter, was Shava or Shaveh.

I apprehend that the "vale of Shiddim" in which the metropolis of this people once lay, is only an orthographic variation
of the same name. In this case, the historian appears to have
transcribed the form of the name literally, from a more ancient
record, perhaps from one embodied in an old and limited alphabet, which, like the Egyptian, did not distinguish such shades
of sound as that between *d* and *t*; whereas, in his personal narrative, he wrote the name as he heard it pronounced in the
country. Both these orthographies are equally well represented
in the Egyptian form of this name, with which Moses was no
doubt very well acquainted.

The origin of the tribe-name Shittim, thus applied by the
Israelite historian to the land once ruled by the Emim, may be
gathered from a remarkable passage in Balaam's concluding prophecy, which is quoted entire at the end of this chapter. The
Egyptian records relating to the SHET'TA furnish a complete
explanation of it, by which the identity of the people is further
confirmed.

In this prophecy, the Emim are alluded to as "the children
of Sheth," in conjunction with the Moabites, among whom the
remnant of the ancient nation had become so intimately blended,
since the Amorite invasion, as to be no longer historically distinguished from them, in the sacred annals, either by Moses or
by their own prophet. From a treaty of peace concluded by
Rameses II. with the SHET'TA, in the twenty-first year of his
reign,[c] we learn that this very name, Sheth נש, was the name of
the tutelar and patronymic god of their land. It is written in
Egyptian, Suth, and Suth-esh. In this very curious document,
not only is the late contest between the Egyptians and SHET'TA
represented as a personal contest between the patron gods of the
two rival nations, but these gods are also introduced as ratifying
the treaty in person, by their signature or attestation at the end!
And if the reader is curious to know under what style and titles
the gods shewed themselves off in such important transactions,

---

c Rosellini, *Mon. Reali*, pl. cxvi.

it is as follows : " The Suth of the fortress of AR·NA ; the Suth of the fortress of ARNA·TA ; the Suth-esh of the fortress of PILKA," etc., etc. ; the same name being thus repeated in connexion with the fortress under his charge, the chieftain of which probably was proxy for his god on the occasion. That the Suth or the Suth-esh thus introduced is neither the name nor the title of a man, is proved by the determinative hieroglyphic sign following the name ; this is neither the figure of a man, nor of a chief, as in that case it would be ; it is the figure of the Egyptian god Seth, which Plutarch informs us was the Egyptian name of him whom the Greeks call Typhon. He is represented with the head of a long-snouted and long-eared unknown animal, which they mistook for an ass. This same figure is used to write ideagraphically the name of the king Seti-Menephtah.

This god's head, with the body of a dog, is also the determinative sign of the name Baro or Baal, בעל, in the historical inscriptions of this period. In the laudatory comparisons with this Baro, so frequently applied by the Egyptian hierogrammatists to their sovereign, we have a sure token that at that time Suth or Baal was a god as highly reverenced by the Egyptians themselves, as by their foes the SHET·TA.

Suth and Baal are nearly synonymous titles ; denoting *a lord* or *master*, the former in Egyptian, the latter in Hebrew. *Sut'n· Keb,* " Lord of Egypt," is the usual formula heading the the names of Egyptian sovereigns.

In the *Papyrus Sallier*[d] there occurs the following remarkable passage :—

" They shall not stand in the land of KHERBU . . . .

Fallen in their blood !

Then shall the revolted chiefs, the fallen of SHET, approach, and glorify the great name of his majesty, saying :

' O thou Ra in thy solar abode, Suthesh the son of Netpe, the great disturber, and Baal who smites his enemies ! Thy terror is in the land of SHET behind thee !' "

The Egyptian author of this historical poem seems here to admit openly, in the terms of this address to the king of Egypt, that Seth, Suth, alias Suthesh, alias Baal, being " son of Netpe,"

---

[d] *Select Papyri* ; facsimiles published by the British Museum. *Pap. Sall. 3,* pl. xxxii., l. 6—9. The passage is thus translated by Mr. Birch, in the introductory account of these documents. I may as well point out in this place an oversight of my own in a reference, which I have corrected in the present section. The ancient papyrus in this collection which includes the geographical fragment so often alluded to in both sections, is not one of the *Sallier,* but one of the *Anastasi* papyri. As, however, I have given the numbers of the plate, etc., this mistake would not have misled any one wishing to refer to the published facsimile of original document.

was brother to Osiris. The myth of Osiris cruelly persecuted by his brother Typhon or Seth, implies the same; and both involve an equally distinct confession on the part of the Egyptians, of the common origin of the Shethite race with themselves, and of their gods with those of Egypt proper.

It is not until after the final dismemberment of this once dreaded race, that the god Seth was blotted out of the Egyptian pantheon, and his name was consigned to execration as the evil genius who so long favoured the cause of the most inveterate enemies of Egypt. Earlier monuments represent him under various forms and characters, as the teacher of kings,[f]—as the patronymic of the dog-star,—as the god to whom one of the five days of the Epact was consecrated, and whose name was borne by several Egyptian monarchs. The assiduity with which the Egyptians erased or defaced his figure, under all its representations, has unfortunately contributed to cast great obscurity over the functions of this god in their mythological system. There is no doubt, however, that his synonym BARO is the Baal of Scripture;[g] and another of his Egyptian synonyms, NUBI, seems to point out his identity with the local god Nebo of Shittim.

The name of ASTRTA, Ashtaroth עשתרות or Ashtoreth, (for the points vary the pronunciation of the name, but the Hebrew radicals are exactly equivalent to the Egyptian characters,) is also mentioned in the treaty above referred to, as the great goddess of the SHET'TA. A chain of connexion singularly consistent and interesting, is thereby established in favour of that people's identity with the race whose metropolis was Heshbon, and whose sway extended to the neck of the Elanitic gulf and over the whole peninsula of Sinai—the Emim, and the cognate Kenite and Amalekite tribes.

In the first place, one of the most noted fortresses of the SHET'TA, was called ATESH. This name is one of the synonyms, or rather local proper names, of Astarte; as is proved by a tablet in the Louvre, described in Prisse's *Monuments de l'Egypte et de le Nubie*, which represents a goddess similar in every respect to the goddess Ken on the tablet of Kaha in the British Museum, save that she bears on her head the cow's horns and globe of Hathor, which are absent in the provincial goddess Ken; and that her name is given as ATESH, instead of "Ken." The identity of Ken with the Assyrian Astarte, in every emblem and attribute, has been sufficiently established by Mr. Layard's designs from the Khorsabad sculptures. And that in the form of

f Burton, *Excerpta Hierog.*, pl. 137.
g Bunsen, *Egypt's Place*, etc., vol. i., pp. 126—129.

Atesh, she is the "two-horned Ashtaroth," patronymic of the metropolis of the Rephaim, is absolutely proved by a fact we gather from the Egyptian sculptures that represent the final triumph of the Egyptian conquerors presenting their captives and the rich spoils of the conquered to the local gods of Thebes; for among these spoils are the sacred vessels employed in the service of the gods, bearing their emblems on the covers; and the cow's head, with the globe and horns, is a frequent device among these emblems, whether the spoils be those of the SHAS'U, the SHET'TA, the RBO, the TAHI, or the LT'N.[k] The religious emblems of all these people are absolutely identical—proving them to be branches of the same people, and agreeing in the external symbols of their worship. Moreover, the SHAS'U who submitted to Rameses II., in his great expedition against the SHET'TA, are represented wearing the same emblem—the horns and globe—on their helmets. The people of SHAIRTA'NA, belonging to the SHAS'U nation, bear the same crest on theirs.

The goddess being thus distinctly identified, it is a very remarkable coincidence that we should recover, in one of her monumental names, Ken, the patronymic of that very branch of the Shethite people who, under the name of "Midianites," in Scripture, took a leading part on behalf of the Moabites in endeavouring to seduce the Israelites to their corrupt religious practices, in order to make friends of them and regain a footing in the lands they had lost. It is still more remarkable, that in one of their possessions, the city of Elath אֵלַת, "the mighty," we should even recover what appears the radical form of another name under which, according to Herodotus,[i] the same goddess was worshipped, namely, the Arabian Ἀλιττα, otherwise Ἀλιλατ, which he informs us is the same as the Babylonian Μυλιττα. Elath is the city I identify with the monumental LT'N mentioned above, among whose sacred emblems that of Astarte is prominent.

So much has been done in a former chapter towards establishing the geographical identity of the Emim of Scripture with the monumental SHET'TA, that very little remains to be

---

[k] Compare the spoils in Rosellini's *Mon. Reali*, pl. xlviii., lii., lv., lix.

[i] Herodotus, *Clio*, c. 131. The etymology of this goddess' name has given rise to much conjecture. The simplest origin for it appears suggested by the passage, Ex. xv. 15 :—

"Then are the leaders of Edom troubled—

Trembling hath seized the mighty of Moab אֵילֵי מוֹאָב."

From which it appears that El (a mighty or powerful one) was a Moabite title of superiority, like Allouph (a leader) of the Edomites. Elath אֵלַת is merely the feminine form of this root.

said in completion of this subject, before we enter upon the few details which scriptural and monumental antiquity unite to afford us concerning their history.

The cities of the SHET'TA which I have been able to trace through the topographical allusions of Scripture or of historical antiquity, to the lands of the Emim, are as follows:

SHEB'T'UN is the first city mentioned in the expedition of Rameses II. against the SHET'TA, and towards which his march was directed.[j] This is the metropolis of the scriptural Shittim, called by the Hebrews, Heshbon. The only difference is in the gender; and, what is very remarkable, in the Egyptian geographer Ptolemy's list of Arabian cities,[k] it is called Ἐσβουτα, which agrees in form and gender with the hieroglyphic transcript. In another part of the same historical inscription, the name is written SHABU, supplying the vowel (an aspirated *a* or *e* = the Greek H), but omitting the final formatives. Thus nothing is wanting to demonstrate the verbal identity of the monumental SHEB'T'UN with the Hebrew version of the name, חשבון, Heshbon.

The four lower lines of the treaty between Rameses II. and the SHET'TA, already referred to, contain a list of their principal fortresses.[l] This part of the monument is unfortunately very defective, as several entire names are broken off at both ends of the lines. Of the eleven, more or less mutilated, which remain, I have found six which can be identified with places in the land once occupied by the Emim.

AR'NA. "The dwelling of Ar," שבתער mentioned in an obscure poetical quotation from the book of the wars of Jehovah, Nu. xxi. 15. Whether this be Ar of Moab, otherwise Rabbah, subsequently known as Areopolis; or whether it be the city

---

j Rosellini, *Mon. Reali*, pl. cii., l. 4, and c., l. 2.

k Ptolemy, *Geog.*, l. v., c, xvi.

l Rosellini, *Mon. Reali*, pl. cxvi., l. 27–30. I am not aware that this important list of names has ever been noticed before. I am indebted to the kindness of Mr. Birch (of the British Museum) for pointing it out to me; as well as for some particulars of the document itself, of which he very obligingly imparted the substance to me, by a verbal translation. No version of this extraordinary relic of ancient customs has ever yet been published.

It is worthy of remark, that the six names I have been able to identify are those of places north of the Arnon—with the exception of Ar-na, if this be Ar of Moab or Rabbah. This was the only part of the land of the Emim known to the Hebrews, and to which the Mosaic and later prophetic lists, exclusively refer. Of the part permanently retained by the Moabites, they knew nothing: yet this is more than half of the original possessions of the Emim. The five unidentified names probably belonging to this unknown part, read as follows:

1. SHISASAPA; 2. SAR·SU · · · (mutilated); 3. SHIHNA(P) · · · (mutilated);

4. TAI (illegible group) TASHERRI .. (final letter wanting); 5. ASHN · · · (mutilated).

Aroer on the Arnon (ערער), a reduplicate form of the same name,
is the only thing doubtful; for the identity of the name itself
is evident.

The fortress of the ARNA'TA is the next on the list. ARNA'TA
is only the feminine Egyptian form of the Hebrew ארנון Arn·on;
and is the name of the river on which the celebrated stronghold
of the SHET'TA, called ATESH, was situated. The picture of this
fortress in the great historical tableau of the expedition of Rameses against the SHET'TA, shews that it was near the mouth of
the river, and almost entirely surrounded by water. This topographical hint concerning the situation of ATESH suggests its
identity with the nameless " *city in the midst of the river*," mentioned, in conjunction with Aroer, as marking the frontier of
the land obtained by the Reubenites through their conquest of
the Amorite usurper Sihon. (Josh. xiii. 16.) On the other hand,
Josephus gives a list of Arabian cities taken by Alexander
Janneus in the wars, which his son promised to restore to the
king of Arabia who reigned at Petra.[m] Among these, he mentions Oronas, as one of the cities of the Moabites. The similarity
of this name to the Egyptian ARNA'TA, is striking; but this does
not clear up the doubt whether the fortress of the ARNA'TA be
the same place as ATESH, "the city in the midst of the river,"
or another place called ARNA'TA = Oronas, after which the river
itself was named.

PILKA. This name is still extant in the castle of *Belka* on
the Haj-route to Damascus. Its scriptural name, however, is
unknown, as it was in the land of the Reubenites, and may have
borne another while in their possession, which it lost when the
Moabites regained possession of the country.

SAR-PAI'NA. This is a compound of צור Zur, a rock or stronghold, and בעון Beôn, (Sept. *Bauav*,) a place in the Reubenite
district. (Nu. xxxii. 3.) The same prefix, SAR, occurs also in
another name in the same list, SAR·SU · · · · too much mutilated
to be identifiable.

KAITAVATA'NA. "The dwelling of Khazavath," corresponds
by its radicals to קרית חצה, mentioned in Nu. xxii. 39, as the
place to which Balak went with Balaam, after meeting him on
the frontier, and from whence they went together to Bamoth-
Baal, the place dedicated to the god of the land, Sheth or Baro,
—before whom the fatal imprecations against Israel were to be
solemnly pronounced. The points transform it into Huzoth.

KATA · · · · · mutilated; it is most probably Kedemoth, where
the Israelites came after passing Bamoth (Deut. ii. 26), and

---

m Josephus, *Ant.*, b. xiii., ch. xv., and b. xiv., ch. 1.

from whence Moses sent messengers to Sihon to ask permission
to pass through his land. This circumstance indicates its position as on the frontier, eastward of Heshbon.

The two remaining names of cities on my list, classed under
the Emim national group, belong to the provinces of Ken and
Amalek. For to the former must in all probability be referred
BARNU'MA, or Kadesh-Barnea, on the border of the great Wady
Arabah, and commanding the Canaanite frontier.

The last, ANUSHU, corresponds to the city Ἰηνύσος of Herodotus.[n] Its site is unknown; but the general indications he
gives of its locality, as on the line of traffic leading to Kadytis,
and as being about three days' journey from the lake Serbonis
which lies at the foot of mount Casius, just where Egypt begins,
point to the eastern side of the Wady El Arish, and consequently place it in the Amalekite district.

From the singular account Herodotus gives of the worship
and costume of the Arabians of Jenysus, it seems they must
have been an isolated remnant of that race. They worshipped
Dionysus (Osiris) under the name of Orotal, and Urania (Astarte)
under the name of Alilat; and "cut away their hair all round,
shaving it off the temples;" assigning as a reason for this practice, that their god was shaved so.[o]

Now it is a peculiarity of national costume, which I have
found without an exception characteristic of all those monumental people whom I have been able to trace to the Rephaim
by means of their cities and names—that they all shave some
part of the head, or beard, or both: and though each tribe does
this after a fashion of its own, yet in one particular they all
agree: *they all shave the temples and the side of the beard.*
Their Aramean and Horite-Edomite dependents, and their
Amorite neighbours, on the contrary, always appear with their
beard entire, and their hair long and carefully trimmed.

We further learn from the Egyptian sculptures that the particular practice of "cutting away the hair all round, and shaving
it off the temples," was characteristic of certain tribes of the
SHET'TA. Among the chiefs represented as hastening in magnificently accoutred war chariots, to aid the city ATESH against
Rameses II., some are conspicuous by a coiffure corresponding
with remarkable exactitude to the above description. None of
their hair is left but a round patch on the top of the skull; and
that is tied up into a tuft, like the scalp-lock of an American
Indian, or twisted into a long pendant braid, like a Chinese
pigtail. If this be the way the god Orotal used to shave for a

---

[n] Herodotus, *Thalia*, c. 5.   [o] *Ibid.*, c. 8.

pattern, we cannot commend his taste; but the pious reverence of the Amalekites for the divine origin of this hideous fashion propably led them to think it very becoming.

The head attire of the SHET'TA of ATESH in the battle-scene of Seti-Menephtah at Karnak,[p] and that of the captive chief in the symbolical group of that king devoting his enemies to destruction, presents a striking contrast to the one described above; and there, the intention of imitating the coiffure of their god is manifest, by comparing it with the effigies of Astarte on some of their sacred utensils. They wore a long thick braid of hair on each side of the face, behind the ear; and the back hair is long, hanging down like that of a woman; it may perhaps be to follow up this strange religious manifestation, that they shaved their beards, or clipped it exceedingly short. While other branches of the Rapha nation proclaimed their allegiance to the tutelar god of their land by the crest of their helmets, the SHET'TA carried out the same idea by their mode of tonsure, as they wore no helmets.

If we now bear in mind that it was in the land of this people that the children of Israel spent thirty-eight years of probation, in the great and terrible wilderness of Parau and Seir, in constant communication with the Edomite and Midianite tribes domesticated among them, we shall then apprehend the full significance of the prohibition given in Lev. xix. 27, in terms precisely equivalent to those by which Herodotus describes the practice of their descendants, the Jenysite Arabians. "Ye shall not round off the corners of your heads, neither shall ye destroy the corners of your beards."[q] Since this practice, as explained by Herodotus, and confirmed by the religious badges and emblems depicted on the Egyptian sculptures, was a distinctive outward token of this idolatrous people's worship and nationality, its adoption, by an Israelite, would of course be regarded as equivalent to an open declaration of religious and national apostasy.

The names of cities above enumerated are given in the third column of the Onomasticon, under the head *Emim Group. No. IV.* Immediately below this column, are two names apart, (40 and 41), which occur in a record of the conquests of Rameses III. They are kept separate from the column, only because I have no criterion for deciding whether they should be referred to the *Emim Group*, or to their Horite dependencies

---

p Rosellini, *Mon. Reali*, pl. lix.

q Compare : לֹא תַקִּפוּ פְּאַת רֹאשְׁכֶם וְלֹא תַשְׁחִית אֵת פְּאַת זְקָנֶךָ——with Herodotus : κείρονται δὲ περιτρόχαλα, περιξυροῦντες τοὺς κροτάφους.

forming the lower part of the *Aramite Group, No. III.*; as they are not mentioned in Scripture, and their sites are uncertain. Their correspondence to two names out of the list of Arabian cities in which Oronas or Orone is mentioned,[r] proves that they certainly were in the dominions of the Shethite race. For Josephus reckons as Arabia, and Ptolemy includes in Arabia-Petræa, all the country east of the Jordan that lay southward of the river Zurka.

TARBUSA is the place called Tharabasa by Josephus, in that list. One cannot easily be misled in the identity of a name with four radicals, all agreeing. LUSS··· is exactly Lussa of the same list: the character wanting, in the hieroglyphic group, is only the final formative, or vowel. If this were the *Αυσα* of Ptolemy, identified by Dr. Robinson with a desert-station east of Wady-el-Arish, it was an Amalekite outpost. The characters however may also be read RSS··· and may possibly stand for Rissah, one of the unknown encampments of the Mosaic itinerary, Nu. xxxiii. 21; in which case it would be referable to the Kenite or the Edomite districts.

CHAPTER X.

Wars of the Emim with Egypt.

If the materials I have thus far brought together before the reader's view are worthy to be accepted as sufficiently satisfactory evidence that the Emim of the Hebrew annals are no other than the daring and dreaded SHETTA of the Egyptian, then the broad outline of their history may be sketched out with something like certainty, by connecting the scriptural and the monumental references to the leading events of their political career, and to the leading features of their social condition.

We gather from Manetho, that when the Phœnician Shepherds first established their power at Memphis, the Assyrians were masters of Asia; and that the chief of the Hyk-sos fortified the eastern frontier of Egypt with peculiar care, being apprehensive that the rival power might make an inroad from that quarter. There was no doubt a reason, founded on experience, for these apprehensions.

For that dynasty passed away—the Hyksos made themselves masters of all Egypt—and an interval, which is perhaps not

---

r Josephus, *Ant.*, b. xiv., c. 1.

overrated at about two centuries, has elapsed, before we meet with the next definite indication of the state of their affairs, in that valuable historical fragment of Genesis xiv., quoted entire in the introduction to this history; and we then find them at open war with a king of Assyria and his confederates.

When Abraham entered Palestine—when Lot chose the royal valley of Shaveh for his residence—the power of the Rephaim in Egypt had perhaps passed its meridian. Thebes was still tributary to their chiefs; for the long and fierce war against them, which ended in the deliverance of the Thebans from their yoke, had not yet begun, since the final expulsion of the Shepherds from the Delta can hardly have taken place before the death of Abraham, according to the system of relative chronology which the identification of that nation compels me to adopt. The uncertainty that hangs over the duration of some reigns in the 18th and 19th dynasties, renders an exact chronological adjustment, on that foundation, hopeless; but a general coincidence of events, of which the respective dates may be fixed within a latitude of twenty years either way, is sufficiently precise for an historical sketch like the present, where a broad and comprehensive view of leading and unquestionable facts is all that we require, and indeed all that the few fragments, snatched from the decay and oblivion of ages, reveal of characteristic and instructive detail.

The invasion described in Gen. xiv., was not the first that the Rephaim had suffered from their Asiatic rivals in power. The Emim tribe had been made tributary to the sovereign of Elam, fourteen years before. This indicates a shade of decline in the power of the race itself; an increasing ascendancy in that of their rivals. The Emim tribe were the section of the nation against which the hostility of the Assyrian confederacy seemed more particularly directed: this would suggest that the task of defending the power of the great political body in the east, had been more particularly delegated to them, while its elder branch strove to maintain it in the south.

The part taken by the great chief of the nation, on the occasion of their unexpected deliverance from their invaders by means of the panic into which Abraham's cautious but unflinching intrepidity had thrown the enemy, teaches us, among other things, that up to that time, the junior branch of the nation and its supreme chieftain acted in concert, under a system of federal discipline which speaks highly in favour of their civil institutions. It also goes far to explain their success, in the immense political ascendancy which their unity of purpose and of action enabled the Rephaim—" the chiefs of the earth"—to obtain, and to retain for so many centuries over the principal kingdoms of the primeval civilized world.

Traces of this people's having once—and for perhaps a long interval of time—exercised a powerful influence over the destinies of Assyria and Babylonia, are by no means wanting; but they are dim and shadowy. Certain gods of the Rephaim are found domesticated beyond the Euphrates. The foundation of Assyrian worship, as far as the monuments shew, seems to have been a pure Sabism; but at a later period, another system has been superadded, with which it does not harmonize. Astarte, Seth-Baal, Nebo, Oannes, in their own land, are not only local gods, but *patronymns* of the people who serve them,—or impersonations of the land. They are forms of the gods peculiar to the nation; and as old among them as the nation itself. When we find counterparts of the gods of the Rephaim on Assyrian sculptures,—when we also find there the name of one of their most formidable tribes, the SHET'TA,—we may count this as a strong indication pointing to the same end as the scriptural account, which presents them at war with the kings of Assyria and Shinar; and with that of Manetho, which presents them as on their guard against aggression from Assyria: that there may have been periods of alternate conquest and depression on both sides, of which the records have perished. Perhaps not altogether; a source of discovery is now only just opening upon us, which may hereafter be found to extend even to the remote ages coeval with the early monarchs of Egypt, the Sesertasens and Amenemhas, who shared the dominion of the Nile with their powerful rivals of the north. But leaving these regions of doubtful speculation, until a ray of sunshine shall have pierced through the cloud of oblivion that hangs over the grave of buried empires, to guide us with a more certain step along the gloomy vista of a past over which forty centuries have closed,—we will now leap over the gap of about three hundred years which separates the intimation of the state of the Rephaim given us at the time of Abraham's migration, from that era of circumstantial monumental records, which presents them to our view with the startling reality of pictorial representation.

The SHET'TA do not appear on this scene upon an independent footing, till the wars against the SHAS'U and their allies of NAHARI'NA have been carried on for a full century, and the power of the elder tribe begins to totter under the inveterate efforts of the Theban kings to avenge the degradation of their fathers by extirpating the children of their oppressors. As auxiliaries to their principals, the Emim doubtless bore their part in the contest. But the records of the immediate successors of Amosis do not afford the same abundance of materials for geographical identification, as that which is so plentifully yielded by the lists of tributaries to Egypt under Seti-Menephtah, and the vaunting historical inscriptions accompanying the pictorial triumphs of Rameses II. and III. The names are few, and the same are often repeated. The city of ATESH is supposed to be mentioned as early as under Thothmes III.; and LT'N, the great emporium of the Aramean Horites, pays the tribute of her rich and varied merchandize to that monarch, though we do not know whether it was then in the power of the Rephaim or not. But whatever part the Emim had borne in the great national conflict, up to the time of the 19th dynasty, was undoubtedly in unison with, though strictly subordinate to, the elder and sovereign branch of their people in Bashan.

Under Seti-Menephtah, they first appear as distinct objects of hostility, though not yet as taking the lead. Their land was less accessible than that of their kindred. It could only be penetrated from the north by the complete reduction of the Zuzim; or from the south, by the conquest of the Amalekite and Horite regions. The tributary list of Seti-Menephtah at at Karnak,[s] goes far to shew that both these points were gained; that this great conqueror had reduced the northern branch of the Rapha nation sufficiently low to command its submission, and had secured the principal passes and stations of the south, Jenysus, Kadesh-Barnea, Elath, Seir, Punon, as far as Atesh on the Arnon; besides those which must remain unrecognized in that list, either because the names are of doubtful reading, or because their correspondents are not to be found in the sacred or classic writers. Such was the relative position of the contending powers, when the mightiest of Egypt's conquerors, Rameses II., ascended the throne, and the fierce and daring children of Sheth rallied all the energies and resources of their nation, to carry on to the utmost of their power the deadly feud of race against race, in which their former chiefs, and now uncertain allies, had almost succumbed.

The celebrated expedition led by the great Rameses against the SHET'TA, in the fifth year of his reign, was deemed the most glorious among the military triumphs achieved by this renowned conqueror. It forms the subject of three vast commemorative sculptures, embellishing his three palace-temples of Luxor, the Ramesseum, and the excavated one of Abou-Simbel in Nubia. I shall refer to the latter in describing the campaign.[t] It is re-

---

[s] Rosellini, *Mon. Reali*, pl. lxi.

[t] *Ibid.*, pl. lxxxvii. The different parts of this design are given on an enlarged scale, in the succeeding plates, to cii.

markable for a curious attempt at combining geographical with
historical delineation, which may perhaps entitle it to be regarded
as the oldest map in the world, in so far that the Egyptian artist
has evidently intended to represent the general outline of the
country invaded by the great conqueror, in conjunction with the
leading incidents of the campaign. But as he probably had
nothing to guide him but the verbal description of those present
at the action who furnished the necessary details, we cannot be
surprised at the bearings not being very accurate. We shall
nevertheless find, from our previous identification of the land of
the SHET'TA by means of the topographical descriptive fragment
of the *Anastasi Papyrus*, that the leading features of the country
are sufficiently well made out in the topographical design of
Abou-Simbel, to admit of our recognizing at once the Jordan,
the Dead Sea, and the Arnon. So that when we endeavour to
refer the leading events of the campaign to their proper localities
according to the indications given to the inscriptions appended to
the design, we discover that the Egyptian artist has forestalled us,
by representing them *in situ;* and when we find the route of the
land of the SHET'TA elaborately described in the records of their
wars with Rameses which constitute the subject of the *Papyrus,*
we also find out the motive of that description—that this was
the route actually followed by the conqueror; that, in fact, these
two geographical documents—the most ancient of their kind in
the world—are complementary to and explanatory of each other;
and the mystery they presented, is finally unsealed and rendered intelligible to us, through a third document almost coeval
with them in antiquity—the early historical and geographical
notices of the Bible.

The tableau is a very oblong parallelogram. The scene of
action is laid on the two sides of a river, which runs from the
left, across it, into a lake situated near the middle of the picture.
The opposite end of the lake receives another river, at the
mouth of which is placed a fortress. The inscriptions give the
name of this river ARNA'TA, and of the fortress ATESH.[a]

The eastern mode of orientation is to place the east in front,
the south at the right hand, and the north at the left hand. It
is singular that these are the bearings of the topographical design of Abou-Simbel, and from the Jordan at the Shibboleth
ford to the Dead Sea, they are geographically true. But those
of the Arnon are not correct, its true course being from east to
west; whereas the Egyptian artist has made it run into the sea

---

[a] In the Egyptian list of names, I give the two forms of this one; col. iv., fig.
20, *a*, is as it is found on the fortress; and 20, *b*, as it occurs in the inscriptions of
Seti-Menephtah, and of Rameses II., in the account of the expedition.

A

from the south. This was done most probably to secure a linear arrangement of his incidents, which could not all have been brought in, had he made the river run into the sea from the top of the picture. For the final scene of action, where the incidents are the most crowded, is just the very part which lies above the Arnon and the city of ATESH.

Having thus planned the field of action, the artist could hardly have given sufficient consequence to the actors in it, unless he had made them a little out of proportion with respect to the landscape. The figures are on a scale of about a foot to a mile! Thus the Jordan dwindles to the relative dimensions of a street-kennel, and the Dead Sea to those of a little fishpond, which the royal chariot-horses galloping along the river's eastern bank might easily stride over, seeing that their legs span an arch of some ten miles. The fortress of Atesh also gains in consequence at the expense of the sea, its picture being projected from the mouth of the river so far out, as to cover nearly all the lake; and even then, it is so much too small for the warriors who defend it, that each of its five towers cannot possibly contain more than two brave men very tightly jammed together into the battlements, and half as high as the towers themselves.

Owing to this unavoidable disproportion between the people and the field of action, and the number of incidents he had to delineate, the artist was reduce to indicate the successive stages of the action itself, by dividing the field into several horizontal lines, along which his groups are arranged. To follow the thread of the story, you must begin at the bottom line, near the prefatory inscription, just below the two encampments of the Egyptian king and of the SHETTA, which are delineated *in situ*. You must then follow the figures in their course along the two lines above this, so as to end with the passage of the Jordan at the extreme left edge of the picture, where what may be called the *first act* of the pictorial drama ends. It consists of the encampment, and preparations for action.

The *second act* begins on the other side of the Jordan; it is the invasion. The king in his chariot, (four times as large as the other figures and chariots, according to custom,) having crossed the river, is proceeding southwards to the country east of the Dead Sea. The SHETTA and their allies are rushing in their chariots across the ford, at the left border of the picture. The line of this important geographical incident is prolonged over the king's head, to the fortress of ATESH, to which their course, like his, is directed.

The *third act* depicts the final rout of the SHETTA and their allics. The royal war-chariot appears a third time, in the parts north of the Arnon. Here we see all the animation and confusion of an Egyptian battle-scene. The king is transfixing his enemies in every direction with his enormous arrows, or riding over them; they tumble about in every imaginable impossible attitude; some run off with their cattle, the dead bodies of others float along the river—there are heaps of spoil, and strings of captives led off in ignominious triumph, among who are conspicuous a group of the remarkable and unmistakeable ᴋᴜᴏ, the indomitable Anakim of Arbâ, the faithful allies of their kindred, the Emim.

The course of events, as thus read off from the picture, is much more intelligible than the narrative of them, which may be extracted, though not without difficulty, from Rosellini's translation. The style of the Egyptian hierogrammatists is so verbose, so loaded with bombastical epithets, metaphors, and eulogies of the monarch, as to be almost unintelligible, even to the learned pupil of Champollion. It is astonishing how small a lump of fact remains, when the froth of adulation and circumlocution which overlays it, is removed. The local names are the most valuable among those facts, since they furnish us with references to the sites whereby the identity of the people and of their land is again put to the severe test of topographical as well as verbal correspondence; and the circumstantial agreement we thus obtain, leaves nothing to be desired.

When we find it stated as the opening fact, in the inscription, that his majesty was staying in the land of ᴛᴀʜ, it is very satisfactory to find that in a map of Palestine, the site of Juttah, a fortress of the Anakim with which I identify the ᴛᴀʜ, ᴛᴀʜɪ, or ᴛᴀʜ·ɴ of the Egyptian monuments, corresponds exactly to the place in the picture occupied by the royal encampment, where the king is represented sitting on his throne and receiving the report of the ambassadors.

When we find in the inscription, that two ambassadors from the ꜱʜᴀꜱ·ᴜ came to the king, and told him that the ꜱʜᴇᴛ·ᴛᴀ were encamped in the land of ᴄʜᴇʀʙ·ᴜ,ᵛ it is not less satisfactory to find in the picture that the place of the ꜱʜᴇᴛ·ᴛᴀ encampment corresponds exactly to the site of Hebron in the map.

This camp is surrounded by palisades. The self-satisfied assurance of the enemy is indicated by the warriors and horses lying down within the enclosure; while others are engaged in games of skill or military exercises. In the middle of the camp is a sacred enclosure, in which four priests are prostrate before a

---

ᵛ I here follow Mr. Birch's quotation, as Rosellini's reading is not accurate.

shrine overshadowed by the wings of two cherubic figures. This
is a very remarkable circumstance; for the date of this event is
about seventy-nine years before the Exodus. It proves the antiquity and universality of this symbolical representation.

When we next find, by the inscription, that the object of
these two SHAS·U ambassadors was to tender their submission to
the Egyptian king, in the name of their nation, and to give him
"an entrance into the country,"—it is very satisfactory to recognize in this incident three valuable coincidences :—

Firstly : That the pictorial description corresponding to this
event, placed at the beginning of the lowest line, just under the
Egyptian camp, shews us that the people there represented as
coming forward to greet the Egyptian chiefs with every demonstration of friendship, were a people devoted to Astarte, whose
crest they wear on their helmets; and Ashtaroth-Karnaïm (the
two-horned Ashtaroth) metropolis of Bashan and head of the
SHAS·U nation, was sacred to that very goddess, whose name it
bore.

Secondly : That the people of Zarthan or SHAIRTA·NA wear
the same crest and costume; and that was also a city of the
SHAS·U of Gilead.

Thirdly : That by knowing who these people were, and where
their lands lay, we understand what is meant by their giving the
king of Egypt " an entrance into the country." For we see by
the picture itself, that the Egyptians invaded the SHET·TA by
crossing the Jordan at the Shibboleth ford. We learn by the
itinerary of the *Anastasi Papyrus*, that the way to the land of
the SHET·TA was through part of the land of the SHAS·U, near
"the hill of the land of SHAVA;" which amounts to the same
thing as the picture,—since we find that part to be the very part
about the hill of *Jelâd* which faces the Shibboleth ford. We
further learn from the date of the expedition, "the 9th of
Epiphi in the fifth year of the king's reign,"[w] that it took place
at a season of the year when the Jordan is too full to be forded,

---

[w] The earliest period at which this expedition can be fixed, is 1389 B.C., and the
latest, 1369 B.C. In 1389 B.C., the 1st of Thoth of the Egyptian vague year, fell on
Aug. 5th, and the 9th of Epiphi on June 10th, of the Julian account. In the 14th
century B.C., June 10th was nearly twenty-eight days before the summer solstice; a
season-position equivalent to May 26th of the Gregorian account now in use. In
1369, the 9th of Epiphi would be five days earlier.

The remark in Josh. iii. 15, that "the Jordan overfloweth all his banks, all the
time of harvest," is illustrated by Dr. Robinson's valuable observations on the state
of the river. (*Bibl. Researches in Palestine*, vol. ii.) The harvest is during April
and the early part of May. Dr. Robinson describes the true river-bed on May 12th,
as full to the brim, and flowing over, so as to wet the bottom of the upper bed over-
grown with cane-brake.

" except at a very few places known only to the Arabs;"[z] and
that by thus favouring the passage of the Egyptian conqueror
through their territory, across the very first ford at which the
river could be crossed, the SHAS·U were rendering him a far
greater service than by fighting for him.

While the SHAS·U were thus sacrificing their brethren to
their own security by a disgraceful unconditional surrender to
the formidable invader, the SHET·TA were endeavouring to nego-
ciate with him; they sent rich presents and proposed terms of
peace. But ambassadors who dared to parley and propose conditions to the great king, were not so well treated as those who
laid their all at the foot of his throne: they were taken up as
spies and beaten; their proposals were of course scouted—and
the war-cry of the tribes was then raised, the camp broke up,
and they all prepared for active resistance.

The king now marched towards the land of the rebels. The
CHERBU and AMAR (Anakim of Hebron or Arba, and Amorites)
and all the southern dependencies of the SHET·TA, came to their
assistance. But when they saw that the plains of Heshbon
were placed in the power of the invader by the sudden defection
of their SHAS·U brethren, the SHET·TA and the allied powers
threw themselves into the mountain fortresses beyond the
Arnon. Rameses laid siege to ATESH, " the city in the midst
of the river," which appears to have defended the valley of the
Arnon. The place held out a long time; but the chiefs were
drowned in attempting to cross the river, and the city then surrendered. The inscription concludes with his majesty's repri-
mand to the rebellious chiefs for the troubles they have brought
upon their allies far and near, as well as on themselves, by their
presumptuous resistance to his power. It is here that NAHRI·NA
and PADI are mentioned: whence it appears that the SHET·TA
were powerful enough to command the assistance of the Aramite
dependencies of their kindred the SHAS·U, even when these were
themselves too weak to venture upon resisting the king of Egypt
on their own part.

This memorable campaign was the first of a long series of
hostilities which only closed with the treaty of peace signed by
the gods of the two belligerent nations in the twenty-first year
of Rameses II. The records of the *Sallier* and *Anastasi Papyri*
advert to several intermediate campaigns; and at this period,
the power of the Shethite chiefs extended very far, if we judge
from the lists of their allies,[y] to whom these documents represent

---

[z] Burckhardt, *Travels in Syria*, etc., p. 345.
[y] *Select Papyri*, pl. xxiv., xxv.; quoted by Mr. Birch in his " Observations on

them as sending for troops to aid them against Egypt. Among
these is KARKUMASHA, generally admitted to be Carchemish on
the Euphrates. Many of the other names are also well known
on the monuments, and those that are identified among these,
will be found in my list: CHERBU, SHAS'U, SHAIRTA'NA, NAHA-
RINA, KATVATA, KESH, which cannot be the black KESH of
Ethiopia (Cushites), as they are much too remote to be allies of
the SHET'TA; they are probably the Goshen settled in Palestine.
One of these names, ARHE'NA, may possibly be יריחו IRHO, Jericho
(now *Riha*), as the Amorites of that part of Canaan are always
associated with both the SHET'TA and the CHERBU in the contest
against Egypt. But many of the local names in these lists cannot be identified with any known to scriptural or to classical
antiquity. This is not surprising, considering how many sites
may have perished in the war itself; and how many besides lay
in parts of the land unknown to the Hebrew historians.

When the Emim and their kindred first became involved in
the long and desolating war with Egypt which only closed with
their fall, the Moabites and Ammonites were as yet an inconsiderable tribe. Their continued increase, while the original race
was sinking, as well as their secluded position on the Aramite
frontier, are circumstances rather favourable to the inference
that they took no aggressive part in the fierce contest between
the two mighty races whose national hatred aimed at nothing
short of total annihilation on one part or on the other,—save
when their land was invaded; for then, neutrality would have
been treachery against the people under whose protection they
had so long dwelt. If the Aramites took up arms on behalf of
the Rephaim, when Egypt attacked them, we cannot suppose
that the Moabites, whose destiny and interests were wholly interwoven with those of the Emim, could remain inactive in the
struggle. But the monumental representations throw no light
on this question; for if the tribe of Moab figures in any of the
contests they depict, we cannot distinguish them from the ancient race by any peculiarity of costume, as we can the Edomite
allies of the southern tribes.

The Amorites are the only Canaanites who appear on the
monuments of Egypt. Their geographical position, as co-residents with the Anakim in Judea, necessarily exposed them to
aggression from any nation at war with the Rephaim; and
would compel them to take a part against the invaders, if their

the Statistical Tablet of Karnac," already referred to, who gives the passage thus:
" The wretched chief of the Khita (*i.e.* SHET'TA), and the numerous lands with him,
the Arutu, the Massu, the Sharu, the Keshkesh, the Arhena, the Katuata, with the
Chirubu, the Ati (sh?), and the Ruka."

own land was attacked. But the singular paucity of Canaanite
names, in the Egyptian lists, is a certain indication that Egypt
had no quarrel with that nation; and that the implication of
the Amorites in the political affairs of the Rephaim, was only
casual. The Amorite colony appears to have established itself
beyond the Jordan, as early as the reign of Seti-Menophtah;
for when that monarch attacked the SHET'TA before ATESH, he
encountered a party of Amorite herdsmen, and put them to
flight; they are represented as scampering off in all directions
with their cattle. Having thus gained a footing in the country,
the Amorites easily ingratiated themselves with the ruling race,
by taking their part against the Egyptians. The Amorites not
only appear in the campaign of Rameses II., but also in those
of Rameses III., since the figure of an Amorite chief occurs
among the portraits of captive chiefs at Medinet-Abou.

The last mention of the SHET'TA on the monumental records
of Egypt, is in the twelfth year of Rameses III., when the Rephaim rose in a body, and made a final but unsuccessful effort
to shake off the dominion of Egypt. The conqueror then swept
through their lands, defeated their combined forces, destroyed
their fortresses, broke up their national polity, carried their
chieftains off in triumph to Thebes, and crushed their power for
ever. The once mighty children of Sheth were thus brought so
low, as to yield the fertile plains of their metropolitan province
an easy prey to the Amorite horde, who now took advantage of
their weakened condition to sieze their depopulated capital, and
establish their own chieftain Sihon, ruler over the land.

The Emim chiefs were too haughty to bend before an usurper whom they had no longer power to resist. They, with the
remnant of the decimated population, withdrew to the mountain fastnesses beyond the Arnon, to the settlements of the
Moabites. These were now become so superior in numbers and
position, that the few dispossessed Emim refugees among them
are no longer considered worth distinguishing as a separate
nation, by the sacred annalist,—whose account of them, in his
own time, runs thus:—

"Distress not the Moabites, neither contend with them, for I will not
give thee a possession from their land, because I have given Ar for a possession unto the children of Lot. The Emim formerly settled there; a
great, numerous, and haughty people, like the Anakim; who were also
accounted Rephaim like the Anakim; but the Moabites call them 'the
Emim;'—אמים—*i.e.* '*the terrible people.*'"

It is particularly worthy of remark that, in this brief notice,
the historian merely states that Moab *replaced* the Emim in
their land (a part of it); but he does not say that "THE LORD

had destroyed them" from before the Moabites, as the Zuzim were destroyed from before the Ammonites. Nor does he, in either instance, attribute the destruction of the ancient race to the agency of the children of Lot, as he does that of the Horim to the children of Esau. A small remnant of the Emim had yet escaped destruction in the time of Moses. This miserable residue of the "terrible people" long survived the downfall of their supremacy. Their baneful influence over the destinies of Israel long outlasted the breaking-up of their polity and disappearance of their name from among nations.

The Moabites requited more worthily than the treacherous Amorites the hospitality accorded to their forefathers by the Emim. They received and protected the fugitive children of Sheth, and continued to pay to the hereditary chieftain of the ancient race the honour due to him as their king, in virtue of their original settlement in the lands under his jurisdiction. The manner in which they are mentioned, either as associated or as politically identical with the "people of Chemosh," in the triumphal ode of the victorious Amorites, quoted by Moses in Nu. xxi. 27—30, would even suggest that the Moabites had taken a leading and active part in the unsuccessful contest against Sihon. But the sacred historian does not intimate whether they did so as partisans of the primeval race with whom their national destinies had so long been blended, or whether as territorial successors of that broken people, and, as such, deeming themselves entitled on that ground to dispute with the Amorites for possession of the metropolitan district which these had wrested from their deposed chieftain.

Whatever doubts may remain as to the precise position of the Moabites and Emim with respect to the Amorites, the supposition that the personage who is styled in Scripture "king of Moab"—"Balak the son of Zippor"—was a chieftain of the ancient race, is not altogether gratuitous; it is strongly supported by the following curious circumstance: In the treatise between Rameses II. and the SHET-TA, the pedigree of the great chief of this nation is given; and the name of his grandfather, which Mr. Birch reads SAPURU, shews us that the name of Balak's father, צפור, Zippor, evidently must have been a *family* name, as characteristic of the last Shethite dynasty, as *Rameses* was of the contemporaneous rival power in Egypt. The first Zippor or SAPURU lived in the time of Rameses I. The last was contemporary of Rameses III.; and, for aught we know, it may be his portrait that figures among the captive princes at Medinet-Abou.

It was therefore to the dispossessed representative of that

ancient royal race, that Balaam, the far-famed prophet of the children of Ammon, disclosed the future destiny of the tribes who either claimed a common origin with the children of Sheth, or who had joined their political body as settlers; and were doomed hereafter to fall under the sway of that very Israel whom the prophet was hired to imprecate. This remarkable prophecy is the only historical clue we possess to the ultimate fate of the Emim. It will therefore close the present section of our history, not less appropriately than it will serve to introduce the history of the kindred tribes it enumerates.

BALAAM'S PROPHECY.

"And now, behold! I am returning to my people: come, I will inform thee of what this people will do unto thy people in after-times."

He then resumed his parable, saying:

"Sentence of Balaam, son of Beor.
Sentence of the man whose vision was sealed.
Sentence of him who now heareth the words of God,
And perceiveth the counsel of the Supreme:
Who—prostrate—with unveiled eyes
Beholdeth the vision of the Almighty.

I see him—but it is not now.
I behold him—but it is not nigh.
      A star proceedeth from Jacob,—
      A sceptre ariseth from Israel,—
      He wounds the recesses of Moab,
      And crushes the children of Sheth!
Edom, too, becometh his domain;
Seir becometh the domain of his foe,
For Israel doeth valiant deeds!
      He (who) descendeth from Jacob
      Will destroy the remnant of the city.

---

‡ נְאֻם בִּלְעָם. נְאֻם is a more energetic term than אָמַר "to say." It generally implies the utterance of a solemn denunciation or sentence. Hebrew, literally: "sentence-pronounced of Balaam." The opening of the three verses with the same formula, in the Hebrew, gives great solemnity to the passage.

שְׁתֻם הָעָיִן same construction, literally: "stopped-up of eye." When the visual organs are meant, the Hebrew has always the *dual* form. When עַיִן is used in a figurative sense, it is *singular*; whether denoting the surface or colour, or a fountain. Here, it stands for the visional powers of the prophet, suspended for a while; and of which, on this occasion, the Almighty had permitted the return. Mark the change in the tense of the participles: שְׁתוּם, contrasted with שֹׁמֵעַ one "actually hearing." קַרְקַר literally, "demolishes."

Then, looking upon Amalek, he resumed his parable, and said :

> First among nations was Amalek ;
> His end is—to perish for ever !

Then, looking upon the Kenite, he resumed his parable, and said :

> Strong is thine habitation !
> Thou settest thy nest in the Rock :[a]
> Nevertheless—Ken shall be devoured !
> How far will Asshur lead thee captive !

[Then, looking upon Og,] he resumed his parable, and said :

> Alas ! who can survive the appointment of God ![b]

> Ships from the coast of Chittim !
> They humble Asshur—they humble Eber—
> Yet he, too, shall perish for ever !"

Nu. xxiv. 14—24.

CHAPTER XI.

The Kenites.

The characteristic features of the country possessed by the Kenites are so well known through the vivid and interesting accounts of modern travellers, especially De Laborde and Dr. E. Robinson, that any particular description of it here would be superfluous. The magnificent dwellings of their metropolis, Petra,—partly excavated in the solid rock, partly hewn away from its face; the wild grandeur of its mountain strongholds, dangerous of access to the traveller and deserted of inhabitants, are now among the most familiar objects in the list of ancient wonders held up for the admiration and awe of modern times.

We have no evidence to decide whether the Kenites were

---

[a] שׂים בסלע קנך, a play of words on סלע *Sela*, the rock, name of the city = Petra; and קין *Kain*, name of the nation.

[b] אוי מי יחיה משמו אל. I here take מ for the particle of comparison ; literally, "Alas ! who can *live more than* the appointment of God !" The force and deep pathos of this ejaculation will be apprehended by the feeling reader, in connexion with the important clause in the introductory sentence, between brackets, which appears to have been lost in the Hebrew text, but is fortunately preserved by the Septuagint ; and is evidently required by the parallelism of the context. The reader will bear in mind that "Og" was the political head of the children of Ammon, in whose land Balaam resided.

original possessors of this astonishing city, or whether they held it by conquest. The promise made to Abraham, before the tenth year of his residence in Palestine—that his posterity would obtain the dominion over the lands of the *Kenites*, contains sufficient proof, in the terms of the promise itself, that this people occupied the Wady Mousa as early as this promise was made; how much earlier, we cannot know, since authentic history ascends no higher. As to their claims over the tract to the south and east of this, there can be no doubt that the whole valley between Mount Seir and the great Arabian continent originally belonged to another people—the Horim; and that these still held it at the time of Chedorlaomer's invasion. A parenthetical reference in Deut. ii. 12, informs us that the children of Esau succeeded to their land; and from the passage in Lam. iv. 21, "O daughter of Edom, who dwellest in the land of Uz," it further appears that the possession thus obtained by the Edomites was reckoned part of the land of Uz, eldest son of Aram. Thus the primitive Horites were a race altogether distinct from the Rephaim, and must have been Aramites.

There is no historical reference to shew whether the Horites ever held the Wady Mousa and Petra also. But whatever the original title of the Kenites to this part of their country may have been, it is certain that their sway, in the time of Moses, extended as far down as the neck of the Elanitic Gulf, and that they were accordingly joint tenants with Edom over the Horite valley eastward of Mount Seir: that their national decadence followed so closely upon that of their neighbours, the Emim, as to shew that they were all involved in the same cause, and shared the same political doom; and finally, that the civil position of Edom among the children of Ken, was like that of Moab among the children of Sheth; a rapidly increasing tribe of wealthy and industrious settlers, at first dependants among a powerful nation; but who, on the decay of their political head, gradually superseded them in ascendancy; and ultimately absorbed into their own body both the residue of the original population, and its name.

The address of Balaam to Balak : "Come, and I will inform thee of what *this people* (Israel) will do unto *thy people*, in aftertimes," is very significant in pointing out the original stock of the nation that ruled over Ken, in his time; since, under the head of "Balak's people," he not only includes Moab and the children of Sheth, Balak's immediate subjects, but also Edom, Amalek, and Ken. It is difficult to conceive what claim the three latter could have to be thus ranked among the people of a Shethite king, unless they belonged to a community claiming direct affinity to his race. The difficulty is not lessened in any way by our supposing Balak a genuine Moabite by birth. This might account for the mention of Edom as his people, in virtue of an original affinity of race; but Amalek—the Amalek Balaam styles "the first of nations "—was certainly a distinct people long before Moab was born; and so was Ken: and neither were ever subject to or connected with Lot's children in any way to justify their being classed among their people.

But a very conclusive fact may be produced in evidence, that—prior to the Edomite monarchy—the tribe of Ken, albeit its rule extended from the torrent Zared to the extremity of the Madyanite coast, was itself only a branch of the Emim; that in this way, they really were a part of Balak's people, and Edom only an allied state engrafted upon them; and that, in fact, the chiefs of Ken ruled only under subordination to the great chief of the Emim. It is stated in Josh. xiii. 21, that the five princes of Midian slain in the war, Evi, Rekam, Zur, Hur, and Rebâ, were נְסִיכֵי *anointed ones* of Sihon, inhabitants of the land; native princes, who had been invested by the Amorite spoiler of the Emim with his delegated authority over their respective tribes. Now a more satisfactory proof than this could not have been given, short of an express declaration to the effect, that the political jurisdiction of the Emim had extended to the land of Madyan; that the capital of this race, Heshbon, was the central seat of their government; that by establishing himself in their metropolis, Sihon the Amorite became, according to the usage of conquerors, lord over all their dependencies, and they must either serve and obey him as tributaries, or fly; that all the provinces of the Emim were become his provinces; their chiefs, his subordinates; and that Ken and all her cities were among the number.

Thus, whether the Kenites whose habitation was so strong—who had set their nest in the Rock-city, Sela of the wilderness—were usurpers in that city or its founders, the conclusion that they were a branch of the Shethite tribe appears irresistible. Therefore, they were fully entitled to be classed by the Eberite prophet among the people of the Shethite king Balak. And although the half-breed Canaanite and Eberite tribe of Esau, who had supplanted the Horite aborigines of the south-eastern valley, were not of their race, they were settlers among them; had cast their lot upon theirs; had lived under their protection when they were yet but a small tribe; had fought for them, and traded for them, and in course of time had grown rich and great enough among them to share their dominion, and could thus, without impropriety, be included also among the people of whom

Balak was the hereditary chief, seeing how important a branch of the Kenite community they formed.

The Kenite nation, as a whole, prior to the Mosaic period, comprehended a mixture of various races, which may be thus classed according to their districts :—

1st. Ken proper, the northern province, which should perhaps be regarded, ethnographically as well as geographically, as the extreme southern region of the Emim; it lay between the brook Zared (Wady *el Ahsy*), the Wady Mousa, the Wady Arabah, and the Horite settlements. Its chief city was Petra.

2nd. The Horite eastern province, which was gradually absorbed into Edom; this should be regarded ethnographically as the extreme southern region of Aram; being the prolongation of "the land of Uz," "mountains of Aram," or "East-country," down the valley that lay eastward of Mount Seir, as far as Elath.

3rd. The coast-region southward of Elath, the Madyanite province, subsequently absorbed into Midian; the original names of its few cities, and the race of the aboriginal inhabitants, being absolutely unknown.

The southern division of Ken, who thus claimed the cities on the coast, included under the collective name of Midianites, in the history of Moses, not only the Kenite rulers of the land, but also the chief tribes of Abraham's descendants by Keturah, who, with their Ishmaelite brethren, had settled on the desert-confines of their territory, as the Edomites originally settled at Bozrah on the borders of Ken proper. The Abrahamite Midianites formed an independent yet valuable part of the political community, inasmuch as their industry contributed to the wealth of the nation while it also laid the foundation of their own. They carried on all the inland trade, of which Petra was the central emporium.

It is very important to establish this distinction between the two members of the Midianite people. For though they afterwards merged into one, like Sheth and Moab, Ken and Edom, yet, in the time of Moses, they were still very distinct in race, in manners, and in religion. The aboriginal Midianites of Ken are the idolaters referred to in the book of Numbers, as the corrupters of Israel. But the Scenite Midianites descended from Abraham are those referred to in the beginning of Exodus. These were still the faithful worshippers of the one true and eternal God; and Jethro, father-in-law of Moses, was their priest. Like the earlier Edomites, they rather voluntarily lived under the protection of the Kenite rulers, than were subject to them. They neither resided in their cities, nor shared in their

worship. They were nomads, dwelt in tents on the borders of
the inhabited districts of Seir and Paran, and lived entirely on
the produce of their flocks and by trading.

In the infancy of the Ishmaelite tribe, its settlement was in
the desert of Paran. Here, therefore, in the holy mountain of
Sinai, was the first patriarchal church of the desert-tribes, which
in the time of Moses was still the common rendezvous of the
children of Abraham, where they celebrated the annual festivals
of their common ancestral faith. Moses, who had resided among
them nearly forty years, was conversant with their customs, and
knew their haunts and fixed stations; and these annual festivals
are the sacrifices he had purposed that the Israelites should go
forth in the wilderness, to join their Eberite kindred in cele-
brating in their due season.

That the national designation of the ancient race ruling over
Mount Seir was Ken, is proved by the prophet Balaam's giving
them that name:

> " Strong is thine habitation !
> Thou settest thy nest in the rock · · · ·
> Nevertheless—Ken shall be devoured !"

And another circumstance shews that it was also the political designation of the tribes who belonged to the body by
settlement or by amalgamation, and by which they were known
among themselves, though the Israelites called the same body
"Midianites." After the conquest, a family of the true Midianite stock of the nation is found registered as "the children of
the Kenite, Moses's father-in-law," (the Septungint has Jothor
the Kenite.) And more than a century afterwards we find the
husband of the heroine Jael designated as "Heber the Kenite,"
notwithstanding the naturalization of his family in Israel for
several generations. But the Hebrews always call this people
collectively "Edom" or "Midian," as they call the remnant of
the Emim included among the Moabites, "Moab,"—without
distinction. They were naturally more conversant with the engrafted Eberite race, among whom they had spent thirty-eight
years of wandering life, than with the aboriginal stock; which
indeed, in their time, was so nearly absorbed under the increasing numbers and ascendancy of Edom and Moab, as to justify
its being sunk in the historian's general designation of the political community.

Several names referable to the Kenite dominions appear in
the triumphal records of Egypt. The Aramean character of the
people—the similarity of their costume, remarkably unlike that
of the Rephaim—shew them to belong to one land, the Horite

province ruled by Edom. The Egyptian form for their land is
shâr=שעיר (Shâir), which the pointing transforms into Seir.[c]

The land of LT·N is one of the names of most frequent occurrence on Egyptian lists; and the costume of the people, very
like that of the shar·u, is well known. I incline to refer this
name to the celebrated ancient maritime city Elath, or El-Paran.
LT are the radicals of אלה, omitting the vowel equivalent to E
which the Egyptians do not generally express, and the N is only
a final formative letter. It is preserved in the classical form of
the name Æla-na. The land of the LT·N·NU is said to be one
of the northern lands at the "extremity of the great sea;"
which exactly describes Elath at the head of the Red Sea.
There were two regions of LT·N, an "upper" and a "lower"
city; and Elath was a double city, consisting of the ancient
port, on the gulf; and Ezion-gaber, which was a contiguous
fortress, probably defending the mountain-pass.

The first station passed by the Hebrews in going round
Mount Seir from Elath and Eziongaber, is called Zalmonah, in
the Mosaic itinerary (Nu. xxxiii.   ); the next is Punon, which,
from its position in the itinerary, must have been situated near
a narrow pass at the head of the Horite valley, half way between
Elath and Petra; for there is another station between Punon
and the torrent Zared. The name, Punon, agrees singularly
well with the monumental *Poun* or *Pour·t*. The fact that this
city was under the civil jurisdiction of the shet·ta race a hundred years before the time of Moses, is clear from the representation of the siege of that city in the sculptures of the
Ramesseum, as an incident of the war against the shet·ta;
where the name is written on the fortress, poun, without the
feminine suffix. The costume of the people is similar to that
of the shar, lt·n, and rmn·n, but those who defend the city
are shaved, like the shet·ta.

The rmn·n are named on the sculptures of Karnak in conjunction with the lower lt·n, as submitting Seti-Menephtah,
and cutting down trees by way of service-tribute.[e] In the remarks on the Onomasticon, I stated that I saw no objection to
Mr. Osburn's reading that name as Hermon. The people who
lived on the flanks of Hermon were Aramites, and their costume
might therefore resemble that of the old Horites. The distance
between Hermon and Elath, however, does suggest a slight
difficulty; as one may doubt that the people of Elath would
have been sent so far to labour for the king of Egypt, rather
than serve him by their personal tribute in their own country.

---

[c] Rosellini, *Mon. Reali*, pl. xlix.   [e] *Ibid.*, pl. xlvi.

The Edomite city, Rimmon-Parez, one of the unknown stations
of Israel in the first of the thirty-eight years' wandering, is
just as likely to be the tributary ᴚᴀᴍⵝ of Seti-Menephtah, as
the remote Hermon. Being the very next station after Rith-
mah, which, in the itinerary of Nu. xxxvi. 18, corresponds to
the Kadesh-Barnea of the history. Nu. xiii. 26, it cannot have
been very distant from either Kadesh or Elath; and we have
found out several names of desert-stations on the Egyptian lists
to prove that the occupation of these was a special desideratum
with the warlike Theban Pharaohs, to keep open their way to
the inimical lands.

I have not been able to recognize any Egyptian form corresponding to the Kenite metropolis; indeed, its original name
is unknown. The Hebrews call it Sela, "the Rock," which
the Greeks translated Petra. Josephus pretends that its ancient
local name was Arekem,[f] and that Rekem, one of the five kings
of Midian, was its chief, and bore the name of his city. If
this statement has not helped us to finding its Egyptian equivalent, it nevertheless grants two valuable facts: firstly, that
Petra was known in ancient times as having formerly been a
city of the people called Midianites in Scripture; and, moreover,
of the idolatrous or Kenite section of that people: secondly,
that it was not unusual for princes of that land to be known by
their territorial names.

Prior to the decay of the ruling Shethite race, the various
provinces of Ken were governed by the heads of the respective
tribes, forming a sort of commonwealth under the jurisdiction
of the great chief of the Emim nation. This we learn from
the case of the five Midianite princes of Sihon. Although the
Amorite conqueror of the nation had invested them with his
delegated authority, they were not arbitrarily chosen to be rulers
of their respective districts; they were hereditary chiefs of tribes.
One of them, Zur, father of the Midianite woman slain by
Phinehas with the Simeonite chief Zimri, in the sanctuary of
Astarte, is styled "head of a people, of a paternal house."

The Edomite section of the Kenite state was at first governed
in the same way by "leaders," אלֻּפִים, who were also the heads
of tribes. We learn from Gen. xxxvi. that two generations of
Esau's immediate descendants became thus, each individual,
"the head of a paternal house." Two generations of "leaders"
are also given as descended from Seir, a Hivite chief connected
by marriage with Esau, and who joined him in his settlement
near Bozrah. He must have been very nearly Esau's contem-

_____

[f] Josephus, *Ant.*, b. iv., c. 7.

porary in age; for while Esau's third wife, Aholibamah, was his great-granddaughter, his youngest daughter Timnâ was concubine to Eliphaz, Esau's eldest son. This double intermarriage precludes a difference of more than forty years in their ages.

This circumstance is worthy of remark, because it leads to a very valuable historical coincidence in the third generation following the two progenitor-chiefs, Esau and Seir. We find a son of Eliphaz by Timnâ becoming a chief among the ancient nation of Amalek, and consequently assuming their name. We find another son of Eliphaz registered as "leader Kenaz,"—reminding us of the unknown race, "the Kenizzites," associated with the Kenites in the promise to Abraham; and though I cannot assent to the opinion some have advanced, that, in this promise, the land was so named proleptically from this Kenaz yet unborn,—it is very likely that Kenaz himself assumed that name from the tribe of which he became leader, like his brother Amalek. The eldest son of Eliphaz likewise bears a territorial name, Teman, "the south," to indicate the province over which he ruled. And to make the case still stronger, the eldest grandson of the Hivite Seir is called Hori, "the Horite," to shew that he was made ruler over the ancient inhabitants of the land, who were so called; while, as those lands were part of "the land of Uz," we find another of Seir's grandsons assuming the title of Uz.

The singular coincidence of five contemporaneous chiefs of a conquering tribe so obviously bearing five local names, appears to indicate the period of the event referred to by Moses, Deut. ii. 12: "The Horim also dwelt in Seir formerly; but the children of Esau succeeded them, when they had destroyed them from before them, and dwelt in their place; as Israel did unto the land of his possession, which the Lord gave unto them."[9]

This is strongly in favour of the conclusion I have already ventured to anticipate, that the descendants of Esau could not have been sufficiently numerous to conquer the Horim alone; and that the Kenites, near whom they first settled at Bozrah, may have partaken both of the victory and of its fruits. Being the old-established race, and the Edomites the new-comers, the Kenites probably employed the adventurous sons of Esau as mercenaries to enlarge their dominions, and requited their services by appointing them to the honourable post of hereditary local governors over the tribes subdued, and even over some of their own. Such a circumstance was well calculated to lay the foundation of the perfect friendly alliance in which we find the

---

[9] Alluding to the recent conquest of the Transjordanic provinces.

B

Edomites continue to the last in their political relations with the indigenous race of Ken.

By supposing the five Edomite chiefs to average sixty years of age when they achieved this conquest, it would about coincide in time with the birth of Kohath, grandfather of Moses. The event would then synchronize very nearly with the death of Jacob in Egypt; and at all events must have occurred during Joseph's lifetime.

No Edomite leaders are mentioned after this victorious generation. Yet, from the birth of Kenaz, son of Eliphaz, the junior of the five contemporaneous chiefs, to the death of Joseph, there is an interval of about 150 years, and nearly 240 to the Exodus, and 260 to the earliest date at which we can fix the beginning of the Edomite monarchy. We may conclude, that during the 200 years that elapsed between the Edomite conquest and the regal state, the eldest sons of the "leaders," or "heads of a paternal house," succeeded their fathers in due course in the local administration of their respective tribes; all these, like the Kenite chiefs, looking to the great chief of the Shethites as their supreme head in matters of state policy. The children of Eliphaz were set over tribes in the southern district, as the territorial names of his sons indicate; while those of Reuel continued in the original settlement of his father, since we find his descendant called "Zerah of Bozrah."

But when the unity of the Shethite nation was finally broken up, by the central seat of its government falling a prey to the Amorite invader Sihon,—when its hereditary sovereign had been degraded to the inferior rank of a mere local ruler among the Moabites, and the native chiefs of the Kenite province were compelled to hold their authority under their conqueror,—the Edomites, in order to remain independent of the usurper, placed a king of their own race at the head of their tribes. The Eberite race now rallied round the new power, and the Edomites became the centre of a powerful federal state, taking the lead among their kindred in political affairs, and maintaining it by the successive election of eight sovereigns. These chiefs were chosen out of the different tribes and cities of the Eberite people; not exclusively from among the children of Esau. This measure greatly extended and consolidated their power by connecting all the tribes. The first of these kings, "Bela, the son of Beor," may have begun to reign about twenty years after the Exodus. The last, Hadad, the son of Bedad, "reigned before there was any king in Israel,"—probably a little before the election of Saul, under whose successor, David, the Edomites were brought under subjection to Israel.

Meanwhile, the destruction and dissolution of the parent Shethite race had brought the Kenite branch to so low and secondary a position before the flourishing and increasing race of Edom, as to be no longer regarded as a separate nation. Already as early as the close of Moses' career we find them sunk by name among the Midianites. We hear of them no more until Saul's attack on the Amalekites, which reveals to us a small isolated remnant of this ancient race still abiding in the land, keeping aloof from the Eberite race and its government, cleaving to their own kindred, and dwelling in the cities of Amalek. It was reserved for David, the Star descended from the patriarch Jacob, the Sceptre ruling over the mixed community of Israel,—to wound the power of those claiming descent from the patriarch Moab, and to crush for ever the last residue of the Shethite community, to whose evil influence the turbulence and disaffection of Moab and Edom were mainly due. Moab became tributary to David (2 Sa. viii. 2). The Edomite monarchy was overturned, Israelite garrisons were placed in its strong cities, and " Seir became the domain of his foe." (2 Sa. viii. 13, 14).

Thus was the prediction of Balaam accomplished, and the promise vouchsafed to Abraham fulfilled. The limits of the kingdom of Israel at last included all the lands of the Rephaim, and of their Aramean and Eberite tributaries, from Carchemish and Damascus, to Elath and the frontier of Pelesheth; and the dominion of Abraham's descendant, Solomon, extended "from the river of Mizraim to the great river, the river Euphrates."

CHAPTER XII.

The Amalekites.

The Amalekite branch of Balak's people occupied the labyrinthine strongholds of the great Sinaïtic desert. By this we may judge how effectually their detached communities which dotted the few green spots scattered over this inhospitable peninsula, placed the land of Egypt within the power of their allies; while conversely, they were a barrier of protection to their kindred against Egypt; since no army from that land could cross their ground without their good will.

We must not measure the power and prosperity of the ancient Amalek by the miserable condition of the wandering Arab tribes now dwelling in the desert. That land yields little to an isolated people depending on its produce for subsistence. But the Amalekites of old were an outlying branch of a nation who owned the richest and most fertile regions of Palestine. Placed on the frontier as the sentinels of the whole nation, and in constant communication with them, the Amalekites could want for nothing which their brethren were not able to supply, in return for the protection their desert-stations afforded, both to their military and commercial enterprise.

But as the parent nation sank, the Amalekite branch declined. As their power failed by the dispersion of their kindred in Palestine, they became jealous and suspicious; and in this frame of mind wantonly attacked the Israelites as they were passing through the Amalekite settlement of Rephidim, to rejoin their Midianite brethren in faith. The Hebrews never forgave this act of aggression. For Moses, in Deut. xxv. 17—19, solemnly records the injury, and the injunction to avenge it: "Remember what Amalek did unto thee on the way, when ye came forth from Egypt; how he encountered thee on the way and smote in thy rear all the feeble behind thee, when thou wast faint and weary; and he feared not God. Therefore, it shall be when the Lord thy God hath given thee rest from all thine enemies around thee, in the land the Lord thy God giveth thee to possess as an inheritance, that thou shalt blot out the remembrance of Amalek from under heaven. Forget it not!"

During the period of the Judges, when the Amalekites appear as open enemies of Israel, it is always in alliance with the children of Ammon, who act as partisans of the ancient Rephaim, or with the Philistines, partisans of their outcast Anakim kindred. The group of foes is further swelled by the children of the East, and the Moabite, Ishmaelite, and Midianite allies of the dispossessed Shittim, whose cause they espouse. It seemed therefore a political measure necessary to the peace of Israel, that such dangerous neighbours as the fierce and reckless race of Amalek should be subdued at a blow. Samuel accordingly urged Saul to attack them on the ground of the old national grudge. The distinction made between the Amalekites and the remnant of their Kenite kindred, on that occasion, is interesting to record: the latter, who had allowed the homeless Hebrew wanderers to dwell on their borders thirty-eight years unmolested, were specially exempted from the destruction prepared for their brethren. "Saul said to the Kenites, Go, depart; get you down from among the Amalekites, lest I destroy you with them; for ye shewed kindness to all the children of Israel when they came forth from Egypt. So the Kenites departed from among the Amalekites. And Saul smote the Amalekites, from Havilah until thou comest to Shur which is before Egypt. He took Agag the king of Amalek alive, and utterly destroyed all the people with the edge of the sword." (1 Sam. xv. 6—8.)

Notwithstanding the friendly countenance of their Eberite territorial successors, the great bond of unity in action, constituting the power of the Rapha nations, had been irrecoverably broken by the dispersion of the ancient race ; and their power to help each other was likewise broken. The Amalekites, bereft of the support from without formerly derived from their wealthier brethren, and cast for supplies on the scanty resources of their desert-home, had dwindled away to the obscure position of an isolated nomadic troop. The miserable remnant that escaped the destructive onset of Saul, are mentioned as having fled to Mount Seir, where they were exterminated by a band of Simeonites, in the time of Hezekiah.

After this, we should not know from history that an individual of the race remained, were it not for the curious account of the Arabians of Jenysus given by Herodotus; in whose customs, worship, and costume, we are compelled to recognize an isolated troop of this most ancient race, too few to be called a nation ; whose only security, in their desert-home, was the poverty of the land, the barrenness of its impracticable passes, that other nations made a highway for their own enterprise and wealth, But even while we suspect the existence of this small degraded remnant as yet extant in the time of Cambyses, their name is lost : it is sunk in the general denomination of " Arabians,"—the " mixed people."

Thus effectually was the remembrance of Amalek blotted out from under heaven ! Thus did this once powerful tribe— " the first of the nations " originally inhabiting that land— perish for ever under the hand of Israel, even as the Ammonite prophet had foretold.

F. C.

THE REPHAIM, AND THEIR CONNEXION WITH EGYPTIAN HISTORY.[a]

CHAPTER XIII.

The Anakim.

" HEAR, O Israel ! Thou art to pass over Jordan, this day, to enter and take possession of nations greater and mightier than thyself; cities great and fenced up to the skies; a great and haughty people, the children of the Anakim, whom thou knowest,—for thou hast heard: Who can stand before the children of Anak !" (Deut. ix. 1, 2.)

In such a strain of poetic energy does the sacred historian refer to this once mighty nation, that he may awaken in the breasts of his countrymen a noble spirit of emulation. Not less powerful is the impression of their formidable appearance, produced by the report of the Hebrew spies, though the tone of the speakers now sinks to the level of a terror-stricken populace: " The people who dwell in that land are strong, and the cities are fortified and exceedingly great. . . That land is a land that consumeth its inhabitants; and all the people whom we saw there are men of great stature ! And we have also seen *the nephilim* (*expelled* or *refugees*[b])—the children of Anak (who come) of *the nephilim*,—and we were in our own eyes as grasshoppers, and so were we in their eyes !" (Nu. xiii. 32, 33.)

The report of those who explored the land, in the same chapter, conveys a glowing description of its fertility. " They came to the vale of Eschol, and cut down from thence a branch with one cluster of grapes, and bare it between two (men) on a staff; also of the pomegranates and the figs. . . . and said : We came into the land whither thou sentest us, and surely it floweth with milk and honey, and this is its fruit." (verses 23—27.)

The accounts of modern travellers are quite in harmony with this statement. Dr. E. Robinson[c] describes the country about Hebron as covered with fields of wheat; and the mountain slopes, as clothed with olive groves. The vicinity of Nezib, on the western side of the mountain, is also highly commended as " a rich and fertile region, which once teemed with an abun-

---

[a] Continued from the April Number of the *J. S. L.*

[b] נְפִילִם The interpretation of this obscure term by *refugees* or *expelled* will be found in the next chapter on *The Philistines.*

[c] *Biblical Researches,* vol. iii., pp. 11, 19.

dant population, as is shewn by the numerous former sites now in ruins and level with the ground."

It thus appears that the Rephaim of southern Palestine had early established themselves in the choicest part of the country; and took care to protect their possessions by dwelling in strongly fortified cities, which occupied the most commanding positions. The high antiquity of their settlement may be gathered from the incidental notice of Moses, that Hebron, the city of Arbâ, where Abraham lived, died, and is buried, "was built seven years before Zoan"—the capital of the Delta, and one of the most ancient cities in Lower Egypt. (Nu. xiii. 22.)

The claim of the Anakim to be classed among the Rephaim nations is indisputable. They are distinctly referred to that stock by Moses, in his reference to their Emim kindred, in Deut. ii. 11: "A great, numerous, and haughty people, like the Anakim; who were also accounted Rephaim, like the Anakim." And since the evidence that the Rephaim nations beyond Jordan were not Canaanites is so positive, the fact thereby established necessarily proves that the Anakim, being Rephaim by origin, could not have been Canaanites either.

Nevertheless, the ethnographical position of the Anakim has often been misconceived, like that of the Rephaim of Bashan, and much on the same grounds. It will, therefore, be necessary to the complete rectification of this error, that we should enter into a more critical examination of its origin; and that, at the same time, we should define, as clearly as the indirect intimations afforded by Scripture will justify it, the relative positions of the Anakim and the Canaanites. Numerous enough are the hints and casual allusions disseminated throughout the early Bible history, relating to this ancient people, and from which a general idea of their political extension and condition may be arrived at. The ordinary reader, with his mind bent on the progress of Israel which forms the immediate subject of the Bible records, and who merely walks over the beaten ground of this surface-history, is very liable to disregard the substratum of collateral history he now and then lights upon in his course; a substratum fraught with the relics of a primeval social world, cropping out from below in isolated patches, and telling a tale full of meaning to the curious investigator who may be patient enough to explore them, and to hunt up the traces of their continuity.

Hebron, or Kiriath-Arbâ, chief city of the Anakim, is sometimes alluded to in the Bible history as being in the land of Canaan. Whether the insulated position of the Anakim cities among the Amorite children of Heth is a fact sufficient by itself to explain such references as a mere geographical generalization, or whether, in the origin, the whole of the land occupied by the Anakim really had been Canaanite territory, of which the Rephaim had obtained possession, and which they retained by their superior power and political discipline, constitutes a separate question which we will also examine, but which does not affect the one now under consideration; as in neither of these two cases would the *geographical* statement, that Hebron is in the land of Canaan, necessarily draw after it the very illogical *ethnographical* consequence, that, because *some* Canaanites dwelt about Hebron, *all* the people of Hebron—even those who were masters of the city—were Canaanites.

The children of Anak and the Amorites were evidently coresidents in southern Judea. The Amorites not only had many towns of their own on the western sides of the mountain, but they also appear to have formed no inconsiderable part of the population in the cities on the eastern side, which the Anakim held. Each of these Amorite dependent communities had its local chieftain, or *melek,*—a title generally translated *king.* There is no reason to believe that these chiefs were on a different footing among their older Anakim rulers, than we see their descendants under their subsequent Hebrew rulers. In the time of the Judges, we find "Hamor, the father of Shechem," retaining his hereditary title and sovereignty over his own clan; and the Shechemites are even divided in their inclination whether to serve him or the judge of the dominant Hebrew race (Jud. ix. 28). Later still, when the Canaanites "paid tribute of bond-service to Solomon," we find "the kings of the Hittites," as well as those of the Aramites, engaged as the Jewish sovereign's merchants to bring chariots of valuables out of Egypt. (Comp. 1 Kings viii. 20, 21; and x. 28, 29.) And yet later, we find them alluded to as liable to be hired as mercenaries against Aram by the Israelite king. (2 Kings vii. 6.) The part taken by the Amorites, in the wars of the Emim, the Anakim, and the Philistines against Egypt, also presents them in the same subordinate position; while the statement of Scripture history bears out the same conclusion by expressly representing the Philistines as rulers over five chief Canaanite cities. In the contest between the Israelites and the Philistines which follows the conquest, it is equally apparent that, although the Amorites of western Judea are the standing population, the Philistines are masters of every important post in the land; and when Samuel had subdued the Philistines, and recovered the line of frontier from Ekron to Gath, the account winds up with "there was peace between Israel and the Amorites," although

the Amorites had not been heard of whilst the struggle was
raging; which even leaves it doubtful whether they had borne
any part at all in it, while the Philistines were contending with
Israel for lordship over the western Amorite territory,—or
whether they had fought for and under the Philistines, and
without them had not even power of peace and war on their
own soil. From these indications, we may gather that, whether
as aborigines overpowered by a stronger people, like the Amorites of Pelesheth, or whether as tolerated settlers, like the
Amorites of Shittim, their political *status* was altogether subordinate. The *kings*, or heads of tribes, appear to have enjoyed
a considerable amount of local authority over their clans, and
of civil independence in the management of their internal concerns; but subject to a certain degree of political dependance
on the far more powerful race who garrisoned the chief citadels
in their land.

There is no direct intimation of their having paid tribute of
personal service or of property; but as this was usually exacted
by the overruling power, according to the law of nations of
those times, it is exceedingly probable that they did, since they
are found under such a tribute to their subsequent Israelite
subjugators.

Such being the relative positions of two people who have
been so strangely confounded with each other—the Amorites
and the Rephaim,—we shall be able to reconcile with ease certain accounts in the book of Joshua, which would have presented
insuperable difficulties, had these people been the same.

The local chiefs of the Amorites residing about Hebron and
Debir, are counted among the five Amorite kings who combined
against the Gibeonites in Joshua's first campaign. On this occasion, Joshua not only routed their forces and slew their chiefs,
but he also smote, destroyed, and burnt Hebron and her cities,
and Debir and her cities. And yet, six years after, when the
Canaanites of the north have been subdued, and the land is
portioned out among the Israelite tribes, we find that Hebron
or Kiriath-Arbâ, and Debir or Kiriath-Sepher, were still standing; and that the children of Anak, Sheshai, Ahiman, and
Talmai, held these cities; that Caleb himself, as soon as he had
been formally invested with his territorial rights, commanded
the special expedition by which Arbâ, in the portion of his inheritance, was taken; and that his nephew, Othniel, performed
the no less formidable feat of dislodging the Anakim from
Kiriath-Sepher, and capturing their city, for which he was re-
warded with the hand of Caleb's daughter.

It is very apparent that the Amorite quarters of these cities,

the suburban dwellings of a vast dependant population, enclosed
by the outer wall, were alone destroyed in the rapid attack of
Joshua's victorious host in his opening campaign ; but that the
strongly fortified primitive citadels, garrisoned by the children of
Anak, were not included in this destruction.[d] The expulsion of
the Anakim and capture of their fortresses are totally different
transactions, both in point of time and in point of fact. Indeed
the order of the narrative of Joshua (chapters. x., xi.) implies as
much. It relates three distinct sets of events : Firstly, the
campaign against the Amorite league ; in which he swept round
the mountain of Judah, returning by Hebron through the
vale of Eshcol to Gilgal. Secondly, the campaign against the
northern Canaanite combination. "Joshua made war a long
time with all those kings." (xi. 18.) Finally, the general statement of special expeditions against the Anakim. "At that
time came Joshua, and cut off the Anakim from the mountains,
from Hebron, from Debir, and from Anab ; from all the mountains of Judah, and from all the mountains of Israel : Joshua
destroyed them utterly with their cities. There were none of
the Anakim left in all the land of the children of Israel ; only
in Gaza, Gath, and Ashdod, some remained." So Joshua took
the whole land, according to all that the Lord said unto Moses,
and Joshua gave it for an inheritance unto Israel, according to
their divisions by tribes. And the land had rest from war."
(Josh. xi. 21—23.)

After this summary statement, the filling up of its detail
is given in the succeeding chapters. Thus the enumeration of
tribes and kings subdued is an amplification of the summary
of ch. xi. 18 ; and the episode of Caleb, at the allotment of
the lands then subdued (ch. xiv.), is an amplification of the
summary of ch. xi. 21—23, whereby we discover proof positive
that the expeditions against the Anakim were not only posterior to the first campaign, when Hebron and Debir were said
to be taken and destroyed, but were even posterior to the allotment of the lands related in that chapter. Otherwise, in the
first place, if the Amorites and the Anakim were the same
people, and the events identical, how could Caleb and Othniel
have taken their cities of Arbâ and Sepher, since they would
have been utterly destroyed six years before ? And in the next
place, how could the Anakim still have occupied those cities
with a sufficient force to call for a regular siege and a special
expedition to dislodge them, if, *before* the allotment, Joshua

---

[d] Vide Jud. ix. 50, 51, for a parallel case. Abimelech first besieges and *takes*
the town of Thebez ; and afterwards attacks the central fortress.

had already expelled *all* the Anakim from Hebron, Debir, Anab, and all their other cities,—and there were *none left in the land*, except at Gaza, Gath, and Ashdod?

The inference to which these circumstances point is manifestly this :—that the Amorite towns and communities of Hebron and Debir, ravaged by Joshua in the first year of the Canaanite war, must not be confounded with the children of Anak and the "cities great and fenced up to the skies" of Arbâ and Sepher, in which they had for a while securely entrenched themselves. That they were in some sense distinct places—the outer town, and the fortified central citadel,—and that their relative occupants were two distinct people, is the only reasonable explanation of the difficulty presented by the collation of the two accounts. This explanation arises quite naturally out of the ascertained political relation of the inhabitants, and completely dismisses the supposition that the Anakim in any way belonged to the Canaanite stock.

The prophetic denunciation of the ancient seer, that "Canaan should be servant of servants to *his own brethren," first*, had long been working out its fulfilment, when Israel entered the land to accomplish the second stage of the prophecy, by striking at one blow the degraded Canaan a willing servant at the feet of Shem. They had so long held the secondary place, that they were used to the yoke. One effort was made to repel the invader; one hasty, ill-organized combination was attempted. It proved unsuccessful; they yielded to a change of masters, and never sought to cast them off again. Not so the Rephaim; they were of another blood—of another spirit. We have seen two sections of this intrepid race decimated and annihilated, but never yielding a permanent submission to the conqueror. The popular saying so well known to Israel,—"Thou hast heard, *Who can stand before the children of Anak !"*—could not have thus passed into a proverb without a cause. Caleb knew, when he received a nominal authority over the land allotted to his tribe, that although the Amorites of his district were ready to bend and serve, the other haughty race that held its ground in the fortresses, was not. He knew that he could only secure the permanent possession of his inheritance by capturing the strongholds in which the Anakim had entrenched their forces. Otherwise, his posterity must only look forward to dwelling on the same terms as the Amorites had done before them. If weaker, they would be treated as dependants. If strong enough to be esteemed rivals, they would be regarded as allies or as foes, according to the caprice of the Anakim rulers. The nation that could not be subdued must be expelled from the land. When the Canaanite population had been brought under control, special expeditions were framed against the Anakim, under the direction of Joshua; those in which Caleb and Othniel took a prominent part on their own behalf, among the number. By such means, the land was finally cleared of those dangerous rivals.

The subordinate position of the Canaanites to the Rephaim being thus made out, the collateral question,—which race had a prior claim to the land they jointly occupied?—becomes a point of secondary consequence. The indirect evidence of Scripture is divided on both sides of this question. In such a case, a candid historian is bound simply to state the matter as he finds it; and not to give his own prepossessions as a judgment, but to leave the reader to form his own decision from what evidence is producible.

On behalf of the original Canaanite claims upon central Judea, it may be urged that this region is tacitly included within the geographical definition of the primitive and lawful boundary assigned by Moses to the Canaanite race. If, in this definition, the southern boundary is left undescribed, it may be because the line of desert between Sodom and Gaza formed a natural limit easily understood. But it may be also because the Anakim settlements lay along the mountains that form the backbone of the country; so that those of the Canaanites, as far as they extended in the time of Moses, could only have been described by the two lines he draws: a western line along the sea to Gaza; an eastern line along the banks of the Jordan, from its sources at Lesha or Dan, to its final receptacle, the Dead Sea. Nevertheless, it must be admitted that every geographically descriptive reference to Hebron, in Scripture, is coupled with the idea that the land in which that city lay is "accounted to the Canaanite."

This fact leaves it very probable that the cities of the Rephaim alluded to in Scripture as "strongly fortified and fenced up to the skies," were only a line of military outposts, in which they stationed the garrisons that maintained their mastery over the country, and kept up a line of communication with Lower Egypt more direct than the tedious and circuitous route by the Wady Arabah and the Sinaïtic desert. It may be that the Canaanite tribes formed the original population of this central mountain tract,—a pastoral, industrious, unambitious people; who had yielded themselves, while they were as yet few in numbers, to the superior power and discipline of the kindred Hamite race that erected its fortresses and planted its dominion along the heart of their land. It may be that the Anakim thus lorded it over the aboriginal population, as the Philistine branch of the same nation subsequently spread its power over the western district, which is also "accounted to the Canaanite."

But on the other hand, it is equally probable that the two national settlements were coeval; that by the time the junior Canaanites families had spread themselves abroad so far as to reach their utmost southward limits, the Rephaim had already laid the foundation of their supremacy by building their walled cities in the strongest positions among the mountains, leaving the Canaanites to constitute the standing population of the land, but only as suburbans under their control, though they claimed no territorial right in the land, as a paternal inheritance, beyond the immediate circuit of their cities.

We have not even any direct scriptural authority for defining the utmost northward limits of the territory thus occupied by the children of Anak. The most ancient records of the human race only hint at their end;—so utterly lost is their beginning in the gloom of a recordless primeval antiquity. The account of their expulsion merely intimates that they were cut off from their strongholds, in "all the mountains of Judah" and "all the mountains of Israel." But this certainly entitles us to believe that, up to the time of Joshua, they still had possessions beyond the lot of Judah, although the three cities of Hebron, Anab, and Debir are the only ones mentioned by name as belonging to them.

There is, however, definite authority for tracing them as far north as Bethel, under circumstances that even rather appear to tell in favour of their priority of settlement. When Abraham first crossed the Jordan, and arrived near "the place of Shechem," it is remarked that "the Canaanite was then in the land;" as though the presence of Canaanites in that neighbourhood was something new (Gen. xii. 6). Moreover the peculiar locution, "*the place* of Shechem," and the fact, that this place was actually a *grove* at the time—"the grove of Moreh,"—would suggest that the city was not yet built. When Abraham returned to his first resting place, which he called Bethel, after his journey to Egypt, he found the Canaanite and the Perizzite then dwelling (or settled) in that land (Gen. xiii. 3—7). These parenthetical remarks look very much as if the Hivites and Perizzites were at that time quite new-comers in the vicinity of Bethel and Mount Ephraim.

Five centuries afterwards, we find the Ephraimites of the Bethel district complaining to Joshua[d] that their land was in-

___

[d] Josh. xvii. 14, 15. In this passage, as in the next quoted, Josh. xv. 8, the geographical and historical value of these notices is disguised in the common version

sufficient to sustain their population ; and he recommends them to go down to the forest-country in the land of the Perizzites and of the Rephaim, and clear the ground for themselves, if Mount Ephraim be too narrow for them. Here is very direct scriptural evidence that a part of the country about Bethel had been known of old as "the land of the Rephaim," and still retained its name, although, when this was spoken, the Hivites had not only extended their settlements considerably southward of Shechem, even to Gibeon, but were also in possession of the city of forests, — "Kiriath-Ieârim," in the above-mentioned "forest country;" and of Chephirah, a little to the north of Jerusalem ; while the Jebusite tribe were in actual possession of the metropolis, Shalem, which they had called Jebus (Josh. xv. 8, 63.) This city was thus in the very heart of the land of the Rephaim. The valley which leads to it from the south-west, and terminates in the valley of Jehosaphat, almost in sight of the ancient citadel, is always called in Scripture "the valley of the Rephaim." All these circumstances tend to point out the deep-rooted claim of this people to the land. Indeed, no stronger proof of this can be given, than its being called by their name.

It is a very remarkable circumstance, that Jebus, which in the days of Abraham was called Shalem, is only found bearing a new name—that of a Canaanite tribe—in the time of Joshua. Such a change of name did not always follow upon a conquest ; but wherever it does occur, it invariably marks a change of proprietors. The Israelites also occasionally conformed to this usage. The children of Reuben, we are told, rebuilt Heshbon, Elealeh, etc., etc., their names being changed, and gave (other) names[e] to the cities which they built : ". . . and Nobah went and took Kenath and its villages, and called it Nobah after his own name." (Nu. xxxii. 37—42.) The Danites also, when they took Laish, called it by the name of Dan their father (Judges xviii. 27, 28.) Bethel itself was a name given by the Hebrew settlers to a city formerly called Luz (Judges i. 23). The recent alteration in the ancient name of Shalem is thus as strong an indication of its having passed over to the power of the Jebusite children of Heth, as its geographical position, in the very middle

---

by the conventional mistranslation of "Rephaim" by "*giants*." In 2 Sa. v. 18, 22; and xxiii. 13 ; 1 Chron. xiv. 9; and Isa. xvii. 5, it is rendered rightly as a proper local name.

  [e] These names are unknown. When the Moabites recovered the lands taken from their territorial predecessors by the Amorites, and from these by the Israelites, many of the original names were restored : that of the capital, Heshbon, certainly must be more ancient than the Israelite conquest, since it is mentioned upwards of a century before, in the fifth year of Rameses II.

of the line along which the domains of the Rephaim are traceable, is, *per se*, strong evidence that the metropolis of Palestine originally claimed them as its masters.

The few fragments of Manetho's history which have been handed down to us by his copists—though in so garbled a form, through their own preconceived misapprehensions of his statements, as to look more like fable than the valuable historical truths they really are,—these mutilated fragments contain references which, by implication, leave no doubt upon the matter—that Shalem was once the great metropolis of the shepherd-kings. In relating the expulsion of the Hyksos by Amosis, Manetho says that they marched into the country now called Judea, where they built a city large enough to contain so great a multitude, and called it Jerusalem./ He afterwards represents the shepherds of Goshen, who revolted from Amenophis (Menephtah, son of Rameses II.), as sending an embassy to that city for assistance, as though it were well known as the head-quarters of the government. The anachronism of confounding the return of the expelled shepherd rulers to their own metropolis, with its original foundation, may be excused in the Egyptian historian who wrote nearly fifteen centuries after the event, with nothing to guide him as to the personal history of the inimical nations but remote and imperfect traditions. The actual existence of Shalem at the time of Abraham's victory, more than a century *before* the expulsion of the shepherds from Lower Egypt, is sufficient proof that, in this respect, Manetho was mistaken. Nevertheless, the error itself virtually implies that the city was known as having belonged to that people. This indeed, among other circumstances, may have misled Josephus into confounding the exode of the shepherds in the reign of Amosis, at the beginning of the eighteenth dynasty, with that of his own people during the reign of Menephtah, near the close of the nineteenth. It may also have beguiled him into his clumsy attempt at identifying the principal actors in great political revolutions of Egypt, with his own forefathers, whose part in them, as far as we can gather from what he quotes *verbatim* from Manetho, amounted to nothing more than an unsuccessful endeavour to free themselves from an unjustifiable bondage, by joining the oppressed captive race of Lower Egypt who revolted against Menephtah. For it appears that ever since the accession of the nineteenth dynasty, when the wars with the people of Palestine broke out again under Seti-Menephtah I., the Hebrew nation had been involved in the servitude to which the indigenous

/ Josephus, *Contra Apionem*, l. i., c. 14.

tribes of Goshen were subjected as a conquered people, in common with the remnant of their Hyksos abettors.

Another remarkable instance of evidence by implication, that the great metropolis of the Shepherd race of Palestine was situated in their province of Anak, is found in Manetho's dynastic lists. He calls the fifteenth dynasty of "foreign kings who also took Memphis," *Phœnicians*. I shall have to instance other confirmations besides the present case of Bochart's important suggestion, that the Greek form Φοινικες is derived from the Hebrew ענק, ôNK—read according to the primary value of the letters without the points—and with p (the Egyptian article) prefixed : Φ-οινικ-ες is exactly equivalent, verbally and grammatically, to הענקים *the Onkites*, or Anakim. For the present, we may safely admit the resemblance of *form*, and the consequent etymological inference, that, from the extensive influence this powerful nation obtained over the whole *land* of Palestine, its *people* collectively became known to subsequent generations as the Onkites or Phœnicians, without distinction of race; and then, by a further extension of the same idea, the name of Phœnicia became the Greek equivalent of Canaan, or—to speak more correctly—a conventional geographical substitute for the Hebrew patronymic.

Now although Manetho calls these six kings of the fifteenth dynasty *Phœnicians*, as coming from the land of ôNK or Anak, because their chief royal city was Shalem in the province of Anak, it is nevertheless manifest, by his historical narrative, that they were of the *Royal* Shepherds—Hyksos—or chief tribe of the Zuzim, whose particular province was Bashan ; for the names of these kings in the lists, and duration of their reigns, substantially correspond to the names quoted in the detailed account extracted by Josephus from his history, of the wonderful manner in which they gained a footing in Lower Egypt, without fighting ; the ready submission of the population, and their final election of a king from among their race, who established his court at Memphis. All this implies, as clearly as historical records can speak, that the sovereign chiefs of the elder Shepherd state—that of the Zuzim, who were regarded by the other tribes as the political and military head of their national confederacy, and who took the lead in the conquest of Egypt—had fixed the seat of their government in the most central point of their extensive domains, which was Shalem in the province of Anak.

The part taken by the king of Shalem, when the allied Asiatic kings who had invaded the Rephaim were suddenly discomfited by Abraham's well-directed expedition, is another instance pointing to the same conclusion. For had this king-priest been no greater a personage than the local chief of the particular tribe of Rephaim called Anakim, there are no suffi-cient grounds apparent in the historical account of the transac-tion in Gen. xiv., why he should be presented with a tenth of the spoils which the enemy had taken from another tribe of Rephaim called Emim, and which Abraham had rescued and restored to them; neither can we satisfactorily make out why the king of Shalem should receive this tenth so evidently as a right conceded by the Emim chief of Sodom. But the moment the important fact comes in by way of explanation, supported by sufficient extrinsic evidence, that the king of Shalem was the supreme chief of the entire nation, and the local chiefs of tribes were his subordinates, the whole transaction becomes perfectly intelligible, because we understand the mutual relation of all the parties concerned in it. As feudal lord of the land in which Abraham had settled, Abraham paid him this tribute. As head of the national body to which the Emim belonged, the chief of the Emim sanctioned it. As head of the state in religious as well as in temporal concerns, according to the primitive pa-triarchal order, Melchizedek received the tribute, both as a votive offering of gratitude from the givers for the rescue of the goods, and as an acknowledgment of his lordship over the goods rescued.

Besides these numerous tokens that Shalem was the metro-polis of the whole nation, and not of the children of Anak only, we have a direct intimation to the same effect in some occasional references to Hebron, which indicate that city as the metropolis of the Anakim. For instance (Josh. xiv. 15) : "The name of Hebron, formerly, was the city of Arbâ, he who is the great man of the Anakim;"[9] a primitive and very expressive equiva-lent for the chieftain of the tribe. It further appears that this dignitary bore the name of his city as a title of supremacy; for we have again, in Josh. xv. 13, "The city of Arbâ the father of the Anakite, this is Hebron." The primeval city, or rather citadel, seems to have been the true city of Arbâ, the original foundation; and the local name, Hebron, (the *confederacy*) may have been subsequently given to the collective group of this citadel and its Amorite suburb—all that was included within the outer wall. Both names, however, are more ancient than

---

9 הָאָדָם הַגָּדוֹל בָּעֲנָקִים הוּא. "The great man among the Anakim is he." The common translation (*which Arba*) *was a* great man among the Anakim, is a misin-terpretation ; "*which Arba*" is not in the text ; the emphatic pronoun of actual existence, הוּא *he is*, cannot be rendered by a past tense, and the definite article ה pre-cedes הָאָדָם *the* man.

the Israelite establishment, since both are found on Egyptian monuments a century older than the conquest, under the corresponding forms RBO and CHERBU or CHEBRU, denoting the same locality and people. The *proprietary* name, "the city of Arbâ," was dropped when the Anakim lost the dominion over the place; but the *local* name, Hebron, was retained.

It is a striking peculiarity that the recurrence, both of local names as names of persons who were chiefs of the places, and of the title "father" of the place, is very frequent indeed in the genealogies of the tribes of Judah and Benjamin who succeeded the Rephaim in a land where such local names and titles had been a matter of long-established custom; whereas there is not a single instance of these peculiarities in the genealogical lists of the other tribes.[h]

There is monumental evidence that Shalem still bore its original name in the time of Rameses III., up to the fifth year of his reign, when the submission of SHALĂM'U'NA and of several Philistine cities are recorded as among his greatest triumphs. From this, we gather that the encroachments of the Hivites and Jebusites on the northern quarters of the Anakim, were very recent in the days of Joshua. The same might be inferred from the ease with which the Israelite host were able to rout the confederate Canaanite communities; shewing how little their power in the land was consolidated.

We shall be better prepared to trace the progress of Rameses III., and his conquests in the land of the Rephaim, when we have gone through the next section of this history, relating to the Philistines, who occupy a conspicuous, though not very honourable position, in the monumental memorials of the last Egyptian war against the Rephaim. In the present, we will limit ourselves to establishing the identity of the few local names referable to the land of Anak which the historical inscriptions afford; and this, at the same time, will bring the history of the Anakim up to the period of Rameses III., and of the final catastrophe of the nation.

Some among the grounds of local and verbal correspondence on which I was led to infer the identity of the formidable RBO people who appear so conspicuously in the sculptures of Medinet-Abou, with the Anakim of Kiriath-Arbâ, have been already stated. The geographical proximity of the Anakim and Philistines is one among many corroborative proofs of this identity;

h Refer to the following passages:—1 Chron. ii. 24, 42, 44, 45, 49—51; iv. 3—5, 11, 12, 14, 17, 18. In the Benjamite district:—1 Chron. viii. 29; ix. 35. Among these are numerous instances of individuals assuming territorial names.

for the appearance of both these people on the same monuments, under the names of PULSA·TA and RBO, as engaged in the same wars, whether for or against Egypt, proves at least that they must have been near neighbours.

The earliest mention of the metropolis of Anak on monuments, occurs in the time of Rameses II., in the expedition against the Shethite Rephaim already referred to, when we meet with its local name, CHERBU=Hebron, in the explanatory inscriptions; RBO=Arbâ, also occurs in the legend affixed to the body of the chief drowned before ATESH, as a prefix to his proper name. The captives of this people are distinctly recognizable by their remarkable costume.

The name of another city of the Anakim, called TAHI, and sometimes TAH·N or TAH·N·NU, appears on the monuments at a much earlier period, and more frequently, than the former. Its radical Egyptian form, TAHI, exactly corresponds to the radical Hebrew form יטה ITAH, which, with the points, is read Iuttah. The site is still extant by name in *Yuttâ*, a village about seven miles south of Hebron, on the border of the desert of Judea. Iuttah was one of the Levitical cities.

The costume of the TAH·N·NU people is already a strong proof that this was their fortress; for even if we had not found a site near RBO, corresponding to their name, the resemblance of their costume to that of the RBO people would have sufficed to point them out as a tribe of Anakim.

But there is another remarkable circumstance which, if it would be of little value by itself, cannot be overlooked when added to this double correspondence of locality and costume. I have already had occasion to notice how the two synonyms of the same city, Arbâ and Hebron, are rendered into Greek by the Alexandrian translators of the Bible in a manner more closely resembling the Egyptian versions of those names, than the pronunciation assigned to them by the modern *pointed* Hebrew text; viz., RBO, ארבע 'Αρβοκ; and CHEBRU חברון Χεβρων. In the first name, they render the true primary vocal power of the final guttural ע; in the second, they, like the Egyptian, give a strong aspirated guttural power to the initial ח.[i]

Now in the Septuagint version of יטה Itah (Iuttah), the result of a similar comparison is still more remarkable. They seem to have purposely gone out of the way of the Hebrew

---

[i] In another name, Heshbon חשבון—where the same letter has only a vowel power, with a very slight aspiration absorbed by the next radical, and the Egyptian SHEB·T·UN does not express it; the Septuagint likewise disregard it, and have not even given the sign of aspiration to the initial, 'Εσεβων. Ptolemy the same,—in his form, 'Εσβουτα.

radical form, *by making additions to it,* in so pointed a manner
as to suggest a suspicion that, up to their time, popular tradition,
in Egypt, might yet have handed down a remembrance of the
true situation of the lands once tenanted by her enemies, and
that they availed themselves of the knowledge. For Iuttah is
only mentioned twice in the Bible; in the first instance that
occurs, the list of Judean cities, Josh. xv. 55, they render it
'Ἰτὰν, like the Egyptian composite form TAH'N; and in the
second instance, the list of Levitical cities (Josh. xxi. 16), they
imitate the *peculiarly* idiomatic Egyptian form TAH'N'NU, by
rendering it *Tavù.*

From its having been made a Levitical city, we might conclude that Iuttah was formerly a place of consequence. Its
prominent position on the border of the desert, facing the entrance into the vale of Eshcol, so as to shelter Anab, Debir, and
all the southern cities of the valley, must have made it a post of
great importance to the children of Anak; and being the first
of their cities on the line of march towards Hebron, it was
necessarily the first frontier-fortress that an enemy entering
from the south would attack. Accordingly, in case of invasion,
the whole force of the nation would be concentrated on that
critical point. Iuttah was therefore the scene of frequent en-
gagements. Every Egyptian conqueror who has any sculptured
memorials of his prowess to boast of, has recorded a victory
over the TAH'N'NU as one of his greatest triumphs.

The statistical tablet of Karnak,[j] one of the most ancient
systematic records of Egyptian conquest extant, introduces the
Anakim who garrisoned the fortress of Iuttah, at the very
opening of the list:

"In the twenty-ninth year, then his majesty (was in the land of TAH)
about to molest all the abominable lands in it in the fifth expedition with
his force; then the fortress of the UA·UA·[k] was captured by his majesty
. . . . those who were the good, surrounding his majesty, did all as
appointed, and his majesty went to the treasury of offering and received
the pure and good things of . . . (name lost) with bulls and steers and
waterfowl . . . . . brought by the descendants of the vanquished of that
land, one chief of the fort, 329 men, 100 ingots of gold, tin (?), copper,
and vases of brass and iron. Then was the loading of the ships . . . .
all other good things as his majesty went on his return towards Egypt
. . . . in triumph: after that his majesty sacked the fort of the ARD·TU
of its corn, and smote all its arms: after that his majesty went to the

---

j From Mr. Birch's dissertation; *Trans. R. S. of Literature,* vol ii., 2nd series.
k The Egyptians often double monosyllabic names. This, like the KSH, must
not be confounded with a negro people of a similar name. AU is also found in the
Asiatic series of the list of Seti-Menephtah at Karnak.

land of TAHI in triumph . . . . their fine wine in their waters . . . . . . likewise their corn of . . . . navigating their waters, their infinite . . . .
for bread of offering ; honey 6428 measures of wine, (metals) 618 bulls,
3636 goats,[1] bread, corn, flour." . . . .

Although a name and several words are missing in the
above first line of this valuable memorial, it is sufficiently intelligible to yield several confirmations of the identity of Iuttah
with the TAHI therein referred to.

Firstly, we need only look at a map of Palestine to see that
the ARD'TU and UA'UA collocated with TAHI both find their correspondents in the Canaanite city Arad, very near Iuttah, and
in the ‎עוים‎ Avvim of the south-country, neighbours of the Philistines (Josh. xiii. 3) ; whose district, according to Moses (Deut.
ii. 23), had been seized by the Caphtorim who came forth from
Caphtor—the shepherds expelled from the Delta, who established themselves near the Philistines in the Goshen of Judea.

Secondly, the produce of the land, as described by Dr. E.
Robinson (quoted in the beginning of this chapter), agrees
equally well with the rich booty of *corn* and *fine wine* carried
off by the victorious Egyptians.   Kiriath-Anab, the city of
Anak in the vale of Eshcol, covered by this very fortress of
Iuttah, is literally *"the city of grapes;"* and the vale itself
received its name from the luxuriance of the sample-clusters
brought back by the spies (Nu. xiii. 24).

Between the decisive conquests of Thothmes III. and the
close of the eighteenth dynasty, the historical monuments of
Egypt merely affirm from time to time the tributary state of a
few among the inimical tribes, but relate no fresh victories, and
all memorials of the kind disappear prior to the close of that
dynasty.

The course of active warfare begins again with the nineteenth dynasty, after Seti-Menephtah had again driven the
SHAS'U from Pelusium.   This time, hostilities do not cease from
reign to reign, until the enemies of Egypt have been exterminated.   The children of Anak were not inactive in the last
deadly struggle.   On the contrary, while, from their geographical position, they were sure to be the first attacked, the
Egyptian annals concur with Scripture in testifying that they
were the last to yield.   One of the earliest triumphs of Seti-
Menephtah was a signal victory over the TAH'N'NU ; a cast of
the battle-scene is hung above the staircase leading to the gal-
lery of antiquities, in the British Museum.   A long train of
captives, and a rich array of spoils, were presented by the

---

[1] This item indicates a mountainous country.

Theban king to his gods in the temple of Amun. This is the first known representation of the children of Anak and their manly, picturesque costume, of which a description will be given with the rest in the concluding chapter of this account.

The records of the successes obtained by the great Rameses II. over the Anakim, are equally rich in graphic particulars. In the sculptures of the Ramesseum, he is represented killing one chief of the TAH·N·NU with his own hand, while his foot rests on the neck of another. This symbolical method of denoting complete subjugation was apparently customary in Palestine (comp. Josh. x. 24). There is monumental evidence that Rameses II. had made himself master of the principal fortresses of Anak, prior to his invasion of the Shethite Rephaim in the fifth year of his reign. For it was in the land of Iuttah that his force was at first encamped; and he afterwards seized the camp of the Shethites in the land of Hebron or CHERBU. This incident is represented in the Abou-Simbel tableau of the expedition, where the Egyptians are evidently in possession of the camp, and are rejoicing in security over the booty; and the mention of Caphar-barucha (near Hebron) in the Anastasi papyrus itinerary, as " CAFIRI, the *house of Ramessu*, the fortress of the CHERBU," further corroborates the fact that the king, at this time, actually was in possession of the place. Indeed, if he had not previously made himself master of the whole route through Judea, he could not have penetrated to the land of the SHETTA (Shittim) that way. The ready surrender of the SHAS·U (Zuzim) on that occasion, also argues that he had already obtained such advantages over their kindred, as to leave the intimidated SHAS·U no hope of a successful resistance.

Driven from their capital by the Egyptian conqueror, the Anakim, seeing that the camp of their Shethite brethren had also been taken, followed them across the Jordan, to aid them against the threatened invasion. The people of Hebron and the Amorites bore an active part in the fight before ATESH. The few incidents thus selected for pictorial illustration by the Egyptian hieragrammatists—not because they embody all the notable deeds of their sovereign, but because those were the deeds which most glorified his name, whether from the importance of the victory, or from the prowess and celebrity of the conquered foe—those incidents speak highly for the dauntless bravery of the Anakim, and for their immoveable fidelity to their brethren and to their national cause.

The CHERBU or CHEBRU, alias RBO, and the TAHI or TAH· N·NU, are the only monumental names traceable, with any certainty, to particular cities mentioned in the Bible as situated in the Anakim territory. But the name of the nation itself is of frequent occurrence, whether in memorials of conquest or in tributary lists, during the whole period of the warfare. The name which heads the Asiatic series in the great list of Seti-Menephtah at Karnak (vide *Onomasticon*, plate, col. v., fig. 27) is the full group which stands for the land of the Anakim; though it is oftener written with the last character of that group only. The full group reads: MNA'T'UN[m] * * * *land of the shepherds of* * * * I here express with * * * that last character, the figure of a neck-collar or bracelet. It is not a letter, but an ideagraph, the *sound* of which has not yet been determined, though its *sense*, when it occurs alone, as a name, is generally taken to denote the hitherto unknown *land of the shepherds*, from its following in the present group a series of phonetic characters which have that signification. On this account it has been assumed to be only the *determinative*[n] of that group. But in the progress of this enquiry, I have found reason to believe that this is only a *part* of the truth. The following decisive facts will help us to attain the whole. They contain in themselves such a clear indication of the *particular land* the unknown character stands for, that this essential point, once obtained, may perhaps in its turn give us a clue to the true reading of the character.

In the first place, the proof that this character denotes *geographically* Southern Judea—*i. e.*, the land once belonging to the Anakim, is, that in the list of the conquests of Shishak, at Karnak,[o] it denotes the land invaded by that monarch when he went up against the king of Judah. Now we know from the Bible that the domains of Rehoboam were the lands of Judah and Benjamin; and also, that Shishak penetrated as far as Jerusalem, from whence, according to the custom of Egyptian conquerors, he carried off as spoils "the treasures of the house of the Lord, and of the king's house." (1 Kings xiv. 26.) In their memorial, the Egyptians have not changed the name of the land, though it had fallen under the rule of a different

---

[m] Vide for this group *Onomasticon*, col. v., fig. 27, Anakim group.

[n] An explanation of this term may be of use to those who are not familiar with the peculiarities of Egyptian writing. Egyptian proper names are sometimes spelt with letters, and sometimes written with syllabic characters, or with a single ideagraphic character; but in all cases, the grammatical formatives of gender, number, etc., are followed by a peculiar symbol by which we know whether the name be that of a man, woman, god, chief, house, or land. This symbol is called the *determinative sign*. The *three mountains* at the end of the proper names in the *Onomasticon* are the det. s. of *a foreign land*.

[o] On the south wall; here, Champollion read IUTAH'MALK, *Kingdom of Judah*, in the list of names. Rosellini, *Mon. Storici*, pl. 148.

people. That land is the hill-country of Judea, which belonged to the Anakim, and geographically includes Jerusalem.

In the next place, that character denotes *ethnographically* the land belonging to the people of which the RBO, TAH·N·NU, MASHUASH, and Philistines were sections; *i. e.*, the land of the Anakim. There are several evidences of this. Firstly: in the long inscription (subsequently quoted) it forms the *name* in the group which stand for the proper name of the land invaded by Rameses in his first expedition,[p] and this name is immediately followed by the well-known group TAH·N·NU as the particular locality of the battle; the notices of this victory, in the presentation of captives, also state that the contest took place in the land of TAHI,[q] and the prisoners are the RBO. Secondly: in the war which closed with the twelfth year of his reign, Rameses III., when presenting long chains of RBO and T·AKKAR·U captives to Amun-Ra, is congratulated by the god for his victory over the people whose name is written with that character—and the RBO of Arbâ are Anakim.

In fact, these two tribes, the Anakim and the Philistines of Scripture, or their subdivisions, are the only people ever mentioned on Egyptian inscriptions, as directly referable to and as forming a part of the collective body implied by the name for which that character stands. This quite tallies with its use to express the land invaded by Shishak. The inference from these instances, both of positive and of negative evidence, is obvious: that it is not the land of the shepherd-races generally, but only *that particular part of it occupied by the children of Anak*, which is the region expressed in Egyptian inscriptions and memorials, either by the full group MNA·T·UN * * * (neck-collar or bracelet figure), or by that figure alone with its appropriate grammatical affixes. Its geographical and ethnographical *sense* is "the land" or "race of Anak"—although the *sound* or proper name it represents, may be unknown.[r]

When the Egyptians meant to express the land of the

---

p Vide the group 27, b, col. v., Anakim group, of the *Onomasticon*. The character is the *proper name* written ideagraphically, followed by the sign of *gender*, then the det. s. of *a race*, a man and woman, with its *plural* sign, three strokes=u, and the det. s. of *a foreign land*. "Land of the race (or nation) of * * *."

q Rosellini, *Mon. Storici*, pl. 135.

r The following suggestion of its probable reading occurred to me from the interpretation given in Chevalier Bunsen's vocabulary of the Egyptian word *anka*, "to clasp." The Hebrew root ענק *ánk* has the same radical signification, and its noun denotes a collar or an ornament of some kind, that fastens round the neck. According to the genius of the Egyptian and Hebrew languages, the name of any *clasping object* derived from this root, whether a bracelet or collar, would be called an *ánk*, and the figure of the object would thus become an ideagraph to denote the name of a synonymous region; as a throne *(hes)* writes the name of Isis; a hawk in

shepherd-people generally, or the shepherd-race collectively, without any particular reference to distinctions of district or tribe, they employed another epithet, the origin and etymology of which are unknown,—the TEMAH·U. This may be regarded as the Egyptian equivalent to their Biblical name ' Rephaim.' It occurs frequently in the conquests of Rameses III., where it can have no other sense. In his first expedition, he is said to have conquered all the lands of the TEMAH·U; but we find, by the details of the conquest, that it includes Jerusalem, besides several Anakim and Philistine localities. Again, when Rameses was starting on his last expedition, Amun-Ra says he goes before him "to prepare his way in the lands of the TEMAH·U;" yet on his return we find among his trophies and memorials of victory, not only the names of the Anakim and Philistines, but also those of all the other tribes of Rephaim and names of localities in their lands.[1]

The tombs of the Theban kings are embellished with figures, which from their costumes and epithets are evidently intended to represent the subjects and foreign vassals of the sovereigns doing them homage. In that of Seti-Menephtah, there are four nations, bearing the following epithets :—1. The RT·U *"the race"*—the Theban Egyptians. 2. The NAHS·U or *"rebels"*— the aboriginal negroes of Ethiopia, who were always revolting. 3. The SHEM·U *"Shemites"*—the Aramites. 4. The TEMAH·U, who here represent the Rephaim, claimed as subjects of Theban Egypt by right of conquest. The costume of the SHEM·U, in these groups, is the type of the Aramean Horites; and that of the TEMAH·U is—even to the minutest detail—that of the monumental RBO and TAH·N·NU. In its leading features, it also resembles that of the SHET·TA; and a still more ancient memorial, which will be described in the sequel, points out that costume as the original national costume of the Rephaim.

The Philistines are so deeply involved in the last struggle of the Anakim with Egypt, that, before we conclude our notice of the fortunes and fall of that remarkable people, it will be desirable to trace out their primary connexion with Pelesheth, so far as the limited materials furnished us by a few passing allusions

a square, the name of Hathor, or as we might write *Turkey* ideographically, by a figure of that bird. If this suggestion were admissible, we should have in Manetho's " Phœnician Shepherds," both a literal and a grammatical equivalent of the hieroglyphic group in *Onomasticon*, fig. 27, col. v.; MNA·T·U·N ANKA, " People of the shepherd-land of Anka." MNA denotes a shepherd or herdsman.

[1] In the expedition of Rameses II. against the SHET·TA, the two ambassadors of the SHAS·U who come to tender their allegiance are styled in Rosellini's version, " brethren shepherds of the race MAHUT." This name seems a transposed form of TMAH·U.

to them in the sacred authors are able to afford a shade of assurance on a subject avowedly so obscure.

CHAPTER XIV.

The Philistines.

The Philistines are first introduced to our notice, by name,
when Abraham passed through their land on his return from
Lower Egypt. At that time, they do not appear to have been
an important tribe as to numbers; for their chieftain, Abimelech or "*the Royal Father*," considered Abraham's retinue as
quite on a par with his own, and was glad to secure the friendship and alliance of the wealthy patriarch by the compact of
Beersheba. They had not acquired much additional importance
in the days of Isaac, since we find them jealous of his prosperity, and in fear that he was becoming mightier than they. (Gen.
xxvi. 14—16.) This state of things would indicate, at the time,
their very recent separation from the parent tribe out of which
they had sprung.

All the habitable lands beyond Gaza, the Mosaic limit of the
Canaanites, were the original apanage of the Mizraimite race, of
which we have, in Gen. x. 14, a positive affirmation that the
Philistines were a sub-tribe. The valley of Gerar must therefore have marked the northern limit of the primitive Philistines'
original location. Their extension southward is unknown, but
cannot have been considerable, since the very name of their
tribe, "Pelishtim," points out that this branch of the Rapha
people had taken up a maritime position.[t] To look for them
inland beyond the valley of Beersheba would be fruitless; all
scriptural references to the mountain and desert strongholds
southward of Judea, indicate as their owners the Amalekites, a
branch of the Shethite Rephaim, and suggest that these were
the original population: "The Amalekites, Geshurites and Ge-
zerites were of old the inhabitants of the land as thou goest to
Shur, even unto the land of Egypt." (1 Sam. xxvii. 8.) The
chief cities of Amalek, ravaged by Saul, come under the same
geographical description: "Saul smote the Amalekites from
Havilah till thou comest to Shur which is before Egypt." (1 Sam.
xv. 7.) The report of the spies (Nu. xiv. 29) gives out that the
Amalekites dwelt in the land to the south of the Anakim and

---

[t] פלש to roll over, describing the action of the waves on the shore. Pelesheth
פלשת "seashore-land."

the Amorites. No room is therefore left for the Philistines, but the maritime district connecting the Delta with Canaan proper.

Their extension inland being limited to the valley of Beer-sheba, is one circumstance pointing out the origin of their establishment; for this valley is only a continuation of the vale of Eshcol through an opening in the Judean hills, and it extends westward to the sea.

All the country intersected by this line of wadys, and further east to the border of the naked mountain-desert, is described by recent travellers as a vast tract of low undulating swells clothed with luxuriant pastures. It was therefore admirably adapted to the wants of a tribe whose chief wealth was cattle. A corresponding description of this country occurs in 1 Chron. iv. 39, 40: "They (the Simeonites) went to the entrance of Gedor, eastward of the valley, to seek pasture for their flocks; and they found rich and good pasture, and the land was extensive, quiet, and at peace. But they of Ham had formerly dwelt there."[u]

The Philistines of the Mosaic period are not altogether the same people as those contemporaneous with Abraham. An important accession to their numbers had accrued to them from a kindred stock, on the expulsion of the Hyksos from Egypt. A great number of emigrants from the Delta were among the number, and it seems that these established themselves in the pastoral region of the Avim, and subsequently extended themselves northward, becoming intimately blended with the Philistines. From that time, they are no more heard of as a separate nation, though the prophets, many centuries after, intimate their subsequent connexion with the Philistines, as a well-known fact. Jeremiah says (chap. xlvii. 4),—

> "For Jehovah ravageth the Pelishtim,
> The remnant of the abode of Caphtor."

And Amos likewise (chap. ix. 7) considers the Philistines as the descendants of a people whose deliverance from political annihilation in Caphtor, he places in poetical parallelism with the corresponding deliverance of Hebrews:—

> "Have I not brought up Israel from the land of Mizraim,
> The Pelishtim from Caphtor, and Aram from Kir?"

Which is a palpable allusion to the great army of shepherds who marched out of Egypt after capitulating with Amosis, and who established themselves in Palestine. Those who belonged

---

[u] "They of Ham," *i. e.*, the Amalekites, whom these Simeonites destroyed, and pursued the remnant into Mount Seir, whither they had fled.

to the Rephaim nation, returned to their tribe. Those of Lower Egypt who accompanied them, settled in the south ; and we subsequently find the district in which they settled bearing the significant name of Goshen.

With the addition of such a large body of warriors to their former numbers, it is not surprising that the Philistines, whom we saw, in the days of Abraham and Isaac, an inconsiderable pastoral tribe, should have suddenly become sufficiently powerful to take and retain possession of five Canaanite principalities on the coast northward of Gerar; so as to be found, in the time of the Judges, one of the most warlike and formidable nations of Palestine, the terror and scourge of the twelve tribes of Israel.

I apprehend that the offspring of this colony of expatriated Caphtorim from Goshen, are the people alluded to under the description of "the children of Anak descended from the *nephilim*," in the report of the terrified spies. This word, from the root נפל to fall, sink, settle, cast down, etc., has been translated by *giants* in our common version, quite as inappropriately as "Rephaim." The associated reference to the stature of the people may have beguiled the translators into admitting this misinterpretation of a term to the true sense of which they had no historical clue. One secondary sense of the root נפל is "to settle," which some critics assign to it in Gen. xxv. 18 : "Ishmael settled in the presence of his brethren."[v] Perhaps the idea in the text we are analyzing may be the same, and the derivative noun נפיל may mean *one who is settled*. It is also likely that this noun, which is of the perfect participial form, like the corresponding form ἐκπεπτωκως of the Greek radical πετ (=πιπτω, I fall,) may be susceptible of a corresponding extension of meaning ; inf., to *fall out*; perf. part., *one who is cast out*, an exile, refugee.[w] In order to include the ideas implied in both these possible derivations of an ambiguous root, we may venture to translate it by *refugee*, viz., a person cast out from one place, settled in another. "We have also seen the refugees—the children of Anak who come of the refugees: and we were in our own eyes as grasshoppers, and so were we in their eyes !"

This compound race being here called "the children of Anak," is one circumstance which points to that branch of the great Rapha stock as the parent of the primitive Philistine subtribe, rather than to the direct elder branch. This also agrees

---

[v] Others suppose it to mean, he sank, fell, *i. e.*, died ; so our authorized version.

[w] Some interpreters assign to נפלים the signification of *robbers*, people who *fall upon*—assault—others. The grammatical form is against this interpretation ; as, if that were its sense, the form would have been the *present* participial, נפלים Nophlim.

better with the geographical position of their earliest known settlement, which, as I remarked before, was neither more nor less than a continuous line of communication kept up from the pass that leads out of the vale of Eschcol along the Wady-es-Sebâ, and through the ancient stations Raphæa and Rhinocolura, to Pelusium on the eastern frontier of the Delta.

Another still stronger token that the Philistines claimed original affinity to the tribe of Anak, is found in the peculiar head-dress of the nation. It consists of a helmet surmounted by a circular crown of tall upright feathers, precisely like that characteristic of the Egyptian goddess ÂNK, whose name, in Greek inscriptions, is rendered 'Αvoυκις. This is the same name as Onka, the Phœnician Athene; and this goddess was so evidently the patronymic of their original land and nation, that her Phœnician name is better rendered by the primary Hebrew or Phœnician power of the letters composing their national tribe-name ONK ענק, than by the modern Hebrew conversion of it into Anak. The Judean branch of the Rapha nation assumed the religious denomination of "children of Onka,"—Onkites or "Phœnicians," to distinguish their family from the elder tribe, whose local patronymic was the goddess Ashtaroth; just as the southern transjordanic branch assumed the religious denomination of children of Suth or Sheth, Shethites or Shittim, to distinguish theirs. And the junior province of Pelesheth wore the badge of ÂNK or Onka on their heads, in battle, to shew their affinity to one tribe, and to distinguish themselves from the others; just as the Zuzim of Bashan are found wearing the badge of ÂSTRTA or Ashtaroth on theirs, and for the self-same reasons.

If we feel thus far warranted in regarding "the Pelishtim, who came out of the Casluhim," as a junior branch parted off from the parent stock of Anak at a comparatively late period, we shall easily apprehend the prime cause of their unrelenting animosity towards the Israelites, whom they regarded as interlopers in the domains of their injured brethren of Anak. The part we always find them taking in the later political movements of Palestine, as allies of the Amalekites and Ammonites, are perfectly in accordance with the same view.

If we regard them, not only as a nation of kindred extraction with the Mizraim of Lower Egypt, according to the evidence of Scripture; but also as kindred to those Rephaim who occupied Lower Egypt in the time of Abraham, and ruled it according to the usages of their own nation, as the traces of the local worship of the Philistines, and their personal peculiarities and costume in monumental representations, suggest, we shall

also understand the resemblance of certain customs in both
lands, casually disclosed to us in the narrative of Abraham's
journies to both, which appear more like a repetition of the
self-same adventure in other words, than like two accounts of
separate transactions.

But if, according to the more commonly current notion, we
look upon the Mizraim as colonists of no other country but
Egypt; the position of this outlying tribe, dwelling geographically and politically apart for unnumbered centuries from the
rest of its kindred, isolated from all the concerns and institutions of Egypt, forms, it must be admitted, an ethnological
anomaly exceedingly difficult to explain.

We may seek to evade the difficulty by following the opinion
wrought out with great labour and ingenuity by some of the
most distinguished scholars in archæological research of Ger-
many, who assign to the Philistines an origin altogether foreign
to Palestine. But in that case, we must be prepared to set aside
the scriptural affirmation, that they are an offset of a particular
Mizraimite family; we must sacrifice the unequivocal statement
of an ancient contemporaneous historian, who had the main
facts close at hand from his immediate ancestors, in order to
make way for conjectures originating in analogies of language,
names, and religion, which certainly are very striking and very
significant; but which are fortunately susceptible of being con-
strued the other way. It has yet to be shewn, and can be shewn,
that the facts from which the foreign origin of the Philistines
has been argued have been read backwards in that conclusion;
that the uniform traces of settlement and tradition dispersed
over the Mediterranean coast region by Pelasgic, Phœnician,
and Egypto-Phœnician colonies are rather indications that they
were founded by a nation whose original homestead was Palestine; that instead of bringing their religious traditions into the
East from the West, these nations carried them out into the
West from the East; and that the Philistines themselves are
only a remnant of several branches of that nation, reunited into
a political body which long outlived the nominal extinction of
the others, and the expulsion of its head from their own territories.

Thus only, while strictly following the Bible as far as it will
lead us, and construing all extrinsic evidences in conformity
with its fundamental statements, can we avoid the error of taking
a part for the whole,—as Movers, for instance, when he identifies
the Hyksôs invaders of Egypt with the Phœnicians, who—as
the Onkites or Anakim—were only a member of the great confederate shepherd body, and not even its head;—or the other

error of mistaking the branch for the root, with Calmet and his followers, who would trace the Philistines originally from Crete, at the suggestion of Ezekiel's parallelism of the Cherethites and Philistines. If Crete really was called so, after the Cherethites, it is just as likely that it was because a colony kindred to the Philistines was established in that island. Would not the city *Phœnice* of Crete (Acts xxvii. 12) be thought just as likely to owe its name to a Phœnician commercial station, than to have been the original centre of the Phœnician people? If there was a *Caphtora* in Crete, and another in Cappadocia—and a *Goshen* in Palestine,—is it not much more likely that these isolated settlements in the midst of nations altogether foreign in race to the scriptural Caphtorim of Mizraim, may mark out the refuge of their dispersed remnant, rather than their original homesteads?

The Philistines do not appear by name on the monumental annals of Egypt until the time of Rameses III. It is only after their union with the refugees from Lower Egypt, and their establishment in the Canaanite cities of the coast, that they acquired sufficient political consequence to become independent of Anak, both as a state, and as a subject of hostility on the part of Egypt. Before that time they may have fought in the ranks of the Anakim, and thus would be included under the general denomination of that people, the "MNA" or shepherds of * * * (Anka?)

Nevertheless the Philistine people are not unrepresented in earlier memorials. In the Luxor version of the attack of ATESH, among a row of figures in a boat approaching the city, we discern some attired in the peculiar high crown, and short kilt and corslet, of the Philistine. A people whose name reads KESH or GSH were among those whom the SHET'TA summoned to their assistance on that occasion. As it is utterly impossible that these should be the black KSH-KSH of the land Cush or Ethiopia beyond the cataracts, who are always represented as negroes, and whose name is written with the same characters, it is most probable that the land of Goshen is thereby intended. Not the original Goshen of the Delta, whose land had become part of the Egyptian dominions, but that of the expatriated Goshen of Palestine colonized among the Philistines, who ultimately spread their dominion northwards, even to near Gibeon. (Comp. Josh. x. 41; xi. 16.) And if the descendants of this immigrant body became the bulk of the Philistine population, we must not look for any other costume in a pictorial representation of them, but that of the Philistines.

The monumental form of the Scripture local name Pelesheth

is PULSA·TA. The radicals are exactly the same as the Hebrew form פְּלֶשֶׁת, and where the vowels differ, the Septuagint form again gives us an approximation to the Egyptian version which cannot be accidental—Φυλιστιειμ, in Gen. x. 14; the only instance in which they render the proper name at all.[z]

In another Philistine dependency, Ekron, עֶקְרוֹן, we may safely recognize the T·AKKAR·U people, a conspicuous name on the Egyptian monuments, constantly associated with the PULSA·TA, and whose costume is exactly the same. The modern name of the place is *Akir.* The prefixed *T* is probably the article, equivalent to the Hebrew prefix ה in הָעֶקְרוֹנִי, "the Ekronite," which the Egyptians took for part of the name, as the Greeks did the φ in Φοινικες, *Phœnicians.* The Septuagint have again imitated in their form Ἀκκαρων, the Egyptian *expedient* of doubling the *k*, in order to imitate the rough guttural sound of the Hebrew ע, for which they had no true equivalent.

Three more names of Philistine people are found in the same monumental series. One, written under a row of prisoners taken with the PULSA·TA, and wearing the same costume, reads TUINUNA, for which I cannot recognize any equivalent in the scriptural lists and notices. The two others are in the long inscription of Medinet-Abou, and the names have for their determinative a Philistine prisoner. This leaves no choice as to the region in which we must look for their equivalents. The first, ASHAK·NA, agrees with עֲזֵקָה, Azekah, a city of note at the head of the vale of Elah (Josh. x. 10, 11; 1 Sa. xvii. 1). The other, ALAIU, is most probably Aïalon, אַיָּלוֹן (now *Yalo),* in the same neighbourhood.[y] Both these places are situated between T·AKKAR (Ekron), and SHALÂM·U·NA (Shalem), mentioned in the same inscription.

CHAPTER XV.

Final Wars of the Anakim with Egypt.

Having thus far gone through the technical analysis of the names, we are now prepared to follow up the incidents to which they give us a key, in the most important series of campaigns

---

[z] In all the historical references, the Septuagint paraphrase the proper name by οἱ ἀλλοφυλοι, *those of another tribe,* i.e., different from the Canaanites, or the Hebrews.

[y] Azekah and Aïalon were noted strongholds, and are both named among the fortresses repaired by Rehoboam to strengthen his frontier against Shishak (2 Chron. xi. 9).

conducted by Rameses III., leader of the twentieth dynasty; which laid the Rephaim of Palestine prostrate among the surrounding nations, opened the gates of the land to the children of Israel, and transferred into their hand the yoke of Canaan.

The Rephaim of Bashan had bowed before Rameses II. The Emim had braved his power twenty years, and ended by making peace with him. Exhausted by a prolonged furious warfare, both nations were glad of a truce. A new generation arose, and a new king reigned in Egypt, Pthahmen or Menephtah, the Amenophis of Manetho, a weak prince, who was entirely under the control of the priests. They persuaded him to open a fresh series of persecutions against the oppressed race of Lower Egypt. These unfortunate captives were removed from the land, and sent across the Nile to labour in the stone quarries that are opposite Memphis. After a while, they were allowed to occupy the deserted city which had formerly belonged to their ancestors, Avaris the city of Typhon. Here they contrived to organize a plan of revolt, and sent for assistance to the descendants of their exiled forefathers, who had joined the branch of the great Shepherd-body seated at Shalem.

Such an opportunity of regaining their power in Lower Egypt was not to be cast aside. Manetho relates that the Shepherds of Shalem sent a large army to the relief of their kindred; and that king Amenophis was afraid of fighting against the gods by opposing them in battle, because a priest, called Amenophis, the son of Papis, had prophetically announced to him that the ill-treatment of the captives of Goshen which he had countenanced would be avenged by their obtaining the dominion of Egypt for thirteen years. Accordingly, as soon as the Shepherds appeared, Amenophis provided for the safe keeping of the sacred animals, and of the images of the gods; he committed to the charge of a trusty friend his son Sethos (who is also called Rameses), then only five years of age; retired from before the invaders without an attempt at resistance, and withdrew with thirty thousand men into Ethiopia, where he remained until the appointed period of thirteen years had expired. He then came forth from Ethiopia with a great force; and his son Rameses came also with an army; they together attacked the Shepherds, overcame them, and pursued them to the frontier of Syria.[a]

On the part borne by the Hebrews in this last Egyptian revolution caused by the Shepherd contest, it would take us beyond the range of our immediate subject to dwell. The only

---

[a] Josephus, *Contra Apionem*, l. i., c. 26, 27.

apocryphal feature in the account, is the prophecy of the priest Amenophis, and the superstitious king's alarm at contravening a divine decree. This looks very like a tale devised by popular tradition to cloke over the pusillanimity of Menephtah, who doubtless was much more frightened at the idea of fighting the terrible human foes who now presented themselves in warlike array on his border, for the second time since their expulsion, than of contending against the gods by upsetting their prediction. Well might the saying go forth throughout all Palestine as a popular proverb: "Who can stand before the children of Anak?"—when their force of twenty thousand men, by merely appearing on the frontier, sent the Theban king, with an army of thirty thousand picked warriors, off beyond the cataracts, terror-stricken—fugitives—without striking a blow!

But the young Rameses retrieved the honour of Egypt; he proved himself worthy of his illustrious grandfather. When he led the army that expelled these invaders, he was only eighteen years of age; and as the thirteen years' interregnum caused by the Shepherd-invasion are reckoned in the nineteen years and six months of his father's reign, he must still have been very young when he ascended the throne.

His first known armament, after his accession, is that dated in his fifth year. Within seven years, he finally restored peace to Egypt, and crushed her foes for ever. We will now go through the occurrences of these seven years, by following the monumental records on which they are depicted.

Inasmuch as the country about Jerusalem was so decidedly the scene of the great wars conducted by Rameses III., we are thus far authorized to infer that the reduction of the two eastern tribes by his predecessors had thrown the weight of political ascendancy upon the Phœnician branch; and that the Anakim took the lead in this last invasion of Egypt, which—after a brief triumph—proved the signal for their destruction.

The pictures representing the triumphs of Rameses III. bear no dates. The first dated document is the long inscription on the south wall of the inner court of the palace at Medinet-Abou, which appears to explain the four tableaux sculptured on the other walls of the same court.[a] The references to the king's most remarkable deeds, and the names of lands and nations reduced, will enable us to follow up the leading incidents of this war; and as the royal historiographer who recorded those deeds has not indulged in quite such towering flights of eloquence and circuitous mazes of poetical imagery as his predecessor who

---

[a] Rosellini, *Mon. Storici*, pl. 135—138. Long inscription, pl. 139—140.

glorified Rameses II., he will be found by so much the more intelligible to our more matter of fact understandings, when transferred to a familiar modern dialect. I will take advantage of Rosellini's valuable interpretations of the inscriptions, to select from them the most characteristic passages, as illustrations both of the style of thought and expression in those remote ages, and of the historical occurrences they propose to embody. There may be some interest in knowing that we have the narrative as much in the Egyptian hierogrammatist's own words, as a translation admits of.

"In the fifth year, under the sacred presidency of Horus-Phrâh, the mighty enlarger of Egypt, the guardian of power, the victorious arm which has subdued the impure TAH·N·NU, the lord of Upper and of Lower Egypt, Amun-mai Rameses (III.), who has crushed the inimical TAH·N·NU, and ravaged their dwellings," etc., etc.

(We may here pass over a long complimentary oration to the king, in the style of the above specimen, and proceed to the narration of his deeds.)

"In the night, the king Rameses smote the lands of the foreign foes. He returned to Egypt, and distributed the offerings among the priests, and presented the vanquished as an oblation to the gods, the submission to his grasp of the impure race of the land of ANKA, the TAH·N·NU. His archers smote the enemies, as terrible bulls among the sheep; his horses were like hawks!

"By the renown of his name, he conquered the lands of the TEMAH·U. He reduced to submission the *T and the B*M*U[b] lands, and laid the land of MASHUASH desolate. The carnage was stopped, their hearts being filled with contrition. Their princes prayed with their lips, and he refused not to grant their petitions; they prayed to that god, lord of lords, the great man of Egypt, and he, in the midst of victory, accepted the supplication of the foreign lands and of their princes who humbled themselves to the great king of kings.

"His Majesty had come to the land of the perverse TEMAH·U; and his arm was stayed by their prayers from distressing the land by siege. Praised above all the other Phrâhs be the clemency of his Majesty!

"The terror that he, bull-like, inspired, was as the quaking of little kids. The blows dealt by his Majesty to the confines of the land glared before their gates like flames of fire: from the place where he struck and smote down the ramparts, the defeat was marked by dead to the right and to the left. His Majesty compelled submission with his own members, like *Mentu*.[c] The king Rameses led off the slaves and caused the dead to be numbered." * * * *

After another long description, which may be omitted, of

---

[b] In these two names, the * stands for a character either obliterated or unknown.

[c] Mentu, or Muntu-Ra, is the Egyptian Ares or Mars, god of war.

the mercy the king shewed to some prisoners, whose lives he saved after ravaging their country and levelling their walls to the ground—and another fragment, partly illegible, partly destroyed, in which the names of ASHAK·NA (Azekah) and ALAIU (Aïalon) remain among those mentioned, we have a fierce description of the contest with the RBO :—

> " By the great spirit that came from Egypt, the land of RBO (Arbâ) was a conflagration before and behind, and the gods themselves caused those to perish who went beyond the gates of their city; and those who were saved were brought to Egypt; Ra having commanded that the ruler of Egypt, looking on them, should conquer, like the sun, guardian of the pure race." (*i.e. the Egyptians.*)

After this, comes a fragment that we may abridge, in which the submission of SHALÄM·U·NA[d] is mentioned; the king carried off the flocks of the conquered. After this, " the foreigners of the great island (?)[e] came to be presented in their captivity to Amun Ra because of the smiting with which he (the king) had smitten their land, passing before their gates on the face of the waters like a duck." These are named the PULSA·TA (Philistines) and T·AKKAR·U (Ekronites). Then comes another defective fragment, and SHALÄM·U·NA is again mentioned; closing with a very animated description of the king's personal valour.

> " He fought among shoutings, the lord of might who threw the whole land into consternation ! The great lord of victories, king of the Upper and Lower regions, in his smiting and in the fulness of his triumph over the barbarians, was as a lion, and his roarings went forth thundering ! He passed with his wings over the land of the waters; he purified the abode of iniquity."

This document concludes with a long and very pompous eulogium, which we lose nothing by passing over.

If the four pictures in the same hall as this inscription represent the leading actions it describes—as is most probable from their subjects—a general account of them will shew that the two great triumphs they commemorate are the surrender of the Philistines, and the victory over the Anakim.

The Egyptian king must have gone by sea along the Philistine coast, landing near Ekron; he opened the campaign by an attack on the northern Amorite dependencies of the Anakim and Philistines. This we gather from the names which have

---

[d] This name is here (line 50) written SHALÄM·U·NA; but in line 56, it is written simply SHALÄM·U.

[e] Rosellini's rendering " isola " is doubtful. A *maritime land* is certainly implied; and we know that Pelesheth was not an island. But Rosellini had not identified any of these names. The knowledge of a fact is often necessary to a right interpretation of some among its forms of expression.

survived destruction, of MASHUASH, ASHAK'NA, and ALAIU. Having taken these fortresses, the reduction of SHALĂM'U'NA in the neighbouring region, followed. The union of valour and clemency displayed by the young conqueror, and so energetically extolled by his hierogrammatist, were not without their influence on the chiefs of the land on one side; for the Philistines of the coast, as well as those of Ekron, tendered their submission. The land of the Philistines proper—Pelesheth or PULSA'TA, "*sea-shore land*"—is several times descriptively referred to, where Philistines are represented : "the foreigners of the great island;" (?) "the parts of the great island (?) that are separated from the two Egypts;" "the land of the waters;" "those who dwell in the maritime lands." The Philistines became his auxiliaries; and he now passed round the mountain and attacked the Anakim, on their own frontier.

This is exclusively the subject of the four pictures. It is also the great feat forming the exordium of the inscription. Nevertheless it must have been the last incident of the campaign; for, since the Philistines appear on the side of Egypt in the battle-scene, their submission must have preceded the attack of the Anakim represented in that scene. The order of events is by no means preserved in the long inscription; indeed this is hardly to be expected, since it evidently was not intended as a consecutive narration, but rather as an eulogy interspersed with allusions to those deeds for which the royal conqueror is being glorified; the most glorious, which are pictured on the walls, being the first mentioned.

From the inscriptions accompanying the battle-scene, we learn that the event occurred in the land of "the impure TEMAH.U race (Rephaim)." From those over the picture in which the prisoners are brought before their conqueror, we further learn that the land of TAHI (Iuttah) was the scene of the engagement; nevertheless the captives are all called the people of RBO (Arbâ);" that a thousand prisoners were taken alive, and that the trophies of the dead, when numbered, shewed that three thousand had been killed. The nocturnal assault alluded to in the long inscription seems to explain this enormous loss, and the confusion of the people who were attacked; these are represented in the battle-scene all unarmed, and appear evidently to have been taken by surprise. The other two pictures of this series represent the captives bound, strung together by a rope tied round their necks, and dragged in triumph before the Theban gods. In all these, the RBO and TAH'N'NU are not distinguishable from each other by their costume.

The expression put into the mouths of the MASHUASH princes addressing the king, is very remarkable,—"*the great man of Egypt.*" It is one of those undesigned coincidences which fall in with so many more direct evidences gathered from the agreement of names and localities, in proof that they were a people accustomed to call their supreme chief by a similar title. (Compare "the great man of the Anakim" of Arbâ, Josh. xiv. 15.) And while the fragments we have already quoted are proof direct that the race called TEMAH'U to which the MASHUASH belonged, includes also the people of RBO or Arbâ, the conclusion is further borne out by the analogy of their costume.

The sculptures arranged round the walls of the great external hall of the palace are more numerous; but the subjects all relate to the same people. The principal entrance is flanked on both sides by a triumphal scene, representing Rameses III. leading a line of prisoners—or rather a series of local names enclosed in the castellated oval, indicative of a *conquered region*, to which are added heads and hands, by way of personifying the symbol of conquest. Immediately below this list, is a line in which the date, the twelfth year of the king's reign, is still legible. There are other imperfect traces of dates.

As none of the pictures in this hall are dated, we cannot know which belong to the last expedition of Rameses III. against the enemies of Egypt in this year, or which may be referable to earlier intermediate expeditions. We may be certain, however, that the war was carried on incessantly during those seven years, from the number of the subjects. A general statement of the latter will suffice; for any attempt at arrangement, in the absence of dates and narrative inscriptions, must be too conjectural to be of any value. One subject of great interest represents a pitched battle against the T'AKKAR'U (Ekron). After submitting to Rameses III., in his first expedition, and helping him against the RBO, they revolted. He marched against them, and on this occasion commanded the assistance of the Rephaim of Bashan, who are recognized by their costume and "two-horned Ashtaroth" helmets, as the people who aided Rameses II. against the SHET'TA (Emim). The Rephaim are fighting with the Egyptians against the Ekronites.[f]

Another remarkable subject, unique of its kind, is a terrible naval engagement. The same people figure in it as in the former; but the people of Ashtaroth occupy their natural position as enemies of Egypt, and are fighting in the Philistine

---

f Rosellini, *Mon. Storici*, pl. 127, 128.

ships with their kindred.[g] It is probable that this event was
posterior to the other; and that the temporary submission of the
chief Rephaim, manifested in their acting as auxiliaries to Egypt
against the Philistines, was the fruit of victories obtained in
intermediate expeditions, when the other tribes of Rephaim
were attacked in turn, and either crushed or reduced to final
obedience. The list at the entrance of this great hall contains
names belonging to several Rapha districts and dependencies,
and the chiefs of the *Harem* chamber series of portraits are
those of all their principal tribes; though the bands of captives,
and all the triumphal presentation scenes remaining to be described in this hall, refer exclusively to the Anakim and Philistines, who took the lead in the war. The " address of Amun-Ra,
king of gods," to Rameses, on his departure, names the whole
Rapha race as the object of the last expedition:[h]

> " I go before thee, O my son, lord of the two worlds,
> 　Sun, guardian of truth, beloved of Amun ;
> 　I grant thee (to subdue the foreigners) all
> 　Traversing the lands of the barbarians, victorious.
> 　May thy valour cast down their princes !
> 　I go (to prepare) the ways in the land of the TEMAH·U,
> 　And will go through it with thee, preceding thy coursers."

The importance of this expedition is known by the great
preparations that were made towards it. The next picture represents the distribution of arms and mustering of forces.

The return of Rameses to Egypt, and arrival at the fortress
of MAGADUL (Magdolum), when the conflict was ended, is another interesting picture.[i] His ministers come forth to meet
him, and he is addressing from a throne, standing, those who
have distinguished themselves in the war. The Ashtaroth-
crested people are fellow-prisoners with the Philistines in this
subject. The main body of captives are next presented to the
gods of Thebes. These are the RBO and the T·AKKAR·U.[j] Amun-
Ra thus addresses the king :

> " Be thy return in rejoicing !
> 　Thou hast smitten the barbarians :
> 　Thou hast laid them all prostrate . . . . slaying . . . .
> 　Thou hast (struck terror into the) hearts of the ANAKIM !"

Other pictures represent the rest of the prisoners; one con-

---

　　　　　　　[g] *Ibid.*, pl. 131.　　　　　　　[h] *Ibid.*, pl. 124.
　[i] *Ibid.*, pl. 132, 133. Magdolum is a station of the Antonine itinerary, xii. M. P.,
nearly south of Pelusium, on the frontier. The site is still extant as a mound with
ruins.
　[j] *Ibid.*, pl. 134.

sists of three rows of Philistines, led by a colossal portrait figure
of the king; under one row is written "the chiefs of the land
PULSA'TA," under another, the unknown name TUINU'NA. The
date of the victory to which this subject refers, is uncertain.

Besides these memorials, two fragments greatly mutilated,
figured in Champollion's monuments,[k] give a representation of
a battle scene and capture of a city belonging to a people wearing the Horite costume.

The list of cities captured by Rameses III., inscribed on the
entrance of the great hall, as well as that of the captives of the
Harem chamber, may be regarded together as an epitome of
this monarch's warlike deeds, to which the names of the tribes
figured in the sculptures may be added, as signalizing the most
glorious among those deeds. They will be found—so far as
they are recognizable—to range over every district in which the
Rephaim ruled. The first list is as follows:[l]

TASA'TA.	Doubtful.	הצית Tizah was a Moabite city (1 Chr. xi. 45).
RURI or LULI.	Doubtful.	ערער Aroër might be written so.
PETR*.	Pethor.	Aramite city, belonging to Rephaim
TIR.NA or TIL'NA.	Unknown.	
TARBUSA.	Tharabasa.	Edomite city, subject to Rephaim.
ATU*.		
{ KARNA or	Karnaïm[m]	Metropolis of Bashan.
{ GALNA	or Golan?	City of Bashan.
HAIR'NA.	Haran.	City of Padan-Aram, subject to Rephaim.
LEBNU'T.	{ Libnah	Southern Judea, } subject to
	{ or Lebonah?	Central Judea, } Rephaim.
CHIBUR.[n]	Hebron.	Metropolis of Anakim.
ATAR.	Edrei (Adar-âi) ערדא City of Bashan.	

---

[k] Champollion's *Monuments*, vol. iii., pl. 227, 228.

[l] Rosellini's copy of some among these names is not accurate. This list is taken
from a repetition of the subject in Champollion's *Monuments*, vol. iii., pl. 204.

[m] The double force of the Egyptian characters for GK and LR, makes it impossible to decide which of these two cities the group figured in the *Onomasticon*, col. i.,
fig. 2, represents. At first, I thought it might be Golan; but the alternative of its
being Ashtaroth-karnaïm has claims not to be passed over. The complete subjection
to Rameses III., in which we see the people of Ashtaroth, is rather strongly in favour
of the latter supposition; the city is called simply *Karnaim* by Josephus, and the
omission of the final dual or plural form is not unfrequent in modern names of ancient
sites. We have two instances in the land of this very people, the SHAS'U or Zuzim:
Mahanaïm is now a village called *Mahneh:* and Betonim, *Batneh*. There is no
other city named in the Bible that this group GALNA or KARNA will stand for, but
Golan, or Karnaïm.

[n] Vide *Onomasticon*, col. v., fig. 29, a, b. It was necessary for the convenient
grouping of the hieroglyphic characters in this name, that the b and n should be
together; this causes, in one transcript, the inversion of a radical,—CHIRBU—in
another, the transposition of the vowel, CHIBUR.

RSS or LSS.   { Rissah   Cities of Paran, Amalekites.
                   { or Lusa ?
AIAHA or IIHA.   Unknown.

The portraits of the captive chiefs are sculptured in relievo
on the basement of the Harem chamber, apparently supporting
the upper wall, like Caryatides.[o] Each figure has a legend before him with the name of his city or land. They are so placed,
that every Asiatic alternates with a negro. The series of Asi-
atics is as follows :

The chief of RBO ....Arbâ, otherwise Hebron or CHEBUR.
————————— MASHUASH ...Μααχως?[p]
————————— SHET·TA ......Shittim.
————————— AMÄR ....Amorite.
————————— T'AKUR'I .. ...Ekron.
————————— SHAIRTA·NA ...Zarthan.
————————— SHA*.* ....
————————— TUIRSHA ......Tarichæa (Josephus). (Not mentioned in
                          the Bible.

These two lists testify that Rameses III. not only captured
many cities not previously conquered by his predecessors, which
he added to the already existing lists of tributaries of Egypt,
but that he also had the glory of numbering among his prisoners
the chieftains of each of the three Rapha nations, besides several
provincial rulers.

When we add to this the local names in the historical inscriptions,—Shalem, the great metropolis of the Rapha nations,
—Pelesheth, and its Amorite dependancies of Ekron, Azekah
and Aïalon, besides Iuttah,—we shall have before our view the
full extent of territory over which the last conqueror of the
Theban race swept triumphantly during the brief space of seven
years, and from which its ancient rulers—the TEMAHU or
Rephaim, were cut off from among the nations. Bashan became
a tributary of Egypt, till its lands were conquered by Israel and
its people were absorbed into the Ammonite community. Shittim was laid open to the Amorite spoiler, and its people sank
into the Moabite colony. Anak nominally survived the desolation for a brief space—but only to be expelled by Joshua, and
dispersed among the surrounding Canaanites.

Egypt finally triumphed over her enemies. Her last con-

_____

[o] Rosellini, *Mon. Storici*, pl. 141—143.

[p] This name is not found in the Hebrew text of Joshua's list of Judæan cities
(ch. xv.) ; but it seems to have been accidentally lost out of the text, or altered by
the misreading of copists. The Septuagint have the name Μααχως, in ver. 10,
which consists of letters represented by the Egyptian group read MASHUASH.

queror, returning home, was able to boast before the tutelar god of his own land, that he had "laid their lands waste, and burnt their fortresses with fire;" but she had paid dearly for her triumph. The memorials of victory which have been preserved are all on one side; Egypt has not recorded her defeats. We must by no means suppose that she always had the upper hand in the warfare. The very long period over which these memorials are spread—three centuries at least, from the expulsion of the shepherds to their final overthrow—is a fact in itself that strongly testifies to the contrary; that the task of uprooting the power of her enemies was a very hard task; and that before it was accomplished, the victory had perhaps cost Egypt more than the political advantages were worth. For it was not a war of ambition against a richer and weaker state, with no ostensible motive than the aggrandizement and wealth of the empire by the exaction of tribute. It was a deadly feud of race against race; a bitter protracted act of national vengeance, in which sometimes the one party, sometimes the other, prevailed,—while both were equally resolved to perish before they yielded.

The only two instances recorded by Egypt of some of the Rapha tribes having joined her against their own brethren, are no genuine exceptions to this feeling. Their submission in both cases was but casual. It was a temporary sacrifice of patriotism to the expediency of the moment, extorted by the power of Egypt from the partial exhaustion of the yielding party. But as soon as the Egyptian army had withdrawn from the land, or as soon as time had healed the wound of the bleeding nation, and the act of resistance was again become barely possible, the galling bond was cast off, and the forced and uncertain ally resumed his genuine character of an inveterate foe. The SHAS'U surrendered to Rameses II. without fighting, and bore arms against their Shethite kindred; because they had suffered such severe losses in the war against his predecessor, that they felt their power of resistance unequal to the invading force. But so far were they from being true allies of Egypt, that the notices of subsequent wars recorded in the Sallier and Anastasi papyri, and dated within ten years after, present the SHAS'U cities as sending their contingent of troops to aid the SHET'TA. In like manner, under Rameses III., we see that the Philistines, located so near Egypt as to fall the first under the power of a fresh invading force, are ready to give way and join Egypt as soon as they see two of their inland strongholds, Azekah and Aïalon, in the power of the conqueror. But this cannot be regarded as a national alliance. So evidently was their national inclination constrained, when they took up arms against their brethren of

Anak with Egypt, that almost immediately after, we see them seize on the first opportunity of casting off their compulsory renegade character, and turning against her. The alliance of the SHAS'U with Rameses II. was equally contrary to their national predilections. For the same series of pictures which exhibits them fighting against Pelesheth, also exhibits her warriors contending with Egypt under the Philistine banners, and includes their chieftains among the captive enemies of Egypt.

Each of the three Rapha nations in its turn bore the brunt of warfare; they all succumbed in succession—they all fell together in the last unsuccessful effort. But the children of Sheth and the children of Anak continued to the last true to their cause and to each other. Their patriotism is free from the stain which clings to the name of the Zuzim and the Philistines. No array of power—no constraint of circumstances—was ever sufficient to overbear their faithfulness to each other's cause as brethren, or to turn their hands against each other. Together they struggled—and together they sank—side by side.[q]

                                                                    F. C.

---

[q] As there were two noted conquerors named Rameses, who both bore the epithet of Amun-mai, "beloved of Amun," the reader who may desire to refer to the plates and works quoted in this notice might be perplexed as to the identity of the king in question, without the following explanation:—

Some authors—Champollion and Rosellini, for instance—call Rameses II. the Great, Rameses III.; and the Rameses of Medinet-Abou, his grandson, Rameses IV. There is a doubt as to whether the Great Rameses had a brother of the same name, who reigned five years before him, or whether the name attributed to him be only another cognomen of Rameses II., who changed his titles. As this question is undecided, but the Great Rameses is most generally called Rameses II. by recent authorities, I have conformed to this arrangement.

Again, it is as well to guard against another possible source of confusion in the arrangement of the dynasties, by stating that when Champollion and Rosellini wrote, the nineteenth dynasty of Manetho was supposed to represent the line beginning with Rameses III. of Medinet-Abou (whom they call IV.), but that lately, the most learned and judicious Egyptian scholars have seen the propriety of identifying that dynasty with the immediate successors of Rameses I., and beginning it with Sethos or Seti-Menephtah I. In the Manethonian system, a change of dynasty does not imply a change in the line of hereditary succession, but a change or revolution in the state of things. The three shepherd invasions caused as many changes of dynasty, though Amosis, leader of the eighteenth, was son of the last king of the former Theban dynasty; though Seti-Menephtah, leader of the nineteenth, was son of Rameses I., last king of the eighteenth; and Rameses III., leader of the twentieth, was son of Menephtah, last king of the nineteenth. These three kings restored the Theban dominion, and are therefore considered heads of *a dynasty,* or *condition of power.*

(A supplementary paper on the Costumes of the Rephaim, and their Religious System, will appear in the next number, and conclude the Series.)

THE REPHAIM.

Plate II

Pantheon

THE REPHAIM

PANTHEON OF THE REPHAIM.

DESCRIPTION OF PLATES.

PLATE I.

Fig 1. The Shethite Ashtaroth AT'SII; from a tablet in the Louvre.
2. The Phœnician Pataïkos, or PTHAH.
3. Sheth as RENPU; from a tablet in the British Museum.
4. Onka as Anath or ANTA, the Neith of the Anakim.
5. Dagon, the Philistine form of Oannes or AON, from a Punic coin in the British Museum.

Consecrated vessels from the spoils of the Rephaim, exhibiting a selection of their most remarkable forms and symbols :—

Fig. 6. Patera, with the emblem of AON, the sacred bull Mnevis.
7. Vase, with a crowned lion, emblem of the king of gods, KHEM, Chemosh-Molech or Baal-Khammon. 8. Patera, with sphinx-figure of Ashtaroth. 9. Vase, with the emblem of Renpu. 10. Patera supported by the emblem of Anath.

PLATE II.

Fig. 1. The Egyptian AT'HOR, with a cow's head and globe and horns; counterpart of the Ashtaroth of Bashan.
2. The Egyptian SET, son of NU'T'PE. 3, 4. Names of SUT and SUT'SII in the treaty with Rameses II. 5. Name and figure of Baal, BARO, from inscriptions of the same period. 6. Heads of Sheth and Horus united in one body.
7. The Egyptian ANK lady of the land of NTH, counterpart of the Phœnician Onka. 8. Name of T'NTH ANK. 9. Phonetic name of NTH, with her symbol as determinative. 10. Head of Neith bearing her symbol. 11. TEMAHU chief of the children of Anak, TAHI tribe, bearing the same on his limbs.

Sacred symbols :—

Fig. 12. Crux-ansata, surmounted by emblems of Ashtaroth and Renpu. 13. Vase, with head of unknown bird. 14. Crux-ansata vase supported by emblem of Renpu. 15. Horn for pouring out libations to the Queen of Heaven. 16. Patera supported by the emblem of SEB or Chronus, father of the gods. 17. Ashtaroth-headed vase. 18. Crux-ansata without figures.

THE REPHAIM, AND THEIR CONNECTION WITH EGYPTIAN HISTORY.*

CHAPTER XVI.

Religious System and Pantheon of the Rephaim.

In endeavouring to bring under a systematic arrangement the few fragments of half-obliterated record that we may yet be able to render available in illustrating the religious forms and ideas of the Rephaim, it will be best to abstain from conjectures on their system of theogony and symbolism. Whatever is conjectural is unprofitable to our purpose. We are not framing a theory, but seeking to recover a lost history. All details connected with the worship of this people, which illustrate Scripture or receive illustration from it—all those which assist in confirming their identity with the subjects of the Egyptian monumental records—and all those which tend to exhibit the original connection of their system with the oldest forms of the Egyptians, and thereby to indicate the common origin of the two contending powers,—such are the points to be as prominently brought out as the limits of the materials at hand will allow. The more recondite meaning of the sacred emblems which constitute the image-gods of antiquity, and of their attributes, would only lead to speculations on a floating basis, and to conclusions incapable of tangible demonstration. If we find substantial grounds to establish that the fundamental Osiris and Isis of the Mizraimite pantheon were also the basis of that of the Rephaim, while their secondary forms only are peculiar, an important fact will have been elicited ; and the religious monuments of Egypt will as clearly point out the beginning of that nation, as her historical monuments reveal their end.

The sources from which we may gather all particulars of the worship of the Rephaim that are susceptible of recovery are :—

1. Their religious symbols, and the effigies and names of their gods, on Egyptian monuments, occurring either on detached commemorative tablets, or in historical subjects and inscriptions.

2. Proper names peculiar to the lands we have identified as their lands ; referable to and manifestly derived from the same gods.

3. Occasional allusions in the Bible to the same gods, and to the religious practices of the people.

4. Similar allusions in ancient profane writers.

These data are of no interest, and are often unintelligible, when viewed separately. They are all complementary to one another. It is only by bringing the facts obtained from one source to bear upon those gathered from another, comparing those that are analogous, and reuniting those that are obviously connected in their origin, that we can obtain a whole sufficiently complete to be accepted in illustration of history.

Certain votive tablets are occasionally found in Egypt, chiefly in tombs, bearing figures and names of gods different from those of the Egyptian pantheon, and obviously of foreign origin, but of Egyptian workmanship, as, for instance, the tablet of Kaha in the British Museum. The great number of noble captives brought to Egypt during the Theban wars will account for the occurrence of those monuments. Such captives were not always prisoners taken in battle ; these, after being dragged in triumph, chained together and handcuffed, behind the conqueror's car, were presented to the Theban gods, and then consigned to the task-master, to expiate, by a degrading servitude, the crime of having lifted their hand against the majesty of Pharaoh. Instances occur, however, when the chiefs of the invaded lands offered no resistance, but disarmed the conqueror's wrath by offering themselves up voluntarily, ' to be presented in their captivity to Amun-Ra,' like the Ekronites and Philistines to Rameses III. Such captives were of course very differently treated. Their forts were indeed laid low, and their cities subjected to tribute : the proffered submission of the chiefs to the form of following the royal train and appearing before the gods of Thebes, was accepted, and the ceremony fulfilled, but under circumstances of great leniency, and involving no personal discomfort or degradation. When they reached Egypt, they were honourably treated ; the parallel cases of Daniel, Haman and Mordecai, and Nehemiah, in the Jewish captivity, even show that it was not unusual for such strangers to be invested with offices of distinction in the royal service. And this service did not necessarily entail any interference with the private devotion of these exiles.

As the Rephaim were the object of the whole long series o Egyptian wars, we might have expected, *à priori*, to find their gods occupying a conspicuous place among these mysterious memorials of an unknown worship found in Egypt. We will give a separate account of all those which can be thus recognized by their names.

Astuta, *Astarte*, or *Ashtaroth.*

The tablets in the Louvre and British Museum, representing this goddess under the secondary names and attributes of Atsu and KEN, are the most ancient delineations of her extant in the world : they belong to the period of Rameses II.

They are only provincial forms of Ashtaroth ; and, even at that early age, they exhibit a marked departure from her primeval type, in depicting her with a human countenance ; for the original Astarte, the 'two-horned Ashtaroth' of the Rephaim, was figured with the head of a cow, with a globe between her horns. In this form, we find her graven image among the effigies of various gods surmounting the gold and silver vessels consecrated to their worship, which the Egyptian conquerors, according to custom, carried away from the sanctuaries of the Rephaim with other spoils, and presented to the temple-gods of Thebes. Sanchoniatho assigns as the reason for her being delineated under this form, that it was emblematical of her supremacy.[a]

Sacred symbols are the written language of ancient religions, which invest its forms of outward expression with a permanent character, both in virtue of their consecration to ritual uses in the sanctuary, as exponents of the abstract ideas they were framed to embody ; and also, through a commendable veneration on the part of later generations, for the ancestral teachers who first instructed them through the medium of such emblems.

Accordingly, when we find the Ashtaroth of the Shethite tribes bearing, on private memorials, attributes different from those consecrated in their sanctuaries, we cannot but ascribe to the latter representations priority in antiquity over the former. We understand the variations presented in the more recent forms as intentional departures from the primitive type, introduced either from a desire to give more explicitness to the attributes they symbolize, or in order to superadd, either by appropriate emblems, or by a different descriptive name, the notion of new attributes ascribed to the divinity they represent. To the same cause, also, we may easily trace that progressive departure from their prototype, which is rendered so evident in the Egyptian gods by the manner in which one divinity is found gradually sliding into another, dropping first its own attributes, and then its name, till its original character is completely superseded. This sort of gradation is exemplified in a very interesting manner by the history of Ashtaroth, whose transformations, by the gradual development of one fundamental idea into a connected series of typical forms, may be systematically traced to their respective periods in their respective lands, through-

[a] Cory, *Ancient Fragments.* Ex. Eusebius, *Præp. Ev.*, l. 1, c. 10. For the identity of the cow-headed type throughout the nation, compare, in Rosellini's *Mon. Storici*, the spoils of the SHAS'U, or Chief Rephaim, pl. 52 ; those of the Anakim of TAHI, pl. 56 ; those of the Emim, or SHET'TA, pl. 59 ; and those of the Elathites, or LT'N, pl. 48.

out the wide geographical range over which the influence of her peculiar people extended, not only in the days of their dominion, but even of their dispersion.

We found the normal type of Ashtaroth to be, *a cow-headed female figure bearing a globe between her horns.* Its design is immediately brought under our view, in the Egyptian representations of the spoils taken from the Rapha nation ; for these are undoubtedly matter of fact copies from the original sacred utensils themselves. Nothing, therefore, can be more satisfactorily authenticated than the *genuineness* of this type. The *sacredness* of the type, and its consequent *antiquity*, are thereby attested ; and also its *universality*, by its identity in the sanctuaries of the whole nation. A corresponding testimony to its universality at a later period, and to its being of old the time-honoured form under which the worship of the goddess had been introduced into the land of Canaan, is further afforded by the allusion to her in the book of Tobit (i. 5) as τῇ Βὰαλ τῇ δαμάλει, *Baal the heifer*, to whom all the tribes of Israel who had apostatized offered sacrifices ; and, finally, similar representations of her, on Phœnician coins of a much later date, testify to its persistency. From all this, it appears that the national goddess of the Rapha race—the patroness of their first settlement, and especially (by name) of its metropolis, Ashtaroth-karnaim, or *the two-horned*—was, in the origin, no other than the particular form of the Mizraimite Isis known in the Egyptian pantheon as Athor, ' the abode' (or mother) of Horus.[b] The most ancient representations of Athor are those with a cow's head, enclosing the disk between its horns, precisely like the emblem among the spoils of the Rephaim. She was also represented with a human head bearing the horns and disk ; in this resembling the Shethite Astarte, Atesh.

Isis herself, in her own name, is often found bearing the emblem of Athor, either with or without the cow's head. Of the very few things certain in Egyptian mythology, none are more so than the sameness of these two impersonations. So obvious a derivation of Ashtaroth from Isis in the form of Athor is therefore an incident of great importance, as pointing out a period, however remote in the world's history, when the religious systems of the Rephaim and of the Egyptians met in one ; before those changes had been wrought in either system by the several foreign influences which superimposed astronomical associations and animal-worship on the Egyptian system ; and which degraded the simple cosmogonic idea

---

[b] Plutarch gives this as the signification of her name (*De Is.* s. 56), which its hieroglyph explains : a hawk (emb. of Horus) *within* a square, emb. of a house or abode, ḤT or ḤeT ; whence ḤT-ḤOR, or ḤeT'HOR, the abode, receptacle, of Horus. (Vide Wilkinson, *Anc. Egyptians*, vol. iv. p. 387.)

embodied in Athor by attributes and rites of unspeakable depravity in the other.

In the absence of any equally ancient full-length representation of the primitive Ashtaroth of Bashan, we must remain content to accept the well-known figure of the cow-headed Athor as the nearest approach to her emblem ; since we have at least a satisfactory verification of its authenticity, both in the effigies of Astarte which occur on the spoils of the SHAS·U people identified by so many tokens with the Zuzim of Scripture, and in the recurrence of the same emblem on their helmets, as a religious and national token.[c]

We are more fortunate in possessing the contemporaneous image of the very ÂSTE·TA, goddess of the SHET·TA, who is mentioned with SUTH, or SUTH·SH, as ratifying the treaty between that people and Rameses II. It is the middle figure of the triad sculptured in relief on the upper part of the tablet of Kaha. The Shethite tribe, whose tutelar goddess she was, bore her name, KEN קן, as the senior and metropolitan tribe bore that of their tutelar god Sheth, שת, or SUTH.

The proper name of this goddess is equivalent to a Hebrew translation of the Egyptian component HT or AIT, in the Mizraimite proper name Athor, the abode, receptacle, container, of life. קן is derived from קן, a primary root which, under the forms קנה and קנן, covers all the compound acceptations of our simple verb *to hold*, viz., obtain, contain, retain. The power of the play of words on this proper name, in Balaam's denunciation, is rendered doubly impressive by its evident allusion to the patron goddess and city of the nation :—

Thou settest בְּפֶלַע {in the Rock, קִנֶּךָ {thy nest,
{in Sela, Petra {thy ken,
Nevertheless, Ken shall be devoured !

As patroness of a junior tribe, Ken has not the horns and globe worn by Atesh. Moreover, her signature by proxy, in the treaty, exhibits her punctilious regard for the etiquette of precedence, by coming after the SUTH or SUTH·SH of the senior tribe. Her hair is dressed like that of the statues of Athor ; but she is naked. She stands on a lion, holding in her left hand two serpents tied together, and in her right, a circle formed by the curved stems of a lotus-flower and two buds, which she presents to her consort, Khem, or Chemosh.

---

[c] Four plates, illustrating the consecrated symbols and the costumes of the Rephaim, will appear in the next number of this journal, with the concluding part of the present series. The reader will be referred to these plates for figures of all the gods described in this chapter.

All these emblems are so different from the primeval type of Athor, that we would not have recognized her relation to that goddess without the connecting link afforded by the additional globe and horns of her counterpart AT·SH in the Louvre tablet. This evidence, however, is decisive ; were it less so, it would be confirmed by the name of the goddess.

The title of Ashtaroth on the Louvre tablet is ' AT·SH, goddess, lady of heaven, queen of gods.' This legend explains her title, ' the queen of heaven,' in Sacred Writ, and the epithet Urania, or Aphrodite-Urania, by which the Greek writers distinguish her from their own Aphrodite. Her territorial appellation, as Ken, makes her out especially as the Urania called Alilat and Alitta by the Arabians ; and as the Babylonian Mylitta, whose worship was introduced into Chaldea by the Arabians and Assyrians.[d]

Some sculptured figures of gods, found at Khorsabad, and given in Mr. Layard's great work on Nineveh, very distinctly establish the derivation of the Assyrian Astarte from the Shethite AT·SH and KEN. In one of these subjects, she sits on a throne, holding the mystic circle. Like AT·SH, she has two horns. She wears the Assyrian costume and crown, surmounted by a round ornament, equivalent to the globe. Another form of the goddess is more like AT·SH and KEN ; she stands on a lion, holding the circle, and also has two horns, and a star within the disk on the crown of her cap. These representations are much more recent than the Egyptian tablet that gives us her prototype, Ken.

The account given by Herodotus of the profane customs by which the Babylonian Mylitta was honoured, loses much of its incredible character, when, even at so early a period as the residence of Israel in Shittim (Num. xxv.), we can already trace analogous customs prevailing in a land under the particular tutelage of the same goddess Astarta, who, under the secondary forms of Atesh, Ken, Alilat, or Alitta, was protectress of the four Shethite provinces, Shittim, Ken, Amalek, and Elath. The catastrophe of the Midianite war proves that the people so called were deemed the principal agents in working out the scheme of corruption suggested by Balaam. The daughters of Moab were only put forward on the occasion as the tools of a political movement. From their kindred origin, and the brotherly feeling the Moabite tribe had manifested towards Israel on their passage through Ar,[e] they were judged more likely to succeed in alluring the children of Israel to break down the bar of religious separation that kept them aloof from the indigenous population.

It may be deemed no small addition to the antiquarian value of

---

[d] Herodotus, *Clio*, 131.　　　　[e] Deut. ii. 29.

our Museum-tablet, that the goddess who appears upon it should thus prove to be the heroine of two transactions so memorable in antiquity as those in which she figures as the imaginary witness to the most ancient international treaty in the world, and as the stumbling-block of Israel in Shittim.¹ But any shade of incredulity that might still remain as to this most interesting coincidence, must give way before the actual admission by Josephus—already referred to—that the idolatrous Midianites were the people one of whose five kings, Rekem, was the king of the city of Arekem, afterwards called Petra : when, on the other hand, we had already ascertained, from Scriptural references, that this very city, Petra or Arekem, was the stronghold of the Kenites, and that the Kenites themselves were subjects of the ruler of the metropolitan province, Heshbon in Shittim.

The degraded attributes of the southern Astarte, combined with the fact well known to antiquity that Athor was her primary form, may explain the selection of their Aphrodite by the Greeks, as the conventional synonym for the Egyptian Athor, although these two impersonations have not a discernible attribute in common. Some connection is indeed traceable between those of Astarte and the Grecian Aphrodite ; even though the latter has been veiled under a garb of imaginative grace and poetic beauty totally alien to the primitive framers of her Eastern prototype.

We have no direct proof in Scripture that the more corrupted worship of Ashtaroth had gained a footing among the Rephaim beyond the domains of the Shethite tribes ; unless the local names of Kinah and Ken in southern Judea (Josh. xv. 22, 57), and Kenath in Bashan (Num. xxxii. 42), are to be taken as indications that she had some votaries in those quarters. The very little we know of the primary Phœnician Astarte rather shows that, while her original form of Athor was never materially changed, the incidents of her mythical history draw her still nearer to the primeval source, by their close approximation to those of the bereaved Isis

---

¹ Our common version of Amos v. 26, 27, gives the noun כִּיּוּן *Chiun,* as if it were a proper name ; and from the resemblance of this to the name of Ken, it has been conjectured that Ken was the Midianite goddess alluded to. It is rather curious that a conjecture founded on an etymological error should turn out true in the fact ; for Ken *is* the Midianite goddess, but on other grounds. Even if כִּיּוּן were here a proper name, it would not apply to this goddess, whose name is written with different letters ; neither would it suit her as an epithet, 'the burning object,' the incandescent, implied by its root, כוה, to burn = και-ω (see Isa. iii. 24 ; Exod. xxi. 25). The application of this epithet will be shewn in its place ; here, I will only remark that the Scriptural name corresponding to the monumental ᴋɴ, קֵן, which gives its etymology, and the land and history of the goddess, is written with a ק, and the final ן is radical ; whereas in the epithet *Chiun* the initial is כ, and the ן final is a formative.

of Mizraim mourning the untimely death of her lord. Indeed the Greek fable of Venus and Adonis was so evidently derived from the Phœnician version of the Isidian myth, that it has retained the title of the god אדן, Adon, *the Ruler,* as a proper name, though his original relation of husband is changed to that of a lover. The proto-Phœnician Osiris in this peculiar character bore the name of Thamus ; and according to Gesenius, the mournful rites by which his supposed decease was celebrated are alluded to by Ezekiel : ' He brought me to the entrance of the northern gate of the Lord's house ; and lo ! there sat the women weeping for Thammuz ' (viii. 14). The reference in Ps. cvi. 28, to the backslidings of Israel in Shittim, apparently relates to the same subject :—

> ' They became united to Baal-Peor,
> And ate the sacrifices of the dead,'

inasmuch as the Syrian Belphegor, the local Baal of Peor in Shittim, exhibits many attributes of Osiris in the Plutonic character the latter assumes after his death.[a]

However slight such passing allusions may appear, they assume a deep significance, considered in connection with the Mizraimite origin of the goddess to whose mythical story the allusions apply ; and with the local character of the fabulous beings themselves, who figure in it as home-gods, not as importations ; as absolutely identified by their names with the oldest and chief settlements of the land in which they appear as subjects of the allusions. But this argument must be reserved as a separate topic, to be resumed when the whole of the pantheon has been disposed of. Then only can its force be appreciated.

Khem. *Chemosh.* *Khammon.*

Chemosh next claims our attention, as he is not the special patron of one tribe of Rephaim, but the great god of the whole nation. The Scriptural references to his name represent him as the Dispenser of Good, both to the Ammonites in virtue of their incorporation with the residue of the Zuzim, and to the Moabites amalgamated with the small remnant of the Shethite tribe.

The character and attributes assigned to this god may be seen by the tablet of Kaha, in which he appears as the consort of Astarte-Ken. They in no wise differ from those of the Egyptian Khem of the Mizraimite pantheon, whose name was afterwards changed to Amun-Ra. A little allowance must of course be made for some mannerisms in the treatment of the costume, which is wholly Egyptian : ascribing them to the conventional rules imposed by custom upon the artists who executed these subjects. But

---

[a] Selden, *Syr. Syntag.* i. c. 5.

characteristic attributes cannot be brought within the pale of such
allowance. Those of the god's companions, Ken and Rempu, are
so *un*-Egyptian, that the sculptor's total departure from the formulæ
prescribed in Egypt strongly argues that he wrought from a description, following no familiar exemplar at home; and that,
consequently, had the fundamental attributes of Chemosh been
different from those of the Egyptian Khem, he would have been
obliged to make them different, since he has made those of Astarte
so different from their prototype, the Egyptian Athor. As on the
contrary a figure of Khem of the most orthodox Egyptian construction was chosen by the artist, and accepted by the devotee
Kaha, as a representation of his god Chemosh, it must be because,
in their significant emblems, their identity was obvious to and
admitted by both.

The variation between the typical name KHEM, and the Chemosh
of the Rephaim, may be thus explained :—As the tutelar god of
the Shethites is styled indifferently SUTH or SUTH·SH on the same
monument, and their city on the Arnon, AT·SH, named from the
goddess, is often written ATI, or AT·T,[h] it thereby is demonstrated
by two authentic precedents found in the same land, and referable
to the same dialectic principle, that the final ש in these names is
no part of them, but only a mutable suffix or enclitic, whose
grammatical or etymological power is unknown; and the emblematical hieroglyphic of the Egyptian Khem being here used
for the name of Chemosh (כְּמִיש) in this tablet, shows that it sufficed
to express it.

Towards the close of the 18th dynasty, the phonetic name of
Khem was systematically erased from every inscription in which
it occurred, and the characters for AMN were substituted. Sir
Gardner Wilkinson limits the date of this change to the reign
of Amenoph III.;[i] and Chevalier Bunsen has further noticed that
where the compound form AMN-RA is found, the former name only

---

[h] By the elision of the mutable ש from this name, the radical remains AT, or
AT·T, which is the first component of Athor (vide note [b]) 'א, with the fem. particle,
and exactly equivalent in sense to קֵין, the *abode* or *receptacle*, but expressed in a
term common to the Shethite and Egyptian dialects; whereas קֵין is not Egyptian.
If it be not irrelevant for a suggestion to occupy the place of an illustration, may
not the Phœnician form Thamus itself be a similar compound? By dropping the
enclitic ש, it leaves תֹם, the Complete, Perfection, Integrity, root of the Egyptian
god ATHUM, or THUM, a title of Osiris after his death, as judge of the lower world.
Chevalier Bunsen quotes the following remarkable passage concerning him from
Lepsius' *Book of the Dead:* 'I am ATUM, making the heaven, creating beings,
going into the world, creating all generations which produced the gods, self-created,
lord of life, renewing the other gods.' The very same enclitic letter recurs in
Baal·is, name of an Ammonite king, Jer. xl. 14. A fabulous king Thamus also
appears in the primeval legends of Egypt.

[i] Wilkinson, *Anc. Egyp.* vol. iv. p. 243.

is over the erasure, and RA is unaltered. The suffix RA, the sun, is the addition peculiar to the Egyptian system, in which cosmogonic and astronomical elements are blended in one impersonation, a mixture totally unknown to the Rapha pantheon. We find among them nothing but the Mizraimite forms of the cosmogonic ideas. Their Khem-osh is like the Egyptian Khem, the primeval Osiris, as the Universal Parent of all created nature, manifested in the generative power by which the existence of the animate and inanimate is continued. It is an extension of the creative idea embodied in the primary PTAH (פתח) of the Mizraimite system, he who causes the opening or entering-in of existence, the active principle of original creation, who was therefore regarded in the proto-Phœnician mythology as the Father of all the other Cabiric theophanies.

In the old Egyptian pantheon, Khem was the consort of Maut, *the mother*. In the tablet of Kaha, Chemosh appears in an analogous relation to Isis-Athor in the character of Ken, the dwelling or receptacle of the power typified by the god. Their offspring, RNPU, forms the third member of this very remarkable group. remarkable from its being obviously composed on the genuine Mizraimite principle of the Egyptian local triads, in which the third or junior member embodies the development of the agency typified by the other two; the combination of two harmonious principles producing an effect; the active and passive agencies of nature guided by a Supreme Intelligence, and their result.

In the proper name of Khem we cannot fail to recognize the Ham (חם) of sacred tradition, progenitor of the Mizraimite race. Wherefore, this venerated ancestral name may have been purposely selected by his descendants, to distinguish the particular impersonation of divine power represented by that god,—Osiris, considered as dispenser of existence to all animated nature. Not that they worshipped their ancestor under the name or form of a god, but rather a sensible manifestation of divine power rendered intelligible by an emblematical representation, upon which, for distinction's sake, they conferred the name of their ancestor.

Chemosh is doubtless a form, or the proper name of מלך, Molech, he who reigns, '*the king*.' His Egyptian correspondent, or rather substitute, Amun, or Amun-Ra, is generally entitled 'the king of the gods.' This identification of the god by his attributes appears to explain the origin of the custom so often alluded to in Scripture, of 'passing children through a fire unto Molech.' It was originally a symbolical rite by which the people who owned him as their 'king of gods' solemnly dedicated their offspring to the giver of increase, in grateful acknowledgment of the gift. The offering of cakes and incense to the 'queen of heaven' (Jer. xliv. 17),

Ashtaroth, feminine principle of the same divine power, appears grounded on the same idea that the fruits of the earth, in Egypt, were offered to Khem, these two deities being regarded as joint givers of the earth's increase. Accordingly, the Jews in Egypt attribute the scarcity they complain of in their exile, to having left off their propitiatory offerings to the feminine giver of abundance, worshipped by their apostate fathers, kings and princes, in the cities of Judah, and in the streets of Jerusalem. The spoils of the Rephaim (vide the plates referred to in note [a]) present us with the very pattern of the vessels used in pouring out these libations. From their shape, they were evidently made of a cow's horn, emblem of the goddess; and the tip is finished with her head, in a human form. She wears a crown of lotus flowers and buds, and a long curl hanging down the side of her face. The offering was poured out from the broad end of the horn.

The figure of Khem generally has an altar beside it, bearing the offerings of fruit and corn claimed by that god.

There are strong grounds for believing that groups of Khem and Ashtaroth, similar to our tablet, are implied by the obscure references in Isaiah (xvii. 8; xxvii. 9) to הַחַמָּנִים, the Khammanim, and הָאֲשֵׁרִים, the Asherim, which occur together, and are rendered in our common translation *images* and *groves*. The names of Baal and Asherah are found similarly connected (Judg. iii. 7; and 2 Kings xxiii. 4). Gesenius has established that in such instances 'the Asherah' (אֲשֵׁרָה) is not *a grove*, as it is commonly translated, but the proper name of a goddess, a synonym of Astarte.[k] In Hebrew it has a meaning, 'the giver of prosperity,' and was probably her Canaanite name; it is easily recognized in another well-known synonym of that goddess (Hellenicè), Beltishera, *i. e.* Baalath-Asherah, or Asherah, consort of Baal; the very name thus associated with Asherah in the Bible. חמן Kham'n, is found compounded with the epithet Baal, in the following interesting Punic inscription on a votive tablet found by Chevalier Scheel near the site of ancient Carthage, and deposited in the museum of Copenhagen :—

לרבת · לתנת · ורבע   'To the Great One, to Thanath (THNTH)
ל · כל אדן · לבעל · חמן   and to the Lord of all lords, to Baal-
אישנדר · עבד · מלקר   Hamon (KHMN) devotes himself, the
ת · חישוטי · בן · ברמל   servant of Melkarth, Hashoti, son of
קרת · בן · חנא   Bar-Melkarth, son of Hana.'

---

[k] Vide particularly 1 Kings xv. 23: *groves* cannot well be said to be *built* under a high tree. Also 2 Kings xxi. 7, where the qualifying term פֶּסֶל decidedly implies *an object hewn in stone*, which cannot apply to *a grove*, but may mean a statue or a relievo figure of the Asherah.

This form, KHM·N, is obviously the Canaanite augmentative of Khem ; and Bâl-Khm·n is the name and title corresponding to the Molech-Khem·sh of the unknown dialect of the Rephaim, and to the ' Amun-Ra, king of gods,' of the Thebaid ; consequently, the same god is meant, whether the compound be used, or either of its separate constituents ; Baal or Molech, the epithets ; or Kham·n, Khem·ush, or Khem, the specific name. From the distinction suggested by 1 Kings xi. 7, we may perhaps infer that the royal tribe of the Rephaim, territorial predecessors of the Ammonites, had preferably called him by the epithet Molech, the *royal* god ; while the southern branch, represented by the Moabites, had retained the proper name of the same deity.

A lion's head, crowned, appears to have been the emblem of the ' king of gods ' on the consecrated utensils of his sanctuary. This form occurs on an urn among the spoils of the SHAS·U of the Upper MNA region, or Rephaim of Jerusalem. There is a similar urn, with the lion's head uncrowned, among the spoils of the TAHI (Anakim), and of the SHET·TA (Emim). In the latter, the lion is placed between two geese. This may be an intimation of the god's parentage ; as a goose is the hieroglyphic figure employed to write ideagraphically the name of Seb, father of Osiris and Sheth.[m] A lotus-crowned patera, supported by two geese, occurs among the TAHI symbols ; and the same bird surmounts an urn belonging to the SHET·TA : so that the goose is evidently a sacred symbol common to the Rapha nations.

SUTH, SUTH·SH, or *Sheth.*

In the historical notice of the children of Sheth, I partly anticipated on the account of their tutelar god ; especially on his unquestionable Egyptian character and pedigree, granted by the Egyptians themselves. He was the third son of Seb and Netpe ; and consequently, brother of Osiris, Haroeris or Horus the elder, Isis, and Nephthys ; patron gods, with Sheth, of the five days over the year.

On Egyptian monuments, he is represented under several names, as a figure with the head of a fabulous long-snouted animal whose ears are square at the top. One of these gives the phonetic name ST. When he bears the name of BARO—Baal—he has the same head on an equally imaginary animal's body, sitting like a dog, with an upright tufted tail.

Sir Gardner Wilkinson gives a copy of a most interesting seal in the possession of Chevalier Kestner, in which the figure with the characteristic square ears and pointed snout stands for the third

---

[m] Wilkinson, *Anc. Egyp.*, vol. iv. p. 311, pl. 31, fig. 1.

name of the five patrons of the epact ; and this third day was the day dedicated to Sheth. He also refers to the occurrence of the same five names with those of the parent gods, Seb and Netpe, on the wooden cubits found at Memphis.[n] The same figure forms the name of the king whom Manetho calls Sethos ; it also determines the god's name, when written phonetically ST, and the corresponding form SUTH or SUTH·SH of the god who signs the treaty with Rameses II. on behalf of his children. It therefore appears that Plutarch was correct in giving SETH as the name of the brother of Osiris whom the Greeks called Typhon ; and the appropriation of that proper name to the square-eared god is verified beyond a doubt.

Sheth is represented on the sculptures of Rameses II. with the title of NUB·TT, with Horus, putting the double crown on the king's head,[o] and in another subject, pouring life and power upon him ; at Karnak, he is pictured teaching Thothmes III. the use of the bow. Several variants of the square-eared god's figure are given in Burton's Excerpta (pl. 37) ; but all these subjects are purely Egyptian. If the form and emblems under which the Shethite Rephaim represented their tutelar genius under his proper name differed in any essential point, they must remain unknown.

The metaphysical functions of Sheth among his mythical brethren may be deduced with certainty from what is well known of theirs, by their attributes on Egyptian monuments. Osiris was the Divine Agency dispensing good to man ; Horus and Sheth protected him from evil ; the former, by watching over him ; the latter, by enduing him with the power to withstand it.[p] SETH may be regarded as a personification of the *Divine Helper*. I own I cannot assent to the prevalent opinion that this impersonation was primarily meant to embody an evil power or being, under any qualification of terms. He who assists Horus in crowning the king—he who with Horus sheds life and power upon him—he who teaches him *how to use his weapons against his enemies*, a most significant suggestion—he who is called ' Suth·esh the son of Netpe, the great disturber Baal *who smites his enemies*,' and to whom Egyptian hierogrammatists are proud to compare their royal heroes in their character of avengers of their land by the destruction of its foes,—surely *he* cannot, at that time, have been regarded as an *evil* being, in any sense ! Such an idea appears to involve an

---

[n] Wilkinson, *Anc. Egyp.*, vol. iv. p. 415, and pl. 38, part 2, where his name was given Ombo, the force of the characters which compose it being then considered doubtful.

[o] Ibid., vol. v. pl. 78, and iv. pl. 39.

[p] Plutarch thus gives the etymology of the Egyptian name: ' Σηθ φράζει μὲν τὸ καταδυναστεῦον καὶ καταβιαζόμενον,' what *exercises power over* . . . and *overpowers* or restrains by force.

absolute inversion of his attributes. So far from representing the
abstract Power of Evil acting in opposition to Good, even to produce
good, he seems, both by his primary name and secondary forms, to
embody that Good Agency that encourages and empowers frail
humanity to act in opposition to evil, under whatever form it may
present itself. This view of his character explains his constant
association with his brother Horus, who embodied the Divine
Guardian, the Superintending Providence.[q] In the picture of the
young Thothmes III. learning the use of his weapons, the king
holds the bow and arrows, but Sheth *teaches him*—he guides his
hands : the king darts the javelin into a target, but Horus *loves
him*, for the god's arms are most affectionately—though rather
awkwardly—entwined round the neck of his youthful charge.
Indeed the functions of the two *forms* assumed by the protecting
power are so nearly allied, that in one very curious representation
of Sheth they are found united in a double-headed body, the
square-eared Sheth looking one way, and the hawk-faced Horus
the other.

It is not until a much later epoch than that of the above designs
that Sheth, under his own name, became unpopular in Egypt.
The change of feeling towards him was gradually wrought out by
circumstances. As tutelar god of the fiercest enemies the Egyptians ever had to encounter, he first came to be regarded from
a *political* point of view as the foe of Osiris their benefactor, and of
Horus their protector ; his more abstract character being partially
lost sight of. Popular legends now took up this view ; the heroic
compositions of a secondary age adapted the political similitude to
the primeval religious mystery ; and so, by grafting one myth on
another, transmitted his name to future generations as the betrayer
and murderer of his brother Osiris the good. Thus, little by little,
the national mind became so familiarized with the tangible idea
of his *antagonism to Osiris*, that this character ended in super-
seding the metaphysical conception of which Sheth had originally been the type. The Beneficent Antagonist of evil actually
ended in becoming so obnoxious to popular prejudice as the
Malevolent Antagonist of good, that his very figure became an
object of aversion, and every opportunity was sought of erasing
or defacing it on the sacred edifices its presence was thought to
profane.

The representations of Sheth under the title of NUB-TET are
important, as intimating that he and the Egyptian TET (Thoth) are

---

[q] The well known *winged-globe* emblem is one of the secondary forms of Horus;
NON-HT, or HT, *the shelter*. Hence Egypt is described as 'the land of the over-
shadowing wings,' b. xviii. 1. The 'shadow of thy wings' is a frequent metaphor
in poetic Scripture for the providential care of Jehovah.

only considered as various forms of the same emblematical being,[*] TET the *teacher* in general, NUB·TET or Nebo-Thoth, the *lord-teacher* in particular. So that the Egyptian factotum, Thoth, is merely one among several secondary manifestations of the prime exemplar Sheth, brother of Osiris, helper of man, viz., his helper in understanding. According to Sanchoniatho, the Phœnicians professed to have been instructed in letters and all useful things by one called Thautus, just like the Egyptians by their Thoth. And this derivation of Thoth from Sheth seems to illustrate the ancient tradition of the 'pillars of Seth,' on which the elements of their learning were inscribed and preserved.

The identity of Thoth with Sheth in a special character is admitted by the Egyptians themselves. One of the names of Sheth given by Plutarch, is SMU; whereupon, in his chapter on Sheth, Chev. Bunsen remarks, 'it reminds us of Thoth's title Lord of Eshmunein, derived from *Shmun*, the eighth. In a passage of the Book of the Dead noticed to us by Birch, we read " *Tet, otherwise Set.*" This intimates that Thoth inherited many of the attributes of Seth.' And in his chapter on Thoth, the same distinguished author observes on the titles of Thoth, 'Lord of Shmun—Hermopolis—literally, *lord of the Eighth region*; this reminds us of the well known Cabir Esmun of Phœnicia and Samothrace.' (P. 427 and 393.) To these suggestions, I will only add; put them together, and they confirm each other. SMU, given by Plutarch as a title of SETH, is simply ESHMUN, a little mangled by the Greek interpreter; the Phœnician אשמן, derived from שמי, *eight*: for the title of Thoth in his legends, Lord of SHMUN-NU, is written with *eight strokes*; which proves both the orthography and the etymology of the name : ' Lord of the region of Eshmun,' or ' *the Eighth*;' and in so doing, establishes the Phœnician character of the original possessor and patronym of the region appropriated to Thoth. This region is still called Oshmounein : the Greeks called it Hermopolis, *the city of Hermes*, because they *identified* their 'Ερμης, the Interpreter, with Thoth, ' *otherwise Sheth*,' though they *derived* him from the Pelasgic or Proto-Phœnician Cabir Eshmun ' *the eighth*,' who is SMU the synonym of Sheth. The conclusion arising out of these considerations, is therefore clearly this :

---

[*] The ancient Egyptian radical *tt* is exactly equivalent in all its derivations to those of the Hebrew דבר and the Greek λεγ, ' to say,' or speak, whence λογος. The Egyptian Greeks, therefore, made out Thoth to be Hermes, ' the interpreter.'

The Egyptian form of NUB·TT consists of the gold bowl (syllabically read NUB in the title of Amenemha II. on the tablets of Abydos and Karnak), N, and the complementary leg, B, followed by the name of Thoth phonetically written, T and the S. of duplication = TT. The gold vessel seems to have been chosen for its sound rather than the common vessel NEB, because of its greater resemblance to NBU, נבו; but the radical sense of the epithet remains the same, 'lord-teacher.'

Sheth or SUTII is the proper name, the *character-name*, and
represents the primary form of the divine impersonation it denotes ;
while the other character-names are qualifications of that primary,
and therefore secondaries to it.

Sheth, which means ' what exercises power over . . . and overpowers,' is that emanation of the Primeval Osiris, the overcomer of
Evil, which is *the Helper.* Hence he is mythically regarded as
brother to the same Osiris, considered in a more exclusive light as
the Giver, whether of life or of all other good things. And under
that, his primitive and proper name, we find Sheth established in
a territorial character also, as the tutelar god of the Emim, and
patronym of their land and tribe, Shittim or SHET·TA·N, the ' land
of SHET.'

Baal or ' BARO, who smites his enemies,' is a title applied to
him as *Helper of the nation :* whether in Egypt or in Phœnicia.

Thoth or TT, the speaker and teacher, or interpreter, is the
Helper in Wisdom, and likewise a character common to Egypt and
Phœnicia.

Nebo-Thoth, or NUB·TT, is a more exclusive form of the same,
peculiar to Egypt, the imparter of knowledge and power to kings.

Eshmun, Shmun or SMU, *the Eighth,* is simply his ordinal designation in the primeval Cabiric scheme ; for originally, according
to Herodotus, the Cabiri had *no names.*

It is under the latter designation that Sheth was revered by the
Canaanites, his proper name being regarded as the privilege and
heritage of his children. In this way, the synonym Eshmun became
known to the garbled traditions of the post-Phœnician period,
ascribed to Sanchoniatho by his copyists ; but this period only *begins*
with the Hebrew conquest. The name Eshmun occurs on Punic
inscriptions ; an ancient tombstone discovered near the site of
ancient Carthage presents it as the name of a deity patronym of a
man.

קברי הובס עבד חוא בן עבד־אישמן

Grave of Hobas, servant of Hava, son of Abd-Eshmun.[*]

The scriptural form corresponding to NUB נְבוֹ, Nebo, is found as
a local name in the domains of the children of Sheth. Mount
Nebo was the most elevated part of the Abarim or Moabite mountains, in which that tribe pastured their flocks. Its being charac-
terized as the summit of the high-land, ראֹשׁ הַפִּסְגָּה, suggests the
most probable situation of the height called Mount Nebo, as the
watershed which separates the valley of the Zurka from that of the
Arnon, and where the latter and its tributaries take their rise.

---

[*] Falbe, *Carthage.* Hava, *Life,* is a synonym of Astarte.

From this high ground, the vapoury vale of the Jordan might be just discernible, the mountains of Judea looming in the far distance above it. It is a strange coincidence and worthy of a passing notice, that there, on a mountain dedicated by name to the primeval mythical embodiment of the Fountain of Religion and Knowledge, that great lawgiver died, whose books are *our* foundation of religion—*our* treasury of all knowledge in History and Antiquity;—though no man knoweth his grave to this day.

Renpu. *Remphan.*

From his attributes, renpu was undoubtedly a secondary form of Sheth, the Helper as the Avenger, the warrior-god fighting for his children. His figure, in Egypt, is only found on tablets, and does not belong to the Pantheon of that land. It corresponds to the Egyptian Baro or Baal. His characteristic emblem is the head of an oryx or a mountain gazelle, which appears projecting from his forehead. This same head is a very prominent emblem among the sacred vessels of the Rephaim; quite as much so as that of the cow-headed Ashtaroth. In the origin, he was very probably represented with the head of that animal.

In Sir Gardner Wilkinson's illustrations of the Egyptian Pantheon, two single representations of this god are given, which differ very slightly in their accessories. Their Egyptian costume (for they wear the crown of the Upper country) shows that they must have been executed for a devotee residing in the Thebaïd. In the first figure, Renpu is in a walking attitude, armed to the teeth; he brandishes a battle-axe over his head with his right hand, while his left grasps a shield and spear; a quiver is slung to his back. The other figure is seated, and has the battle-axe and shield, but neither spear nor quiver.[1]

In the triad of the tablet of Kaha, Renpu stands on a pedestal on the left of Astarta-Ken. His right hand holds the long spear, his left the emblem of life. He has no crown, but only the simple fillet and tie round his hair, like that of the Horite chiefs; and the distinctive oryx's head projecting in front. But what is most worthy of attention in this representation, is the *form* and *cut of his beard.* Nothing can be more un-Egyptian. It is the peculiar angular clipped beard characteristic of those among the Rephaim race who wear any beard. We need not ask why they affected that particular fashion: *their god was shaved so!*

One of the Khorsabad sculptures given in Mr. Layard's work on Nineveh contains the figure of Baal, in an attitude and with emblems as evidently copied from the attributes of Sheth the war-

---

[1] Wilkinson, *Anc. Egyp.*, vol. v. pl. 69.

rior, as those of the Assyrian Astarte were from the Atesh of
Shittim. The god is walking ; he has an axe in his right hand,
and in his left a bundle of either arrows or thunderbolts. He
wears, of course, the Assyrian costume, and his head is adorned
with a double pair of horns, but the oryx-emblem is absent.
However, as we know from the Egyptian monumental notices
that Sheth, and Baal or ' Baro who smites his enemies,' are the
same god, the one in his proper local name, the other in a special
character, his identity with the Egyptianized Renpu is substantiated by the Assyrian copy of the latter bearing the name of the
one with the form of the other. By tracing this god to his original form and home, we obtain another interesting elucidation of a
very obscure passage of Scripture ; the much-commented and
never-explained Amos v. 26, 27. I have already remarked on
the misappropriation of the epithet כִּיּוּן to the goddess Ken ; I have
therefore only to follow up the clue to its right appropriation.
This is suggested, and as we shall find, correctly, by the Septuagint substitute ʿΡαιφαν, or according to the quotation in Acts vii.
ʿΡεμφαν. These translators, residing in Egypt at a period when
its hieroglyphic writing and mythological system were known matters of every-day teaching, appear to have availed themselves of
the knowledge that the tutelar god Sheth of the Midianite region
was SUTH·SII or Sothis, patronymic of the brilliant dog-star,[u]
and that Renpu or Remphan was particularly his local character
in Ken, to point out the ultimate application of the vague epithet
כִּיּוּן, ' the Incandescent,' to the god it meant, by substituting *his
name*, and thus rendering it perfectly clear *who* was the ' *star-god* '
in the explanatory verse that follows.

> ' The sacrifices, and the offering,
>   Did ye present them unto Me
> In the desert, forty years, O ye sons of Israel?'

HEB.	SEPT.
Ye bore the shrine of *your* ' Molech,'	Ye bore the shrine of Molech,
And the Burning-object (chiun) of *your* images,	And the star of your god
The Star of your god	*Raiphan* (for chiun), *their* images
Which ye made for yourselves.[x]	Which ye made for yourselves.

We need not inquire which of these various distributions is the
most likely to be the authentic reading : that is a question of
verbal criticism foreign to the present subject. All that concerns
us is the fact that SUTH·SII or Sothis was the patron of the dog-
star, the Chiun, כִּיּוּן, or ' Incandescent ;' and that he was also
Renpu, Raiphan, or Remphan ; and that this identity, notorious

---

[u] Bunsen, *Egypt's Place*, vol. i. p. 429.
[x] This may be translated ' Your images of the Incandescent.' ' Your Star-god.'

in Egypt, and well known to the Greek interpreters, dictated their substitution of the *name* Renpu for the *epithet* Chiun (כִּיּוֹן).

The *crux ansata* held by Renpu in the tablet group deserves a remark. As it is the well-known hieroglyphic emblem of life, generally put into the hands of Egyptian divinities, it might here be taken for an Egyptian conventionality. But the spoils of the Rephaim in the triumphs of Seti-Menephtah shut out this supposition, for among these, that very emblem forms a conspicuous object, beautifully ornamented. A vessel among the LT-N (Elathite) spoils is formed by the cross; two kneeling figures of men support the arms, and the effigies of two gods, Ashtaroth and Renpu, surmount the circular upper limb. In another, among the spoils of the SHET'TA (Emin), the cross is supported by the oryxhead of Renpu, but the effigy over the top is obliterated. The specimen among the spoils of the TAHI Anakim is not ornamented with any effigies of gods.[y]

ANK. *Anak, Onka.*

Onka is well known to antiquity as a great Phœnician goddess. Pausanias regards her as the Athene of Thebes in Bœotia, where, like the Egyptian prototype of Athene, NEITH, she was worshipped in a temple without a roof; and her establishment there is quite in harmony with the tradition that ascribes the foundation of Thebes to Cadmus the Phœnician. From what we have seen of the children of Anak, it is manifest that she was the tutelar genius and patronymic of their nation, which by its name עֲנָקִים, Onkites, justly claims to be the original people from whom the appellation Phœnicians was derived, though we find it applied in after-times to a different people.

The costume of the gods is generally borrowed from that of the people. I have already had occasion to notice the identity of the head attire of the Philistians, and that of the Egyptian goddess ANK; the resemblance is not only in the circular crown of upright feathers which crests the cap, but in the form of the cap itself.[z] This indicates a particular locality—Southern Palestine—as the original seat of a divine impersonation, which we nevertheless find extending at the earliest period of Egyptian history to beyond the cataracts of the Nile; since ANK is found there as a member of the northern Ethiopian triad. She was honoured as a contemplar deity throughout all Egypt, though we must go out of Egypt to find her territorial and primary seat. The only Egyptian goddess

---

[y] See note a for references.

[z] Compare the goddess ANK nursing the king, Rosel., *Mon. Stor.*, pl. 62, s. 4. with the battle-scene (127 and 131) of Medinet Abou, and the figure of ANK in Wilkinson's *Anc. Egyp.*, vol. v. pl. 48, part 2.

besides ANK, who wears the same head-dress, is PE or TPE, the personification of the celestial firmament on monuments of the remotest antiquity.

On an inscription of the Ptolemaic period, in the island of Sehayl, immediately below the first cataract, the Greek form of her name is given as ''Ανουχη, called also Εστια.'[a] As the Grecian Aphrodite, in her attributes, was connected with the Athor of the Rephaim, though she had nothing in common with that of the Egyptians—so we shall find the Grecian Hestia (Vesta) connected in hers only with the ANK of the Rephaim, having nothing in common with the Egyptian goddess. Sir Gardner Wilkinson gives a copy of a triad in the temple of Denderah, composed of Isis, Horus, and Nephthys, in which the latter is styled 'NEB'TEI, the Saviour-sister, ANK.'[b] Here, the Egyptians themselves, in an orthodox temple-representation, admit that the mythical Nephthys, sister of Osiris, Horus, and Sheth, and wife of the latter, is one and the same with her who in her territorial character is called ANK. Now, in this identity alone can we understand her being identified with the Grecian Hestia or Vesta. The *name* of Nephthys, which gives *her character*, is in its Egyptian etymology, 'The lady over the abode.'[c] This ascribes the very same character to her, as the Greek 'Εστια, the goddess guardian of the household and domestic hearth. The Greeks recognized this character in ANK, and yet it could only suit *her*, from her being *also* ' NEB'T'EI, the Saviour sister.' The Greek parentage of Hestia also agrees with that of Nephthys, as Seb and Netpe are the Egyptian correspondents of Chronos and Rhea, parents of Vesta.

'Nephthys, the Saviour-sister,' was the consort of Sheth. It was a beautiful idea, thus to subdivide the *Power that averts Evil* into a masculine and a feminine impersonation; the former, as teaching man to defend his person and father-land,—the latter, as presiding over his hearth and home!

Nephthys, the Saviour-sister, ANK, has also another character, in which she assumes a more active office as protectress of her children. This form is also common to the Egyptian and proto-Phœnician goddesses; for Onka was regarded as the Athene of Bœotia, Pallas the warrior, the shield and champion of her votaries; and Neith, the territorial divinity of Saïs in Lower Egypt—Neith, the prototype of Athene, and patronym of Athens, which was founded by a colony of emigrants from Saïs,—even Neith herself was only regarded *in Egypt* as a derivative form of ANK, ANK as

---

[a] Wilkinson, *Anc. Egyp.*, vol. v. p. 26.

[b] Ibid., vol. iv. p. 438.

[c] ' Her name consists of a bowl, called *neb*, placed upon a house, answering to EI or TEI.'—Ibid.

the warrior goddess. A very important representation of her in that character, at Thebes, is given in Sir Gardner Wilkinson's valuable collection of Egyptian divinities,[d] where she is figured with a bow and arrows in her hand; the name on her legend is TH·NTH-ANK. And an equally explicit admission of the identity of Neith with Onka in her warlike character, on the part of her children in Palestine, will be found on the person of the chief of the Anakim who represents the TEMAHU race (or Rephaim) in the tomb of Seti-Menephtah;[e] but if we would feel the full value of its testimony, we must recur to the mysterious prohibition in Lev. xix. 27, which has already received, in part, so striking an illustration in the monumental representations of some branches of that extraordinary people.

' Ye shall not round off the extremity (of the hair on) your heads, neither shalt thou destroy the extremity of thy beard: Ye shall not make incisions in your flesh for a corpse, nor put upon yourselves כְּתֹבֶת קַעֲקַע the writing (or impression) of a token-mark: I am JEHOVAH!'

We know that the *first* of these prohibitions aimed at a religious demonstration we have traced home to the Amalekites: the *second* at the national token of the whole Rapha race without exception. The *third* was probably one of their customs, since it is alluded to as a rite of the priests of Baal in cases of peculiar solemnity.[f] But at what people and at what religious custom did the *fourth* specially point?

The son of Anak, in the Theban tomb painting, bears the answer *on his person*. Details of costume are here given, which would be superfluous, confusing, and irrelevant in an historical subject; but in a representation intended to exhibit the characteristic customs of the races whom the great Theban king claimed as his subjects, it was indispensable to express them. All the minutiæ of his costume are therefore given with scrupulous precision; and, among other things, we observe certain marks conspicuously painted or tattooed on the fore part of the bare arm and leg of this Anakite chief—an unknown object of a very peculiar form, and certainly not put there for ornament, for it is not a flower, nor an animal, nor any natural object that might be regarded as ornamental. It is simply the well-known figure conventionally called

---

[d] Wilkinson, *Anc. Egyp.*, vol. iv. pl. 28, fig. 1. I understand from Sir Gardner Wilkinson that this interesting representation is of Pharaonic age.

[e] Vide Rosellini, *Mon. Storici*, pl. 155.

[f] Compare 1 Kings xviii. 28. Herodotus relates a practice of the Arabians of Jenysus, analogous to this, when they make a solemn pledge. A man, who stands between the contracting parties, grazes the skin of the hand of each with a sharp stone, and with a shred of their garment dipped in the blood he anoints seven stones lying between them, invoking Orotal and Alilat. Thalia, 8.

a *shuttle* by hieroglyphists (though it rather resembles a *bracelet*), which is employed in Egyptian inscriptions to write the name of Neith, or as the determinative of the name when written phonetically, NTH. It is the goddess's *primeval symbol*, and it is the religious and national token-mark of a son of ANK, imprinted on his person.

This fact speaks for itself; it needs no comment. On the walls of their sanctuaries, the Egyptians admit that their great local goddess Neith is only a form of ANK; and the children of Anak boast of their allegiance to her as the patroness of their homestead by bearing upon their flesh before the face of their enemies the protecting name of Neith! [g]

'The statement of Pausanias that Onka *in the character of Athene* was the deity honoured by the Thebans and Gephyreans of Bœotia, is thus doubly verified. The exile Phœnician chief introduced the tutelar genius of his father-land under the form that had been most honoured by his people – their defender in danger. But that, as in Egypt, was only a *secondary* character of 'the Lady over the home, the Saviour-sister, ANK.' She is also to be met with by name in this secondary character on her own soil, under the corresponding forms of ANATH and THANATH, and is figured by that name, ANTA, in Egypt; so that we can place side by side and compare the NEITH-ANK of the Egyptians with her not less ancient counterpart, the Anath-Onka of the Rephaim.

ANTA. ANATH. Thanath.

ANTA is thus a deity analogous to RENPU; a modified form of the Averter of Evil. She bears the same relation to NEB'T'EI ANK, *Protectress of the Homes* of the children of Anak, that RENPU does to SUTH, protector of the children of Sheth; being the patronym of their land in the special character of *Protectress of the national Homestead*. She then bears warlike attributes corresponding to those of the Egyptian Neith-Ank.

ANTA is not a member of the Egyptian pantheon, and is not found in any temple.[h] She is depicted in the lower compartment

---

[g] Since the above was written, Sir Gardner Wilkinson has mentioned to me two other instances he has met with in Egypt of ANK and NETH being identified with each other. I quote from his own communication on the subject:—'That this goddess (ANK), the Egyptian Vesta, was a character of Neith is evident, as we find her on an ancient tablet in the island of Sehayl, as well as in the Temple of Philæ; the former of Pharaonic, the latter of Ptolemaic time. She is called ANK, lady of the land of Neith.'

These two instances are very valuable; 1stly, as corroborating the view I expressed above, that Neith and Ank are only two forms of the same primary character, Nephthys, guardian of the house, wife of the defender of the land; 2ndly, as showing, by the dates of the two representations referred to, the antiquity and persistency of that opinion in Egypt; 3rdly, as proving the orthodoxy of that opinion, by the fact of its being confessed in a templar representation.

[h] Vide also Wilkinson, *Anc. Egyp.*, vol. v. pl. 70, part 1.

of the tablet of Kaha in our Museum, receiving offerings from the
wife and family of that functionary; the upper compartment
being occupied by the great national triad. She sits on a throne,
brandishing the same battle-axe as Renpu, with one hand, and
holding a shield and lance in the other. She wears the crown of
Upper Egypt, like the single figures of Renpu, and for the same
reason, her devotees being residents in that country : but with this
difference, that it is decorated with *two feathers.* A crest of two
feathers we know to be a characteristic point of costume among
some Anakim tribes; they are a very conspicuous ornament on the
figure who bears the hieroglyph of Neith on his limbs. This
being a national peculiarity, it was necessary to introduce it in the
costume of the goddess of the nation. Consequently, the Egyptian
artisan who executed the figure has rather awkwardly tried to
combine it with the conical cap of the Upper country, which
custom required she should wear in Egypt, by fixing the two feathers up the side of the cap.

This distinctive feature of costume suggests, that in order to
distinguish their tribe by some outward token, the Philistine children of Onka had adopted the badge of the goddess of the land
in her domestic character, the simple Onka-Nephthys, the *Guardian ;* whereas the mountain-tribe, who garrisoned the fortresses,
had given the preference to that which indicated her bellicose
attributes, Onka-Anath the Defender.

Among the mutilated sculptures of Beit-el-Wally,[1] illustrating
the early campaigns of Rameses II., there occurs a subject which
enables us to identify the emblem of Anath among the sacred
symbols of the Rephaim. The king is engaged in single combat
with a chief whose imperfect costume makes it uncertain whether
he be one of the Anakim, or of the shas·u of the Upper mna, or
Jerusalem region; the head-dress square-cut behind and short
kilt being common to both. Rameses of course is giving his enemy
the *coup de grace ;* and, as if to show that even the tutelar goddess
of his enemies had forsaken them, she is introduced joining the
king in his attack, under the form of *a dog,* a domestic dog with a
collar on : over its head is the name ‘ Anta the Goddess.’

Now, among the spoils of Seti-Menephtah there is a vase
crowned with lotuses and buds, in three rows, of a beautiful form,
apparently representing the land and the river ; and on the foot
of the vase, supporting it like the other sacred emblems we know
to be gods, are *two dogs.* It is the only instance of this animal’s
being found among these objects, and it occurs among the spoils
of the lt·n, dependency of the children of Sheth. The faithful

---

[1] Rosellini, *Mon. Storici*, pl. 66.

and watchful house-dog is a very appropriate emblem to typify the Protectress of the Homestead.

The name of Anath occurs in the geographical notices of Scripture ; there was a Beth Anath, בֵּית־עֲנָת, in northern Canaan, Anathoth, עֲנָתוֹת, near Jerusalem, and Beth-Anoth in southern Judea.

The form Thanath, תֵּ׳נַתֿ, in which the feminine particle appears combined with the name, is of frequent occurrence on Phœnician inscriptions. It is found on the Punic tablet quoted above ; and shows that the goddess was greatly venerated by the Tyrian colony of Carthage. As Anata and Anaitis, she was also extensively honoured in the land northward of Phœnicia, even to the confines of Armenia.

HOR. HAROERI. *Horus.*

It hitherto appears that four out of the five gods to whom the five supernumerary days of the year were dedicated by the Egyptians, are the types into which the chief and tutelar gods of the Rephaim are ultimately resolvable : Osiris and Isis as the givers of life Sheth and Nephthys as the Averters of Evil. This leaves a reasonable probability that the fifth member of this mythical family—Horus the Protector—was not unrepresented in the pantheon of the Rephaim.

Hor, or Haroeri, brother of Osiris, is also called HT, 'the Shelter,' and HOR-HT, under which names he is figured either with a hawk's head, or as the well known *winged globe*, the Agathodæmon of Egypt. Now, according to Eusebius, the Agathodæmon of the Phœnicians also had a hawk's head ;[k] and this statement is not inconsistent with the fact that among the spoils of their precursors, the Rephaim, there occurs a sacred vessel with the head of a hawk, eagle, or rapacious bird of some kind, on its cover.

Certain local names in their land, by their repetition, would also testify to the worship of Horus. There was a Beth-Horon in Judea, and another in Shittim, and also Horon-aim, the double-city of Hor. On the frontier of southern Judea we find the fortress of Aroër ; another Aroër on the Arnon, on the frontier of Moab ; a third 'before Rabbah,' on the frontier of the Zuzim ; as if frontier cities were specially committed to his guardianship. Whether this form of the Divine Protector was selected by the Amalekites as the watchers of the nation, is a question which may be further suggested by the name they gave to the form of the Universal Osiris they especially reverenced—Oro-tal. The syllable TAR or TAL occurs so often as a mere *addition to the name,*

---

[k] Eusebius, *Præp. Ev.* l. 10. Vide Rosellini, *Mon. Storici*, pl. 48.

among those of the Shethite chiefs drowned before Atesh,[m] that it appears very probable it was only a title or compound, of which the power is not known; and that нон is the radical name of the god referred to by Herodotus in his account of the Arabians of Jenysus.

AON. *Oannes. Dagon.*

The figure of the Chaldean Oannes, discovered on the sculptured remains of ancient Nineveh, is valuable in two respects; firstly, in that it enables us to reunite him by name to the Mizraimite On, his original; and by his form, to the particular portion of the Mizraimite people inhabiting Pelesheth and its dependencies. Secondly, in that the mythical account by Berosus,[n] of the manner in which Oannes first made himself known on the shores of the Persian Gulf, by rising from the sea to instruct the Chaldeans in all religious and useful knowledge, implies that a certain learned and civilised people, who navigated those seas, were the medium of those communications, and taught in his name; whence the great probability that the other gods of the same people, found in company with Oannes, were also introduced by that people.

Herodotus says that the early maritime settlements of the Phœnicians were on the Erythrean Sea. Under that name he of course could not mean the Canaanites, who never extended beyond the Jordan. Neither must we apply this statement to the nation who more strictly claim the name of Phœnicians — the children of Onka — since they were an *inland* tribe of the great parent nation, extending by the Philistine branch to the Mediterranean in quite another direction. These, however, were only part of a whole; a member of that great body whose wealthiest commercial establishments were on the Elanitic Gulf, and whose ships had navigated the Erythrean Sea to the south, while their caravans brought merchandise across the Arabian desert from the north, for many ages before the wilds of Greece had received from their western colonies the elements of her arts, letters, and civilization. Although Herodotus has evidently put one part of the nation for another, his statement is based on a truth; for the ' Phœnicians ' read the ' Rephaim,' and it becomes strictly correct. As early as the period of Thothmes III.—while Joseph was living in Egypt—when the great nation, her rival, was beginning to decline, and its emigrant

---

[m] Out of *twelve* legible names, in the legends over their floating bodies, *four* present this compound: TAR-KANUNASA, TAR-KATI, TEKA-TAR, and SAP-TAR, besides beginning another mutilated name. The reader will bear in mind that L and R are represented in Egyptian by the same character. Rosellini, *Mon. Storici*, pl. 109, 110.

[n] Cory's *Ancient Fragments*, p. 28.

kindred from Lower Egypt were founding settlements in the Pelo-
ponnesus, while those of Palestine were concentrating all their
forces from far and near to resist the Egyptian invading power ; even
so early do we find the name of the Horite city Elath, ʟᴛʼɴʼɴᴜ,
bringing to the treasury of the conqueror the tribute of the wealth
she had amassed in her traffic with the Euphratesian regions of
sᴀᴇɴᴋᴀʀ (Shinâr, שִׁנְעָר) and ʙʙʟ (Babel, בָּבֶל).[o]

Oannes, Ωαννης, thus introduced into the East, is merely the
Hebrew Aon, אוֹן, with a Greek case-termination ; and the Hebrew form is only a transcript of an ancient Coptic word which,
according to Champollion, signifies 'to enlighten.'

Aon was the original name of the god worshipped in the great
sanctuary of Heliopolis, which is called in Scripture by its
name, Beth-Aon, the 'house of On,' as well as by its translation,
Beth-Shemesh, the 'house of the sun.' The language that explains a local god's name, surely points out the nation who first
worshipped him under that name. The primitive Aon was therefore the 'enlightener of man,' to a people speaking the primitive
language, out of which the Coptic sprang ; and such a people were
the Caphtorim of Lower Egypt, whom we afterwards find established among the Philistines in Palestine. Under this pure
spiritual attribute, the Supreme God was known to the ancient
Heliopolitans, and continued to be an object of secret adoration
by the religious conservatives of the land, its priests, who veiled
under the garb of mysteries and initiations the purer Mizraimite
worship of their ancestors, long after the subjection of Lower
Egypt to the Thebans : long after the dominant race had identified
this god with their Ra or Sun, which appeared his most fitting
emblem. Nevertheless, in the popular religion—that of the rulers,
who commanded, and of the people, who must obey—Aon gradually
glided into the mixed Sun-god Râ, of the Egyptian astro-mytho-
logical system ; in the same way that Thoth, the early instructor
of the Mizraim in letters, arts, science, and the division of time,
according to their ancestral traditions, had the moon, the natural
divider of time, placed under his care.

The ancient Mizraimite name Aon is never mentioned as a
synonym of Râ by the Egyptians themselves. Except in the
name of their month Paôni, we only meet with the primeval name
among the kindred races out of Egypt, as that of a contemplar
god worshipped under the same attributes ; or learn its former
existence in Egypt obliquely, from extra-Egyptian sources. As
under the prescribed form of the state religion, he was named Râ,

---

" Birch on the Statistical Tablet of Karnak, *Trans. R. S. of Literature*, vol. ii.
New Series.

and identified with the sun, the physical light,—the sanctuary of Heliopolis, in Scripture is alluded to either as Beth-Aon, the House of Aon, or as Beth-Shemesh, the House of the Sun. And the Egyptian name of the city in the Mosaic period, when the Delta was annexed to Egypt, is accordingly found as רע־מסס Ra-meses, the birth-place of Rā, rendered by the Greeks Heliopolis, city of the Sun. An explanatory gloss of the Septuagint translators, subsequently copied into the text, and thus most fortunately preserved, intimates their knowledge that the Aon of which Joseph's father-in-law was priest was the same as Heliopolis, and their accuracy as to that reference is proved by the priest's official name, פּוֹטִיפֶרַע Pet-Ph-Rā, dedicated to Rā.[p]

Aon, the divine enlightener of men, was therefore the patronymic god of 'the land of Rameses' or 'Goshen.' His outward symbol was a young bull. In the ancient Egyptian language the same hieroglyphic denotes a *bull* and a *chief*.[q] In the Hebrew, likewise, the name of a bull (שׁוֹר) is derived from the root שׂר, to rule. Such is the simple origin of all sacred symbols. It is only our ignorance of an ancient people's language that leaves the import of their emblems a mystery. In Egypt a live animal was substituted for the ideagraph, in after-times: Manetho gives the reign of Kaiechos, second king of the Thinite dynasty, a descendant of Menes, as the era of the innovation that brought in the worship of a living animal-symbol. It formed no part of the original Mizraimite system.

The worship of Aon under the tauriform emblem is also clearly traceable in the land of the Rephaim; Beth-El is called Beth-Aon in Josh. vii. 2, and 1 Sa. xiii. 5. Hosea also alludes to 'the calves of Beth-Aon,' Ch. iv. 15; v. 8; x. 5. The name, as *Beit-In*, is still extant. It was the antiquity of this symbol of local worship at Beth-El which induced Jeroboam to select the spot for its restoration. We now refer to the Egyptian monuments. After the defeat of the SHAS·U in the upper MNA or Shepherd region, Seti Menephtah presents their spoils to Amun;[r] among them is conspicuous a beautiful vase, on the cover of which the emblematical bull is represented, leaping among the water-plants. Another bull, standing on a pedestal, forms the cover of a tall urn among

---

[p] Wilkinson, *Anc. Egyp.*, vol. iv. p. 301.

[q] The root *ka* in Egyptian is *a bull;* and also *to set up;* corresponding to the Hebrew נשׂא, from which נָשִׂיא, *a prince*, literally *a superior*.

[r] Rosellini, *Mon. Storici*, pl. 52. There is also a bull-headed urn among the spoils of the Anakim of TAHI, pl. 56, and of the SHET·TA, pl. 59. These are known from the Ashtaroth urns by the absence of the disk, and the head being in profile. The entire figure of a bull on the top of a beautiful lotus-plant vase also occurs among the SHET·TA symbols.

the same spoils, similar to those crowned with the emblems of Ashtaroth and Renpu. This bull of Aon was the golden calf of the Exodus—the consecrated emblem of the ruler of Goshen; its living exemplar was called Mnevis at Heliopolis, and Apis at Memphis.

The maritime Aon, or Phœnician and Chaldean Oannes, is a symbolical form peculiar to the people of the sea-coast, Pelesheth. It is the Dag-on or Fish-on of Scripture, compounded of דג, fish, and ן, contracted form of the name of the god. I have a copy of an ancient coin in the British Museum, which represents Dagon on one side, and a ship on the other. The god has a human head and arms, and the tail of a dolphin. In his right hand he holds a fish with its head upwards, in his left another with its head downwards. This ingenious hieroglyphic signifies that in the land over which Aon, the enlightener of men, ruled and guided the sun, it began its course on land, in the east (*the front*), figured by the human fore-part; and ended it in the sea in the west (*the back*), figured by the hind part of a maritime creature. It reached its greatest elevation at the *right hand* of the god, *i. e.* the south,—this is implied by the fish looking upward; and it sank below the horizon at *his left*, the north; this is expressed by the fish going down. Such an emblem must have been designed in a country of which it accurately described the geographical bearings;—one with the continent eastward, and a western sea; and, moreover, for the emblem to be intelligible, it requires that the mode of orientation which refers the east to the *front*, the west to the *back*, &c. should be customary in the language of the country. These conditions are fulfilled in Palestine alone,—in the region of the maritime proto-Phœnicians, where we find the Scriptural Philistines, worshippers of Dagon. And they must have introduced it into Babylonia, for there the emblem loses all its descriptive significance, and consequently it never could have been framed in that country.

The Oannes of Chaldea, by the internal evidence of his representation and his Coptic name, confirms the admission of Berosus that he was introduced into that country by foreigners. His figure in the Khorsabad sculptures only differs from the original type in that it wears the Assyrian costume. He has a double pair of horns; his geographical emblems, the human fore part and fish's tail, the right hand pointing upwards and the left downwards, are preserved; but the accessory fishes are absent.

The form of Dagon in both representations illustrates with a singularly circumstantial precision the allusion to the catastrophe of his fall, in 1 Sa. v. 4, ' Behold, Dagon was prostrate with his face to the ground before the ark of the Lord; the head of Dagon and both the palms of his hands being cut off upon the threshold:

only the dagon of him (*i. e.* the fish part) remained.' If such a figure as the Khorsabad subject were cut in stone, and its upper part happened to separate from the stump at the waist, the weight of the two projecting arms would inevitably bring the trunk down on its face; the two hands first, and then the head, being broken off by the fall.

There are two sites extant by name as Beth-Dagon, in Palestine; one near the coast near Ekron, and one east of Shechem.

The Philistine form of Ashtaroth was a feminine Dagon; the Greek equivalents only of her name are known as Atargatis[s] or Derketo. The Atargateum at Karnion is referred to in 2 Macc. xii. 21-26, as a place difficult to besiege or even to approach, taken by Judas. It thus appears that the maritime Aphrodite was a contemplar deity with that of the inland Rephaim, or rather was considered as a local form of the same impersonation. In referring to her temple at Ashkalon,[t] plundered by the Scythians, Herodotus calls her Aphrodite-Urania, without distinction as to her fishy attribute.

PTHAH.

Although Memphis, the capital of Middle Egypt, was the central locality from whence the particular impersonation of the creative power called Pthah first emanated and was accepted by the Mizraimite nation, this god claims a place in the pantheon of the Rephaim as a contemplar deity. It is interesting to find by the geographical reference of Josh. xv. 9, to the 'Waters of Nephtoah,' near the entrance of the valley of the Rephaim, that the primitive Pthah, parent of the Cabiri or great gods of the Pelasgic or proto-Phœnician races, had a temple within a few miles of Jerusalem, prior in antiquity perhaps to the metropolis of Middle Egypt; for נֶפְתּוֹחַ, Nephtoah (read without the points), is letter for letter the same name as that by which Moses designates the Memphite family נַפְתֻּחִים, Naphtuhim, and means 'the abode of Pthah.'[u]

Two forms of Pthah were reverenced in Egypt. Of the Thebanized form we need not speak; that which concerns us is the primeval god, the entrance, opening, or cause of the entering-in of existence, פתח. Under the Theban system of modifying without abolishing the existing state of things in Mizraim, the name of

---

[s] These two corrupted and incomplete forms may perhaps correct one another, and reveal the primitive etymon of the name, Der＝Atar, AT-HOR; and γατ＝דג, *the fish,* reversed, translated by κητος, a marine animal; the maritime Athor, or 'abode of Horus.'

[t] Herod., *Clio,* 105.

[u] Na or No, an Egyptian formative of locality; No-Amun, נֹא אָמוֹן, Thebes (Nahum iii. 8); apparently akin to the Hebrew נוה, and the Greek ναι-ω, to dwell.

Pthah was not changed, though it has no known sense in the language of Egypt; but it was given to a new form of the same god, an upright mummy-shaped figure; and the more ancient character was then distinguished by a qualifying name, Pthah-Sokar-Osiri. The monumental effigies of the god bearing this name[x] shew him to be the Great Lord of the mysterious rites, referred to by Herodotus, whose time-honoured and most sacred effigy was in the form of a pigmy man like the figures called by the Phœnicians Pataikos (likeness of Ptah), which they fixed to the prows of their vessels. If an emblem is understood, its object is fulfilled; but to us it seems a strange expedient to suggest so abstruse and majestic an idea as that of the $\Delta\eta\mu\iota\upsilon\rho\gamma\acute{\upsilon}s$, 'maker of the people' at the entering in of its existence on earth, through so contemptible a medium as an unperfected representation of his own work—an undeveloped human being—a stunted and deformed little pigmy!

The Theban form of Pthah varied the expression of the same conception by a figure wrapped up in bandages—undisclosed; and Sir Gardner Wilkinson mentions a very curious illustration of the notion embodied in this impersonation—the door or opening of the creative act—the Creator designing his work by a representation of Pthah tracing with a reed the outline of a human figure.[y]—F. C.

---

[x] Wilkinson, *Anc. Egyp.*, vol. iv. p. 253, pl. 24, fig. 2.   [y] Ibid., p. 253, pl. 23.

LONDON: PRINTED BY WILLIAM CLOWES AND SONS, STAMFORD STREET.

THE REPHAIM, AND THEIR CONNECTION WITH EGYPTIAN HISTORY.[a]

CHAPTER XVII.

THE Divine forms reverenced by the Rephaim being thus found identical in name and office with those of Mizraim, the common origin of the respective systems proves itself. The Creator manifest in His works was the object of their worship. To obtain a distinct view of the Divine attributes, the Mizraim separated these into so many figurative impersonations, distinguished by appropriate names. In this, they did not differ from the Hebrews, who knew the true God under various names. Their JEHOVAH is the Eternal; their ELOHIM is the fountain of Power manifest in creation; their SHADDAI, the Power exercised over all creation; their ADONAI, the Governor of the world; their ZEBAOTH, the Spiritual Defender of their Theocratic polity. By these various epithets, a Hebrew no more understood five Gods, than a primitive Mizraimite when he distinguished his primeval Osiris, or *maker of being*, from Isis, *the receptacle of being;* and expressed by various appropriate emblems his idea of God the Creator of the world, called Pthah, as distinguished from God the Enlightener of the world, called Aon; from God the all-pervading Spirit animating the world, called Neph;[b] or from God the Sustainer, renewing the world, called Khem. These names did not designate a variety of gods, but the same Divine Being considered as the subject of a different attribute expressed in the name.

We need not digress to trace how these purely abstract impersonations, on becoming multiplied, degenerated into polytheism; or how the use of mnemonic symbols to suggest the attribute they personified, degenerated into idolatry. This is a secondary point, in which the Rephaim erred in common with all heathen antiquity; and beyond our present purpose, which is rather to distinguish the origin and connection of their system with that of Egypt, from the internal evidence of the system itself; to confirm their ethnographical position in the primeval civilized world, as a branch of the great Mizraimite family.

The four manifestations of the primeval Osiris, that are called Pthah, Aon, Neph, and Khem, with their consorts Pasht, Neith,

---

[a] Concluded from the October number of the *J. S. L.*

[b] Otherwise Num, p and m being interchangeable. The resemblance of this name to the Greek πνευμα, *wind, spirit,* is remarkable.

d

Sati, and Maut, constitute the eight great gods of the *first order,* in the Egyptian system. Whereas, their exemplars, Osiris and Isis, under these their own primary names, and considered as belonging to the system of five manifestations known as the family of Seb and Nutpe, are only ranked in the *third order* of precedence; the *second order* being filled by twelve divinities whose various characters show that they arose out of subdivisions—particularizing developments as it were—of those primary generalizations that form the third order. Such is the principle on which the Egyptian pantheon was framed. All we have to show, by adducing a few cases in point, is, that the national deities of the Rephaim are those primary and generalizing forms of the Mizraimite theogony, out of which the Egyptian system itself was elaborated; and consequently that the criterion of rank assigned to a deified form is not its *antiquity,* but its *nationality;* precedence, in Egypt, being given to the patron-gods of Egyptian lands, over those whose domains were extra-Egyptian.

Osiris, who under that popular name only ranks in the third order, is nevertheless the great god worshipped over all Egypt alike; the mysterious being whose real name it was not lawful to utter. Osiris unmanifested, is Amun (*the concealed*), an expletive for that sacred name. In this character, he ranks in order 1, as god of Thebes. Osiris manifested is Khem, the Pan of Thebes, consort of Maut (*the mother*). In this character, his name in Egypt was cancelled; its equivalent, Amun, being substituted. But under that obliterated name we find him the king of gods, in Palestine.

Isis, though only ranked in order 3, is found under that name, with all its appropriate titles, bearing the form and emblems of the great goddesses; the graceful vulture head-dress, symbol of maternity, characteristic of Maut, goddess of Thebes;—or the cat's head, globe, and uræus of Pasht, goddess of Bubastis—both o order 1;—or the globe and horns of Athor, of order 2; she is even found combining the latter emblem with the bowl and house of her own sister, Nephthys, of order 3. All these emblematical beings are therefore Egyptian forms of Isis, though unacknowledged in Palestine. There, her original name is merged into those of her characters, like in Egypt; but, as the great Ashtaroth, *producer of abundance,* she is the primitive Isis herself, antitype of the Greek Demeter or Ceres; and as Ate·sh and Ken, she is equivalent, both in name and office, to Maut and Athor, in Egypt.

Thoth, god of letters, is ranked in order 2; yet we found him to be a secondary form of Sheth the Helper, who only ranks in order 3.

Auk, ranked in order 2, where she is not related to Thoth, we found to be a local name and form of Nephthys, wife and sister of Sheth, and like him ranked in order 3. This same Ank, localized in Egypt as Neith, is then placed among the eight great gods of order 1.

Osiris, Isis, Sheth, and Nephthys, the primary forms, must be more ancient, as divine impersonations, than their derivatives. The mythical family of Seb (*adoration*) and Nut·pe (*the celestial abode*), must therefore exhibit a more ancient phase of the Mizraimite theogony, than that which includes the territorial gods of Egypt proper. Yet the five deities constituting this family *form the whole national pantheon of the Rephaim;* for Pthah and Aon do not appear as patronyms in their land, although these forms received divine honours. Their position in Palestine seems analogous to that occupied by the family of Seb in Egypt.

From this comparison of the leading divine characters reverenced by the Egyptians and by the Rephaim, it is manifest that the latter nation did not borrow their system at second-hand from Egypt, nor Egypt from them; but that the two are parts of a whole framed on a common principle of national agreement, which had become firmly grounded among them before the tribes were divided, and each separated people began to follow up a principle of development—peculiar to itself—from the common exemplar; the Egyptians, by increasing the number of divine functionaries with every shade of distinction in their offices, so that Isis, Maut, and Athor, become different goddesses of different ranks, as also Nephthys, Ank, and Neith; whereas the Rephaim distinguished the secondary shades of difference in the attributes of each primitive cosmogonic form without increasing the original number of five; so that with them, Chemosh, or Khem, is Osiris: Ashtaroth, Atergatis, Ken, are equally Isis; Renpu, Baal, Nebo, are equally Sheth; Anath, and Onka, are equally Nephthys. And this original unity seems to bear out a proposition which, on other grounds of inference (see ante, Ch. IV.), we might have held as doubtful—the common origin of the Rephaim and Egyptians.

The absolute separation between the Palestine branch of Mizraim (including the Delta) and that established on the Nile, must date as far back *at least* as the empire of Menes and the amalgamation of the Sabean element with the Mizraimite cosmogony. Not a trace of this mixture is to be found in the system of the Rephaim; not an indication of it either in their sacred symbols, or in their local names. Whatever corruptions of idea and form their system may subsequently have undergone, they are totally distinct from those by which the Egyptian system is overlaid. Its elements were strangely perverted,—its pure intellectuality became grossly brutalised,—but it exhibits no admixture of foreign elements.

The absence of every vestige of astral worship in the religion of the Rephaim is a fact the more remarkable, that Scripture contains very decisive evidence of its having constituted the idolatry of the Canaanites before they fell under the influence, or power, of their eastern neighbours. In Canaan proper, we still find a few names alluding to that worship. Nor was it altogether eradicated when the Canaanites consented to the divine forms of the Rephaim as superior objects of reverence. But what remained of it was not, like in Egypt, wrapped up in a complicated garb of cosmogonic similitudes; it remained plain, unqualified adoration of the sun and moon. Both forms are found subsisting separately, long after the Hebrew conquest. The children of Israel are not only enticed to the worship of Baal-Hamon and Asherah, but also to that of the 'Host of Heaven.' The kings of Judah burn incense to Baal; and also to 'the sun, moon, and planets.' They give chariots and horses to the sun, at the same time that they make their children 'pass through fire to Molech;' and pour out libations to his consort, 'the Queen of Heaven.' Ezekiel, in particular, brings out the various corrupt practices of the apostatizing Israelites, with a marked distinction in their *kind* as in their *degree*. Even so late as this, though still co-existent, they remained unblended. The idolatrous elders offering incense in their own image-chambers, before the symbols of a degraded worship, is indeed qualified as 'an evil abomination;'—but the prophet regards it as 'a greater abomination than this,' to find the women sitting in the house of Jehovah, not worshipping Him, but 'weeping for Thammuz.' Yet even this profanation of the holy temple is not the consummation of idolatry:—

'Hast thou seen, son of man? thou shalt see *still greater abominations than these!* And he brought me to the inner court of the House of Jehovah; and lo! at the entrance of the Temple of Jehovah, between the porch and the altar, about five and twenty men, with their backs to the altar and their faces to the east, were bowing themselves before the sun, towards the east!' (Ez. viii. 9-16.)

The allusion to the ode of Deborah is also decisive evidence that this was especially the idolatry of Canaan. The pictorial sarcasm that introduces the defender of Anak under the form of her Phœnician emblem, a dog, dragging the chief of her people down by tugging at his garment behind, while the king of Egypt knocks him on the head,—is not more intense in its power of expressing how utterly the gods of the Anakim have forsaken them, than the daring poetic image:—

'Even from the heavens, they fought—
The stars in their orbits fought against Sisera'—

is in declaring how powerless were those objects of an idolatrous worship to save their infatuated votaries, the Canaanite host of Jabin. But, indeed, the Canaanite nomenclature of the four quarters, based on the posture of a worshipper of the rising sun, is as strong an indication as we could desire, that sun-worship was the pristine idolatry of the people in whose language those terms have that significance.

This point being clear, and the distinctness of the co-existent systems equally so, some idea may be formed of the influence the Rephaim must have obtained over the whole land of Canaan, by the fact that their local gods became the gods of Canaan; and even, in some influential states, quite superseded the astral worship. But though Ashtoreth is 'the abomination of the Zidonians,' as well as of Ken, we do not find her the patronym of the Canaanite foundation city, as in Bashan. Though Sheth, as Thautus or Eshmun, and Onka, as Thanath, are reverenced by the Tyrians up to the very destruction of their Carthaginian colony, we do not find those divine forms patronyms of a single tribe or metropolitan city, like Sheth among the Shittim, Onka among the Anakim, Pthah in No'pth (Noph, Memphis), by the Naphtuhim, and Athor in Pathyris or Pathros, by the Pathrusim.

In the remote East, the same phenomenon meets us. The local gods of Shittim are established in Babylon, but they are neither patronyms of the city, nor of the land, nor of the people. Their Baal is not Baal-Kham·n, the universal progenitor, but Seth-Baal or Renpu with axe and thunder in hand, 'BARO *who smites his enemies:*' the god who 'exercises power and overpowers.' Their Hermes bears the surname of Nebo, the assistant of *lords*, not Thoth or Thautus, the popular teacher. Their Astarte is not AT·SH the abode of being, but Mulitta, openly confessing the Arabian origin we could have ascribed to her from her name. All this speaks as distinctly of conquest, as the fable of Oannes teaching and civilizing the brutal savages of the 'desert of the sea' spoke of colonization.[e] When, therefore, we find the dim and confused traditions of Berosus, which do not gain in clearness by being transmitted through the sieves of several intermediate theorists, declaring the intelligible fact that a primeval dynasty of mythical Chaldean kings was succeeded by *an Arabian dynasty,* we only require the concurrent testimony of Scripture, to see through a whole series of changes in that primeval empire, though

---

[e] Whether we take the Assyrian queen-consort, Semiramis, for a genuine or only for a mythical personage, we must not lose sight of the historical indications contained in the tradition that assigns as her birthplace the Philistine city Ashkalon, and gives her pedigree as the daughter of Derketo or Atergatis, the Ashtaroth of Pelesheth.

we cannot retrace its details, or assign the period of the changes. And the Scripture record is not silent. Its testimony is strangely significant, as well as definite. It opens with the notice of the Rephaim, yet in their greatness, though verging towards decline. A chief of Shinar has joined a powerful combination of Assyrians, rivals of the Shepherd race, against the whole body of that race; but the object of hostility is manifestly the Emim—the Terrible people—that one tribe which stands out from the rest, branded as an exception of depravity in religion and morality from the very day of its introduction to our notice. And thus, the united evidence of sacred and classical tradition enables us distinctly to trace the primary source of their perversion to that great city which sacred revelation has marked out as the typical centre of every religious and moral corruption, 'Babylon, the mother of all the abominations of the earth.'

This hints at the beginning of that subversion, both of principle and practice, which the Mizraimite cosmogonic system underwent while transplanted in Chaldea by the tribe which established its dominion there so long. Success, by increasing riches, and engendering luxury, tempts to the misuse of power. To conciliate the population of the wealthy region they had acquired, the children of Sheth may have consented to bring down their religious formulæ to its level, instead of rather exalting and refining those of the people as they found them. Israel and Judah, in Canaan, fell in the same way!

When the power of the Rephaim in the East was broken, they brought back to their native homestead the taint in all its fundamental principles with which they infected their brethren of Palestine; but which they perhaps had not originated:

'Behold,' says Ezekiel, addressing Judah, 'This was the iniquity (הוע perversion) of thy sister Sodom: pride, fulness of bread, and prosperity undisturbed, were hers and her daughters', yet she strengthened not the hand of the humble and needy. They became haughty, and committed abomination before me—and I removed them, because I saw it!' (Ez. xvi. 49, 50.)

Fearful indeed must the social condition of a people have become, in whose city ten righteous men could not be found, to incline the scale of judgment on the side of mercy! And terrible indeed was that '*removal of them*,' to become from thenceforth in every prophetic denunciation, the crowning comparison for the deepest abyss of desolation; so that terms more emphatic cannot be found to express the fall of Babylon herself, the arch-corrupter, than that even she 'shall become as the overthrow of Sodom and Gomorrah,' and that the only possible aggravation to her degradation, is to be taunted in her perdition by those whose ruin she wrought :—

> ' Art *thou, too*, enfeebled, as we ? art *thou* become like ourselves . . .
> The couch beneath thee, worms—the grub, thy covering !'

While the awful visitation was impending which blotted out from the face of nature the beautiful vale of Shiddim, its cities and its degraded population, as corrupt beyond the power of any ordinance, human or divine, to reclaim—the contrast presented by the religious and moral condition of the elder branch of the nation, and its Philistine offset, is interesting to observe. Here, indeed, we find ample proof that there was nothing in the creed of Mizraim derogatory to the majesty of a God whose glorious attributes they reverenced according to the best of their understandings :— nothing debasing to humanity in the outward forms by which they sought to do Him honour. The great chief of the Rephaim dwelling in Shalem is the head of his people as administrator both of religious and social order, according to the primitive patriarchal appointment. He invokes the same 'Supreme God, possessor of heaven and earth,' as Abraham himself. He considers it a sacred duty to acknowledge, in a public ceremony of thanksgiving, his gratitude to that Supreme God for the deliverance of his people ; and to bless Abraham for the service his interposition has rendered to the nation. This ceremony is accompanied by an Eucharistic rite, which most certainly existed as an ordinance of the true patriarchal church before the Mosaic dispensation. For in an instance of equal solemnity, that of the great national deliverance, as soon as the children of Israel have reached the holy mountain in safety, after the difficulties and dangers of their departure from Egypt and desert route, Jethro the priest comes forth to meet his long expected guests ; like Melchizedek, he blesses God for their preservation, and he, with the elders of Israel, Aaron, the elder of his family among them, go up into the mount to offer sacrifices and to eat bread before God (Exod v. 12.). The sacred historian is careful to indicate both the orthodoxy of the rite performed on the parallel occasion by Melchizedek, and the lawfulness of his ministry thereof. 'Melchizedek brought forth bread and wine : (he was priest of the Supreme God) and blessed Abram,' saying :—

> ' Blessed be Abram of the Supreme God, Possessor of Heaven and Earth ; and Blessed be the Supreme God, who hath delivered thine enemies into thine hand.'

Equally unequivocal is the testimony borne in the same holy page to the piety and integrity of the contemporaneous Philistine chieftain. God appears to the Royal Father of this tribe, in the visions of the night, as to the Hebrew patriarchs; not to warn him of any great impending national calamity, but simply to caution him against the unconscious commission of a crime in appropriating to himself the wife of another man. And Abimelech fears not to address the Almighty with an appeal which speaks as highly for the moral character of his people as for his own. 'Adonai! wilt thou slay also a righteous nation? Said he not unto me, "she is my sister?" and she, even she herself, said, "he is my brother." In the integrity of my heart and innocency of my hands have I done this.' And God said to him in the dream, ' Yea, I know that thou didst this in the integrity of thine heart, and I have accordingly withheld thee from sinning against me.' (Gen. xx.)

Manetho's account of the behaviour of the Shepherd rulers in Egypt is perfectly in keeping with the state of religion in Palestine at that time, if we consider that account as emanating from an Egyptian priest deeply imbued with reverence for the most corrupt superstitions to which the primitive Egyptian religion had become degraded at the latter period. The very acts he denounces as sacrilege are precisely those from which we should argue favourably of their religious practices. They did what the Hebrew conquerors of Palestine were expressly commanded to do for the extirpation of idolatry in Canaan. They closed the temples of the false gods, defiled and pulled down their images, sacrificed, and even ate without scruple the sacred animals adored by the Egyptians. They doubtless deemed the religious customs of Egypt idolatrous and debased; and endeavoured, while they were in power, to suppress them. They thereby incurred the odium of the priesthood, and of the people governed by the priests. As this preceded by four centuries Abraham's arrival in Egypt, it is tolerably certain that the tendency to harmonise with his own religious feelings, which existed among the Shepherd people, and so strangely contrasted with the surrounding corruption, was rather the motive that induced him to settle among them, than the consequence altogether of his example and teaching. Nevertheless, the beneficial effects of these, in purifying and exalting the religious ideas of a nation originally so well disposed, by drawing them even nearer to the primitive standard of the patriarchal faith than he found them, may safely be presumed.

Neither do the Canaanites of Judea show any traces of demoralization in the days of Abraham. We are indeed expressly told that the אַי perversion of the Amorites was not then accomplished. Abraham resides among them in the suburbs of the metropolis of Anak. Three of their chiefs are under a special contract of amity with him, and aid him in pursuing the captors of Lot. In the day of his bereavement, his acknowledged character of a religious teacher, נשׂיא, 'superior-one of God,' is urged by the children of Heth as giving him a special claim on their good will and liberality. The choicest family sepulchres are placed at his disposal; the one he offers to purchase is pressed upon him as a gift by the owner. Everything in that land speaks of a social condition orderly, virtuous, and prosperous, at the time of Abraham's residence there.

The degradation of the race who ruled over that land is thus almost as incomprehensible for its rapidity as for its enormity. Soon after Abraham's death, the Shepherd power in Egypt was finally broken. Then began the great war of the races. It must have been during the interval of Israel's sojourn in Egypt that the work of depravation was consummated; but had the body of the nation maintained the high moral and religious ground it held when Abraham dwelt in its land, the sceptre might not have departed from their ruler; that war might never have begun; the Rephaim would not have been cast out of their heritage that it might be given to another.

After the outbreak of the contest with Egypt, the common cause of the tribes brought them into closer contact. They became familiarised with each other's ideas and forms: the evil race corrupted the good. The taint spread with fearful rapidity, especially among that tribe which we find so constantly associated with the children of Sheth, the Anakim; for these are marked out by name, in Scripture, among the evil-doers cast out by the decree of the Almighty.

'Thou hast heard: who can stand before the children of Anak?—Understand therefore this day, that the Lord thy God Himself passeth over before thee: as a consuming fire He will destroy them, He will bow them down before thee; so wilt thou drive them out and destroy them quickly.... Say not in thine heart: "For my righteousness the Lord hath brought me in to inherit this land;" but for the wickedness of these nations the Lord doth drive them out from thy presence. Not for thy righteousness, nor for the uprightness of thine heart, goest thou to succeed to their land: but for the wickedness of those nations doth the Lord thy God drive them out from thy presence!' (Deut. ix. 3-5.)

It is as painful to trace the degradation of principle and feeling thus wrought in a people whose beginning was so great and pure, as it is difficult to seize on the particular processes by which it may have been wrought; the particular point in which the debasement of abstract conceptions began, which started by substituting impure ideas and forms, as representations of actual divinities, for those simple emblems of names originally conferred on attributes of Deity; and which ended by investing the most cruel and immoral practices with the notion of doing homage to those divinities! Among the medley of Phœnician traditions ascribed to Sanchoniatho, there occurs a very remarkable one, which, from the illustration of Scripture it both receives and gives, will serve our purpose better than any other, as a means of tracing a primitive institution through several successive stages of corruption.

When the nation was in imminent danger from war, a solemn and painful ceremony was enacted to avert the calamity impending over the land. The king brought forth his son, his heir, attired in all the insignia of royalty, and in the presence of all the assembled chiefs he offered him up in sacrifice in front of the city walls, to appease the wrath of the offended Deity.

Some commentators have looked on this tradition as originating an obscure and disfigured reminiscence of Abraham's sacrifice ; but we have positive evidence in the Bible itself that such a custom really did exist among the Rephaim, by the incident related in 2 Kings, 26, 27, which occurred in the days of Jehoshaphat, at the siege of Kir-Harasheth. ‘ When the king of Moab saw that the battle was too sore for him, he took with him seven hundred men with drawn swords, to break through unto the king of Edom, but they could not. Then he took his eldest son, who was to reign after him, and offered him for a burnt offering upon the wall.’ Seeing that the Moabites, by their intimate amalgamation with the remnant of the Emim, cannot fail to have inherited most of their usages as well as their lands, we here obtain a circumstantial verification of Sanchoniatho's story, that this painful scene was sanctioned by custom as the last resource of despair, by the whole body of the nation to whom the Emim appertained, and thus it came to be perpetuated among the later inhabitants of Phœnicia, in the same way as among the Moabites.

It would therefore appear that the presumed connection between the ordeal of Abraham and this Phœnician tradition has been interpreted backwards, and that we should be much nearer the truth if we were to regard the previous existence of such a custom, sanctioned by a fierce but generous fanaticism, in the land where Abraham was settled, as the fact which gave occasion to the *special form* it pleased the Almighty to ordain for the trial whereby the stedfastness of the Patriarch's faith was to be manifested as a glorious example to all future generations.

‘ There was a great indignation against Israel ; and they departed from it, and returned to the land,’ adds the sacred chronicle. Certainly the sudden outbreak of religious excitement, produced on a brave and enthusiastic people, at such a manifestation of devotion to the national cause, both on the part of the royal parent who gave his son, and of the son who thus consented

' to die for the people, that the whole nation perish not,' might very well have the effect of stimulating the disheartened people themselves to almost superhuman efforts; and the success achieved by the wild energy of despair would not fail to be regarded as a token that the Divine displeasure had been appeased by the sacrifice, and confirm the faith of the people in its efficacy.

Once a fatal aberration of judgment has let in the false principle of an inherently meritorious or expiatory efficacy in any sacrificial act, we can trace step by step the processes of degradation by which this one, at first perfectly voluntary on the part of its victim, having begun by assuming a right to dispose of human life, ended by degenerating into the barbarous practice of infanticide which the Israelite kings are reproached with having imitated from their predecessors in dominion. When the war-cry of all the tribes was raised against invading Egypt—when, year after year, army after army poured in upon the devoted race, until their land was ' a conflagration before and behind '—its fields devastated, its women and children massacred, its cattle carried off as booty, and its warriors as slaves—when a savage despair had taken hold of a people forsaken of the God whose attributes they had corrupted and forgotten—we can understand how the simple form of consecrating their offspring to its Giver by an emblematical rite of purification, having degenerated into the notion that the God *individually* had *appropriated* the dedicated offspring, ended in the persuasion that he claimed their blood to appease his wrath in the season of national visitation. Thus a form of sacrifice, originally ordained under the pressure of an exceptional public calamity, and required only of the chief ruler of the land, came at first to be regarded as insufficient, and instances were multiplied in the hope of ensuring its efficacy, firstly by the chiefs, and finally by the whole population.

The perversion of this rite suffices to illustrate the march of every other depravation which stains the memory of the Rephaim at the close of their national career. Scripture history is utterly silent concerning them during an interval of four centuries. After placing before our eyes the glaring contrast of their pristine moral condition, as presented by the majestic piety of the King-Priest Melchizedek and the single-hearted purity of his Philistine vassal, side by side with the terrific catastrophe of the Pentapolis, it leaves them to work out their own destiny. It leaves them, neither unwarned nor uncared for, with the virtuous Abraham and his increasing family circle among them on one side, to point out the way of holiness, and exhibit in their own persons the blessings of peace and prosperity that crown those who choose to walk in it; and with the example and admonition of Lot and his sons in the

midst of them on the other side, to point out the application of
the awful warning against national iniquity, vouchsafed even in
the great judgment which rained down fire and brimstone out of
Heaven upon their metropolitan cities! How far these means
may have been effectual in bettering the moral condition of the
race for a season, and drawing them back a little way from the
verge of the precipice, we cannot exactly know; neither how far
and how long the descendants of Lot themselves escaped the
general contamination by keeping aloof from them, as industrious
nomads tending their flocks in the mountains during the grazing
season, and dwelling apart in their own tribe communities when
they returned to winter at home. Neither warning nor example
ultimately availed: the whole mass of the people became corrupt,
and the whole were abandoned to themselves, to perish!

For our admonition, the sacred history relates their original
condition and their final doom; but it does not say *how* they
perished. This we have learnt from the monumental history of
Egypt. But what matters the *how*, in a religious history that
regards God himself as the guide of all sublunary transactions,
and all human determinations only as secondary means? The
Scripture history is very explicit in informing us *why* they perished;
for that is the momentous lesson it behoves man individually, and
nations collectively, to lay to heart: 'FOR THE WICKEDNESS OF
THOSE NATIONS, DOTH THE LORD DRIVE THEM OUT.' It recounts,
under the doubly solemn form of a Divine prohibition addressed
to Israel, every abomination that the most depraved humanity can
possibly imagine to commit, as actually committed by that people,
in idolatry, superstition, cruelty, and impurity. 'Defile not yourselves in any of these things,' concludes the warning Oracle; 'for
in all these, the nations are defiled which I cast out before you,
and the land is defiled! Therefore I do visit the iniquity thereof
upon it, and the land herself vomiteth out her inhabitants! Keep
ye then my statutes and my ordinances, and commit none of these
abominations, neither your own nation, nor the stranger who so-
journeth among you (for all these abominations did the men of the
land commit, who preceded you, and the land was defiled), that
the land spue you not out also, for defiling her, as she spued out
the nations who preceded you!'

CHAPTER XVIII.

Costumes of the Rephaim.

The slight outlines given in plates III. and IV. are only *a selection* of the most striking forms characterising the national costume of the Rapha tribes. They are intended to appeal to the mind through the eye, inasmuch as a verbal description, however accurate and elaborate, would still fail to convey a distinct idea of form: but they are rather calculated to assist those readers who have not time to consult the voluminous illustrations of Egyptian antiquity from which the materials of the foregoing pages were gathered, than to supersede a reference to the original works themselves. This reference is so important, that in describing the costumes of the tribes, my principal aim will be directed to furnishing the reader with a classified index to the original subjects; so that any student, however unversed hitherto in that class of research, may at once find himself furnished with all the necessary materials to judge for himself whether the generic resemblances of costume which distinguish and connect the national groups whose history we have now gone through, and the specific differences which separate one tribe from another, have been correctly indicated, and sufficiently bear out the ethnographical classification they are called upon to sustain.

So long as we knew nothing of the people figured in these monumental illustrations beyond the bare fact that they had been conquered by the ancient Egyptians, we turned over the pages with very little interest. We might perhaps indulge in a laugh over the quaint and distorted attitudes of the combatants, the wry faces of the chained captives, and the ludicrous expedients to indicate the relative personal consequence of the actors in the scene by their size, with an utter disregard of proportion as well as of perspective; but the subjects told us no story we cared about, for the actors were nothing to us but abstractions without either 'a local habitation or a name,' and as soon as the book was closed, the passing impression they made had vanished from our minds.

But the case is widely altered when we have learnt that the personages in these strange old pictured memorials are a people consecrated in our memory by their intimate association with Scripture history; that those Philistines, whose name and deeds are familiar to our ears as household words, even from the earliest teaching of our childhood, are the very people who figure in one picture, and that their fellow captives in another are the formi-

dable children of Anak ; that on looking at another, we may
actually realise the presence of Og king of Bashan as he marched
out to encounter the children of Israel ; or call up a correct and
unquestionably authentic presentation of the redoubtable Goliath
of Gath hurling a boastful defiance in the teeth of Saul's warriors ; while another presents us with a warlike array like that
with which the king of Sodom went forth to meet Abraham ; or
that of Balak the son of Zippor, as he stood on the high place of
Baal, bribing the Eberite prophet to curse the conquerors of the
land of his fathers. Such associations impart a strange and
thrilling interest to these hitherto unintelligible forms, as the
barbaric abstractions they presented are replaced by definite ideas
of national personality, and our knowledge of these mysterious
people's names and history suddenly places them before our eyes
in the new light of old and familiar acquaintances.

In the *onomasticon* which gave the Egyptian forms of their
names I divided them into five geographical groups. Three belong to the Rephaim, one to their Aramite subordinates, and one
to the only Canaanite tribe casually associated with them. Leaving out this solitary case as exceptional, all the rest resolve themselves into two ethnographical groups, totally distinct in origin—
the Rephaim, children of Ham, and the Aramites, children of
Shem. Our plates, III. and IV., exhibit the monumental representations of these nations in their peculiar costumes, from which
it will be evident at a glance that if these groups had been classified according to their *costumes* instead of their *names*, they would
have fallen into precisely the same two ethnographical groups,
the members of each group being characterised by similar generic
peculiarities, and differing only in those secondary details wherein
a difference is to be expected in different provinces of the same
land, or in different tribes of the same people.

The plates in Rosellini's great work on Egyptian monuments
will be found the best to refer to. Although most of its subjects
are repeated in Champollion's more voluminous publication, the
former is more convenient ; firstly, because the religious and the
historical monuments are in separate volumes ; secondly, because
the illustrations are arranged according to the chronological succession of the Pharaohs to whose reigns they belong, two highly
judicious examples of arrangement entirely disregarded in Champollion's work, where subjects of all kinds and all periods are
indiscriminately mixed up together. I would not so strongly re-
commend a reference to the descriptive volumes of Rosellini's
work, in connection with the present subject, as it would rather
confuse than assist its understanding, partly because Rosellini has
not identified or even read off many of the proper names ; partly

because his ventures at identifying a few of those he has read
have no foundation but a deceptive verbal resemblance, and some
of his random guesses are singularly infelicitous; partly because
he followed a now obsolete system of dynastic classification; and
partly because of the very erroneous series of dates, founded on
Champollion's chronology, which he assigns to his reigns and
dynasties.[d] We must set aside, in fact, all that was *speculative*
in this work, and look at nothing beyond its *graphic* portion.
This, whether ill or well interpreted, always remains the same—
a faithful transcript of those vast sculptured designs which constitute the body of the ancient Egyptian annals.

In describing the characteristic costumes and properties of the
three Rapha nations, it will be desirable to reverse the order I
adopted for the historical arrangement, beginning with the Anakim and ending with the elder tribe. The fact that the costume
of the children of Anak was selected by the Egyptians to imper-
sonate the whole TEMAH·U nation, in the typical representations
of the subjects of Thebes in the royal tombs, added to the general
points of resemblance between the attire of this tribe and that of
the children of Sheth, both argue that if we would obtain what is
original and peculiar to the Rapha nation in these respects, we
must look to those two branches of it that were least mixed up
with Egypt and her population, who retained their national characteristics the most tenaciously, and who contended the most
resolutely for their national independence. The Zuzim and the
mixed Philistines of the latter monumental period became half
Egyptianised in their costumes and national predilections. What
we have seen of their history sufficiently explains these later de-
viations from the original national type, which we must look to
much more ancient representations to recover.

§ A. THE ANAKIM.

The monumental illustrations referring to the Anakim are all
included in the following plates of Rosellini's work, *I monumenti
dell' Egitto e la Nubia*, Mon. Storici.

		Ros. Mon. St.
1. Impersonation of the Rephaim nations, or TEMAH·U, in the tomb of Seti-Menephtah, at Biban el Moluk (*Thebes*)		Pl. 155
2. Ditto, in the tomb of Rameses III. . . .		Pl. 158[e]
3. Battle-scene (*from Karnak*)—Seti-Menephtah defeating the TAHI		Pl. 54

[d] The origin of this chronological error has been ably pointed out in Chev.
Bunsen's ' Egypt's Place in Universal History,' B. 1.

[e] In the plates illustrating this tomb, the copyist has misapplied the epithets,
giving that of SHEM·U to the TEMAH·U people.

The costume of the Anakim was remarkably picturesque. The
figures 7, 8, 9, of our plate III., and the heads, fig. 15, and plate
II., fig. 11, will convey a correct idea of its leading forms. Their
limbs were generally bare; for an under garment, they wore a
short narrow kilt, fastened round the loins by a rich girdle, often
with long ends hanging down in front, and finished with a tassel.
Over this they threw a very peculiar kind of mantle, which, in its
general form, may be considered as the characteristic garment of
the Rapha people. It was narrow, hanging straight down without
folds, and open at the side; it was most generally worn by simply
passing it under one arm, and fastening it over the shoulder on
the other side; but the figure 9 of the TAHI tribe in pl. III.,
and the TEMAH'U chief of pl. II. fig. 11, present a slight variation
from this make. This garment was of gay colours, and richly
ornamented, either with stripes elaborately figured, or fancy patterns. That of the chief of TAHI (Ros. pl. 83) is yellow, and is
divided by broad diagonal stripes with water-plants between.
Those of the TEMAH'U (Ros. pl. 155) are figured, some with
palm-leaves laid horizontally across, with a row of spots between
each, some covered all over with marks in imitation of a leopard's
skin. From these figures, which are on a sufficiently large scale
to render details omitted in ordinary monumental illustrations, we
further learn that the Anakim printed or tattooed token-marks on
their arms and legs; the object thus impressed on the TEMAH'U
typical figure is, as we have seen, the characteristic emblem of
his national goddess, Onka-Athene: compare this figure in our
plate II. with the head of an ancient Egyptian Neith bearing her

name, fig. 10, and the names in the legends NT. fig. 9, and T-NT-
ANK, fig. 8. The Anakim sometimes shaved their face entirely,
but more generally they wore a very small pointed beard, only on
the chin. In this respect their practice was common to them and
to the other Rapha nations. Their head-dress is peculiarly their
own. It consists of a long braided lock of hair hanging down
the side of the face, and a helmet in form very different from
those worn by the Rephaim of Bashan. The top sits close to the
head, the front falls partly over the forehead, and forms a sort
of squared flap, from the side being scooped away in order to
exhibit not only the ear and the characteristic pendant lock, but
a rather unsightly square-shaped patch of the shaved temple
above it. The back of the helmet was also cut square, just low
enough to leave the neck free. The details in the helmets of
the TAHI chiefs (Ros. pl. 54) show how it fastened on by a leather
strap passing under the chin; but most of the historical representations omit these minutiæ, giving only the general forms. Not
a vestige of hair ever appears from under the helmet except the
side lock. This, and the round bare skulls of the CHERBU prisoners in pl. 93, who have lost their head-pieces in the fight,
encourages a suspicion that this people shaved their heads, and
that in their civilian costume, apparently that given in the
TEMAH·U tomb-figures, they wore, not their own hair, but a kind
of wig-like head-gear, which the helmets replaced in battle, and
were intended to imitate in form. This head-gear (see pl. 11.,
fig. 11) seems made of small plates or beads strung together so
as to look like ringlets falling from a common centre: the metal
helmets were grooved in a corresponding form. The Anakim of
TAHI sometimes wore a crest of one or two eagles' feathers on
the crown of their head-piece, but there is not an instance of the
RBO wearing any such ornament: on the other hand, the RBO
never appear without the side lock, but the TAHI did not always
wear it.

The chief of MASHUASH wears his lock behind the ear; moreover his round skull-cap and circlet, totally different from the
genuine and invariable Anakim helmet and strap, but strikingly
resembling those of his fellow captive of AMĀR (Ros. pl. 143), indicate that he was the local ruler of an Amorite dependant district, though a son of Anak by race. Other instances of such
blendings of costume will be found to occur in regions inhabited
by a mixed population.

The sculptured representations of the Anakim are very incomplete in illustrating their armour. In the great battle-scene of
Rameses III. they are entirely unarmed; in that of Seti-Menephtah and the TAHI, their only weapons are bows and arrows.

e

The form of their shields, if they ever used any, is unknown. In the scene last referred to it appears that in pitched battles they removed their mantle in order to fight more freely.

In their personal appearance the children of Anak of the monuments fully realise the description of the Hebrew spies, that they were 'men of great stature.' They are generally delineated as tall, spare, and long-limbed, to a degree often bordering on caricature.

§ b. The Emim.

The geographical range over which the rule of the Emim extended was so wide, and the mixture of races they counted as their vassals so various in origin, that we must expect to find a considerable difference of costume prevailing in the different regions of their domains. Yet even these variations are systematic and consistent. The attire of the people of the primary and metropolitan district—the plains of Shittim northward of the Arnon —is only a partial modification of that worn by the Anakim; both are obviously derived from one common primitive type. The southern section of the nation—those at least who garrisoned and ruled the Horite dependencies—appear in garments of a Horite fashion; nevertheless, the Shethite rulers are clearly distinguishable from their Horite subjects and their allies of Edom, by the broad line of national demarcation, the custom of *destroying the sides of the beard.* Indeed, they more frequently shaved it entirely away.

The monumental illustrations relating to the Emim will be found in the following series of plates in Rosellini's work, from which the leading forms of costume are given in our plate IV., upper line of figures.

Ros. Mon. St.

1. Symbolical group: Seti-Menephtah devoting the enemies of Egypt to destruction (*from Karnak*) . Pl. 60
   The kneeling figure in front of this group represents the Emim nation.
2. Seti-Menephtah engaging with the shet'ta and the amãr before atesh (*from the same*) . . . Pl. 53
3. The same king defeating the shet'ta and killing their chief (*from the same*) . . . . . . Pl. 57
4. shet'ta captive chiefs of various tribes presented by Seti-Menephtah to the Theban Gods (*from the same*) . . . . Pl. 59
5. Rameses II. devoting the enemies of Egypt to destruction (*from Abou-Simbel*) . . . . Pl. 79
6. Great expedition of Rameses II. against the shet'ta (*from the same*) . . . . Pl. 87–103
7. The surrender of atesh (*from Luxor*) . . . Pl. 104–107

The Emim differed from the other Rapha nations in that they
allowed their hair to grow long. Those of the metropolitan district wore it parted into three locks, one hanging on each side,
and one down the back. This is the style of the tribe engaged
with Seti-Menephtah, in the battle-scene, Ros. pl. 57, and of the
chief embodying the nation in the symbolical groups, pl. 60 and
79. The head in our Pl. IV. fig. 26, is copied from the former ;
it exhibits to great advantage the physical characteristics of this
tribe, without the repulsive individual traits of the Medinet Abou
captive, whose costume shows that he belongs to the southern or
Kenite region. These wore their hair in a single long lock or
queue, hanging down behind ; see our Pl. IV. fig. 20, which is
that of a warrior slain at the siege of POUN or Punon. Sometimes the hair was simply combed back from the forehead and
confined by a fillet or circlet either of gold or scarlet ; sometimes
the whole anterior half of the head was shaved, the long back
hair only remaining.

The Emim hardly ever are represented with beards ; those who
did not shave the face entirely never exceeded the limits of a
very small tip and moustache.

In the right-hand division of the vast Abou-Simbel subject
(Ros. pl. 103), where we see the chiefs hastening from the south
to the assistance of their brethren of ATESH, we recognise some
of the long-haired tribes, as well as some with shaved foreheads.
Among them also are those who 'cut away their hair all round
and shave it off the temples,' in imitation of the god Orotal (see
our Pl. IV. fig. 16). Their tufted crests so curiously resemble
the tufts on the skull-caps of the Shethites of ATESH, both in the
siege of the city by Seti-Menephtah (Ros. pl. 53 and 57), and
by Rameses II. (Ros. pl. 91), that we are perhaps not very rash
in conjecturing that this peculiar cap, worn only in battle, was
quite as much a religious signal as the two-horned Ashtaroth
helmets of the Rephaim of Bashan, or the Onka-crested ones of
the Philistines.

In the part of the picture above referred to (pl. 103) the colours are still in good preservation. We thereby recover many
valuable details, which convey a rather striking idea of this people's
luxury and splendour. As they are only marching to the battle,
we have the advantage of seeing them in full costume, with their

mantles on, which we see, by Ros. pl. 57, they sometimes took
off for the fight. This mantle, in form, does not materially differ
from that of the Anakim (see our pl. IV., fig. 16, 17, 19). It
is cut a little shorter, richly bordered, and striped in various
splendid colours. This is the attire of most of the chiefs slain
before ATESH. The fig. 19 in our pl. IV. represents one of
these, a chief named TAATUR; fig. 17 is one of the two Shethite
ambassadors brought before Rameses II., who were beaten as
spies: fig. 18 is a somewhat different form of costume; it is that
of the tribe contending with Seti-Menephtah (Ros. pl. 57), and is
taken (with the exception of the head attire) from the chief TAR·
KANUNASA, killed before ATESH. The upper part of the figure
is covered by a close corselet with short sleeves; the charioteers
in fig. 16 have one of a similar make under their mantles, but
apparently folded or quilted: their under tunic is exactly like that
of the kneeling ambassador behind them. The robe of the chief
in fig. 18 is a substitute for this tunic, worn only by persons of
great distinction; it is somewhat longer, and richly bordered.
The Assyrian sculptures display kings and gods clothed in a
similar garment, fringed and bordered: it is in all probability
the אַדֶּרֶת שִׁנְעָר, 'Babylonian garment,' referred to in Josh. vii. 21.
It appears that the corselet was worn only in battle, when the
upper mantle was discarded. The wearing of an under tunic
with the mantle was quite optional, for the Shethite Rephaim are
as often delineated without one—like the TAH'N·NU—as with one
—like the RBO. The material of this under tunic, as well as its
length and the richness of its adornments, were evidently regu-
lated by no custom but the convenience, taste, and rank of the
wearer.

The arms of the Emim were bows and arrows, and long spears.
They carried shields of various forms, which, from their markings
in the pictures, appear to have been made of wicker. They never
appear in helmets, save the close skull-caps above referred to,
worn only in battle, which were either quite plain, or were finished
at the top with a short tail or tuft.

The various battle-scenes in which they appear, represent them
as fighting on horseback as well as on foot. The chiefs used war-
chariots drawn by a pair of horses. These were not very unlike
the Egyptian chariot in make. The horses were magnificently
caparisoned, with embroidered cloths and ornaments of gold, blue
and scarlet. It is difficult to understand how a people presenting
so elaborately luxurious an array could ever have been referred,
on the strength of a half-resemblance of name, to the rude
nomadic troops of barbarians described under the name of *Scythians*
by Herodotus.

§ c. The Rephaim (*of Bashan*) and Philistines.

The costume of the Zuzim is so exactly the same as that of the
Philistines, that one description will suffice for both. They are
depicted in the following subjects :—

Figs. 1, 2, and 3, in our Pl. III. are, respectively, the Rephaim of the
central Judea region, of PAIROU or Pelusium, and of Bashan, from
Ros., pl. 50, 52, and 127. Figs. 10 and 11 are an Amorite and a
Philistine, from pl. 102. Fig. 12 is a Philistine, from a painted
vase in the tomb of Rameses III.

The Zuzim and Philistine costume consisted of a short kilt like
that of the RBO Anakim. It opened in front ; the hem, which often
had a double border, was sometimes straight, but often cut so as to
make the skirt dip in front into a point. Their bodies were protected by a low corselet, quilted, or made of bands or plates, and
reaching no higher than the arm-pits. Sometimes two broad
straps of the same material or pattern went over the shoulders to
keep it on. This corselet was an Egyptian fashion.

Neither the Zuzim nor the Philistines ever appear on the
monumental sculptures in their upper robe. Yet we have ex-
traneous evidence that this garment was also part of the full
costume of both these nations. In a vase delineated in the tomb
of Rameses III., supported by two Philistines, the figures are
attired in a mantle with a deep fringed border, which is worn in

the fashion characteristic of the Rephaim, passing under one arm and fastening over the other shoulder. As it is made a little more ample than the corresponding garment as worn by the Anakim, it does not appear open at the side, but the upper edge laps over the under edge of the opening in a very graceful manner. A Philistine chief in this elegant costume, with his tall feathered coronet, must have presented an appearance equally gorgeous and imposing.

The SHAS'U who surrendered to Rameses II., in the war with the SHET'TA, present a strange exception to the rest, in being dressed exactly like the Egyptian soldiers coming to their rencontre, —in all but their Ashtaroth-crested helmets. Whether on this occasion they really donned the Egyptian uniform,—or whether it was gratuitously bestowed upon them in the painted relievo, as a compliment, to indicate their assimilation with 'the pure race' of Egypt, we cannot decide. It is quite a solitary instance. This incident is repeated in the Luxor version of the memorial, Ros. pl. 106, lower line of figures.

The Zuzim and the Philistines used the same arms, offensive and defensive. The foot-soldiers had either straight double-edged swords, shaped like wedges, or smaller curved ones, single-edged ; they also used battle-axes of an Egyptian pattern. Those who rode in chariots used spears, javelins, and bows and arrows ; they carried large round shields. There is no representation of the SHAS'U in chariots ; those of the Philistines were exactly like those of the Emim ; but the quiver was attached to its side, after the Egyptian fashion.

We observe the same variations in the shaving of the beard among the Zuzim and Philistines, as among the other tribes of Rephaim. Sometimes they wear it pointed, without a moustache, like the chief of SHAIRTA'NA or Zarthan in our plate 3, fig. 13 ; sometimes they wear a moustache and no beard, like the SHAS'U who surrender to Rameses II. (plate 101) ; sometimes they are quite shaved, as the warriors in the Medinet-Abou battle-pieces. The Ekronite chief of the Medinet-Abou portraits has a pointed beard, yet the warriors in the battle-scene have none. But these people never wear a full beard, nor show any hair. The shape of the Ashtaroth-crested head-pieces worn by the Rephaim of Bashan necessarily exhibits the back of the head ; and it is therefore evident, from all the representations of them, that the hair was shaved off or clipped away quite close.

The only difference in the costumes of the Rephaim of Bashan and the Philistines is in the form and symbol of their helmets : yet there is an agreement even in this difference, since both wore the badge of their respective tutelar goddesses.

There is a part of the SHAS'U nation who did not wear the token of Ashtaroth; those against whom Seti-Menephtah made war in their own land (Ros. pl. 49), after expelling their forces from PAIROU (Pelusium). Their city was near a high hill—but its name is lost. The costume of this tribe is given in our pl. 3, fig. 1; but the shapes of their helmets vary considerably: some project behind in a form strongly resembling the head-gear of a captive of Rameses III. at Medinet-Abou, whose name, SHA-.., is partly erased. His likeness to the chief of SHAIRTA'NA is so strong, that he must have been of the same nation; but it must remain doubtful whether SHASU, or SHALAMU be the restoration of the name on his legend. It is more likely to be the latter, because SHALAMU is registered by name among the conquests of Rameses III.; whereas the SHAS'U are not mentioned by that name in his inscriptions, being comprehended under the general designation of TEMAH'U.

The similarity of costume between the Philistines of the later monumental period, and the elder branch of the Rephaim nation, is quite consistent with the Scriptural intimation that those Philistines were a people who had become closely identified with the remnant of Caphtor or Lower Egypt. The dissimilarity in costume between the Zuzim and the two other Rapha tribes, and its approximation in all such points of dissimilarity to that of the Delta, is also fully explained. For more than five centuries they ruled in Memphis; for three out of the five they held all Upper Egypt under tribute. It is perfectly natural to suppose that during such a long lapse of time they took up many Egyptian observances of costume more adapted to the climate of the country, and which they did not afterwards wholly cast off. And when the kindred race of Caphtor, who shared their exile, joined the small Philistine tribe, we can easily perceive how, although the ancient name of the tribe continued, its national characteristics and predilections became modified by the connection of the new-comers with the Rephaim of Jerusalem; assimilating rather with these, than with the Rephaim of Anak or of Shittim, whenever, in their subsequent relations with Egypt, their political interests happened to clash.

But although in the last phase of their national existence, certain outward tokens of nationality were thus sunk, in the elder family of the Rephaim, there is reason to believe that a most valuable record of their primitive type still exists in the well-known subject from the grottoes of Beni-Hassan, which represents an embassy of unknown foreigners, headed by their HK, named ABSHA, and accompanied by their wives and children, bringing gifts to an officer who lived in the reign of Sesertasen II., one of the earlier kings of the XIIth dynasty (Vide Ros. pl. 26 to 28).

This monument accordingly belongs to a period a little preceding the Hyksos invasion, since the 'six foreign Phœnician kings who took Memphis' are now found to have been contemporaneous with the latter part of the XIIth. Manetho limits the rule of the Hyksos in Egypt to 511 years. This interval is quite sufficient, though not too long, for the XVth Phœnician dynasty, the XVIIth of 'other Shepherd-kings,' who laid Thebes under tribute, and their contemporaries, the tributary XIIIth of Thebans, and VIIIth Memphites. By placing the Exodus at the close of the XIXth dynasty, the expulsion of the Shepherds by Amosis or Aâhmes, leader of the XVIIIth, falls at about the time of Abraham's death. Thus we are not exaggerating the antiquity of this curious old Egyptian picture, when we say that it was painted nearly four hundred years before Abraham was born!

A reference to the figures themselves will, I believe, satisfy the inquirer that in all elementary and characteristic forms of their costume, these foreigners strikingly resemble the Shethite and Anakite Rephaim. Figs. 4, 5, 6, in our Pl. III., represent the three principal persons in the procession. They wear the peculiar mantle, striped with rich variegated patterns and colours, and passing under one arm and fastened over the other shoulder, just like the Anakim of RBO and TAHI, and the SHETTA, but a little shorter than the former. Instead of the loose tunic of the SHETTA, our unknown people wear the short close-fitting kilt of the RBO. The only figures showing this part of the costume are the attendants behind ABSHA, who do not wear the mantle of distinction. They are all in their civilian costume, and wear no helmets; but the form into which their hair or wig is trained reminds one strongly of the caps of some among the SHASU of Pelusium and of the upper SHASU country (compare pl. 49, 50). Their beards are very curiously cut and trimmed to a point; the side of it, according to the invariable custom of the Rephaim, is partly shaved away.

Again, the remarkable outline of their profiles is worthy of attention, viz. the *retiring forehead and chin* peculiar to that nation. The latter feature is particularly well displayed in the female faces. Compare the head of the chief woman with that of a RBO captive of Rameses III. next to it, in our pl. III., figs. 4, 5. By the likeness of their features, she might be taken for his daughter, yet an interval of eight hundred years separates these two individuals.

The costume of the women was very like that of the men; but as all the figures are turned sideways, we cannot see whether their tunics or mantles are open at the side. The fringe down the opening of the HK ABSHA's mantle shows that the men wore this garment open. The hair of the women is dressed in the most archaic Egyptian fashion. See the head of Neith in our pl. II., fig. 10. The men wear sandals, the women boots. The chief, ABSHA, carries the hook-shaped sceptre, which by the way is the initial letter in his title הך, a ruler, equivalent to the Hebraized title עוג (Og). The other men carry bows, spears, and a club of a very remarkable shape.

This resemblance in their general characters of person and costume seems to justify our believing that, in the hitherto unknown Beni-Hassan foreigners, whose identity has given rise to so much speculation,[f] we behold an authentic contemporaneous representation of the primitive type of that ancient people, the REPHAIM of the Bible, in its very earliest stage of nationalization, prior to its conquest of Egypt, perhaps even prior to its subdivision into the branch nations known in Bible-history as the Emim and Anakim, since each of these tribes appears to have adopted to itself certain special modifications of the original national costume, sufficiently marked to distinguish one family or tribe from another, yet not sufficiently different from the primary type to obliterate its essentially characteristic points.

§ D. THE ARAMITES.

The last group to be described presents characters of feature and costume so different from those of the Rephaim, that we must have recognised in them another nation of another race, even if their lands had remained unidentified, and their origin unascertained.

The series of subjects in which this race appear, and from which the figures 21 to 25 of our plate IV. are selected, are as follows:—

	Ros. Mon. St.
1. SHEM'U group; tomb of Seti-Menephtah (*Biban-el-Moluk*)	Pl. 155
2. Same, in full dress; tomb of Menephtah (*from the same*). See our fig. 21	Pl. 157
3. Same; tomb of Rameses III. (*from the same*) .	Pl. 158
4. The lower LT'N'NU and RMN'N submitting to Seti-Menephtah, and cutting down trees (*from Karnak*). See fig. 22	Pl. 46
5. Attack of a city, name partly lost	Pl. 46
6. Defeat of the upper LT'N'NU by Seti-Menephtah .	Pl. 47
7. Captives and spoils of the upper LT'N'NU . .	Pl. 48

[f] The favourite hypothesis that the picture represented the arrival of the Hebrews in Egypt is of course demolished by recent chronological research. An interval of seven centuries elapsed between the reign of Sesertasen II. and that event. If the Exodus happened at the end of the nineteenth dynasty, the elevation of Joseph must have taken place under one of the early reigns of the eighteenth; most probably under the regency preceding the reign of Thothmes III., or during his minority.

The epithet SHEM·U, which describes the tomb-figures of the three first subjects referred to, is evidently the primary designation of the Aramite race, 'the Shemites.' In those early ages, when the great Asiatic migration from the region of the upper Euphrates was only beginning to direct itself southward, the Shemites of the eastern line of population were the only tribes touching upon the Hamites of the western line, who were not of the same paternal stock. Thus their early patronymic, 'SHEM·U,' seems, by an easy transition of ideas, to have passed into the language of the Mizraim as a common appellative for *strangers*—those of a different race. By the Canaanites of the West, they were geographically designated 'the children of the East.'

The fundamental points of resemblance between these SHEM people of the tombs and the monumental groups of the succeeding subjects, clearly show that they are of the same stock—that the SHEM·U are the typical figure of which the monumental nations are as many local and unessential variations. The SHEM·U may be the metropolitan tribe, for Damascus and Shem were both names of the same city; and therefore the people bearing that name would be pictorial representatives of the monumental NAHARI·NA (River-land, Aram Naharaim); while those figured in the historical illustrations appear, by the names of their localities, to belong to the southern region of this ancient establishment, and to represent its provincial members, though at a period when its power had been superseded by the Shethite Rephaim, and its population had given way to the Edomites.

The figure in the tomb of Seti-Menephtah does not give the full costume—it only wears the short under garment of inferior people, like the attendants of Absha in the old Beni-Hassan subject; but in the tomb of Menephtah, son of the great Rameses, and contemporary of Moses, we find a repetition of the figure in full attire, with the same name, countenance, and head-dress as the others (see fig. 24 of our pl. IV.). We are thereby enabled to connect this typical figure with the monumental group to which it belongs.

The people comprised within this group all affect the following peculiarities :—

They do not clip or shave any part of the beard, like the Rephaim ; but wear it full and round.

They do not go with their limbs bare, like the Rephaim ; but wear a long robe, which either folds over the person in front, or is twined spirally round the figure, fastening at the waist with a short girdle.

They do not wear a mantle, like the Rephaim ; but the upper part of the body is covered by a short cape, rounded and open in front, which never reaches lower than the waist. The aperture for the throat is sometimes cut and bordered in a peculiar form which gives it the appearance, in the sculptures, of a cross hanging from the neck. In the SHEM·U of the two first tomb-subjects, the hair seems to have been powdered, or enclosed in a white bag or net spotted over with blue. A fillet with a bow behind encircles the head.

The faces of all the people wearing this costume present as great a contrast to those of the Rephaim as their attire. Their profile exhibits a much more upright outline, with a genuine aquiline cast approximating to the Hebrew countenance. See our fig. 27.

Four Biblical names are found in one region, corresponding to the four names of the people whose costume answers to the above description, viz. SHAR, Seir ; LET, Elath ; RMN, Rimmon-Parez ; and POUN, Punon. This fourfold correspondence of name and costume is a coincidence of great value as a test of the people's identity ; while, on the other hand, the general resemblance they all bear to the SHEM of the tombs is a striking confirmation of the conclusion founded on a great number of Scriptural references already quoted—that the original settlers in the Horite valley were an Aramite race.

The individual variations of costume between the people bearing these names are very unimportant, and chiefly consist of a slight difference in the head attire. Some wear the back hair full and round, with the fillet and tie behind : the LET, Elath (Ros. pl. 46, 47, 48), SHAR, Seir (pl. 49), and the Luxor captive chieftain (pl. 141), are so represented. The REMEN, and some of the SHAR, have a close round skull-cap with a flap over the back of the neck, and they seem to have cut off their back hair. The garrison of the nameless fortress in the Beit-el-Wally subject (fig. 24) shave their heads, though their chief wears the SHEM·U coiffure. Some wore the back hair full, but shaved the crown of the head, and cover it with a cap. But amidst all these variations of individual fancy, the great line of demarcation between the Shemite and the Rapha races remains inviolate. None of these people *shave their beards*. The Scripture history constrains us to recognise the Edomite rulers and successors of the Horites in the chiefs of the people whose costume we have described; and it appears established, from the evidence of these interesting representations, that the children of Esau, although in all their political relations they proved themselves true friends and faithful allies of the Shethite people, among whom their first establishment was formed, had not assimilated themselves with that idolatrous race so far as to adopt their external badge of nationality by shaving their beards.

The only exception to this rule would seem to be the shaved garrison of POUN, or Punon, who wear the genuine Horite robe and cape (see our fig. 26); but the monumental picture which records the event, also records the fact that the masters of Punon were of the SHET'TA people, and thus proves the rule to be without exception.

The fortress in the subject (pl. 68) exhibits the female costume of the country, in three women on the battlements: one is beating her head in despair, another offering her child to the victors, or throwing it over the walls. Two of them wear capes like the men; the third, apparently a young maiden, has her neck and shoulders unclothed. Their hair is long, hanging down, and from the shoulders the ends are braided into three tails. See fig. 25.

In these battle-pieces, most of the enemy are represented without weapons. This ingenious Egyptian expedient to suggest their absolute helplessness, unfortunately deprives us of the means of knowing how they really did defend themselves. Here and there we see a figure with a broken bow; and in one of the battles of Seti-Menephtah (pl. 46), a chief is looking out of a circular window or loophole, with one hand on his head, and his sword pointing downwards in the other, as a token of submission. This sword is the same double-edged and wedge-shaped weapon as that borne by the Philistines, and the Zuzim surrendering to Rameses II. in the great picture of Abou-Simbel.

The costume of the Amorites may be gathered from the only three subjects in which they appear by name. In the attack on ATESH by Seti-Menephtah, the city is evidently defended by an Amorite garrison; for although their costume resembles that of the Shethites as to the military uniform—the corselet, and a skull-cap crested with a tail—they have full beards, and moreover are commanded by a bearded chief who wears the same head-attire as the chief of AMAR, captive of Rameses III., in the harem at Medinet Abou (Ros. pl. 143). The same *bearded* people, in plain long robes, accompany the Philistines coming to aid the Shethite garrison of ATESH against Rameses II., in the Luxor subject, from which the figure 10 in our plate III. is taken; and we know from Scripture, on the one hand, that the Philistines ruled over an extensive Amorite district, and could therefore command the services of its population in case of war: on the other hand, the AMARU are mentioned by name with the people of CHERBU (Hebron), in the Egyptian inscriptions of these subjects, as allies of the SHET'TA in the war. Finally, in the captive chief of Rameses III., a distinct idea of the physique of this race is handed down to us. This chief has a longer face than the Rephaim, and a much straighter line of profile. The Ekronite chief is not unlike him. The Amorite has a fine long full beard, and the sides of his face are not shaved. His hair is arranged precisely like that of the SHEM'U and LET people, and bound by a similar fillet and tie. As the Edomites themselves were half-breed Canaanites, descendants of Seir the Hivite, co-settler with Esau, it is interesting to find the similarity of their respective fashions thus in harmony with their origin.

F. C.

LONDON: PRINTED BY W. CLOWES AND SONS, STAMFORD STREET.

THE REPHAIM.

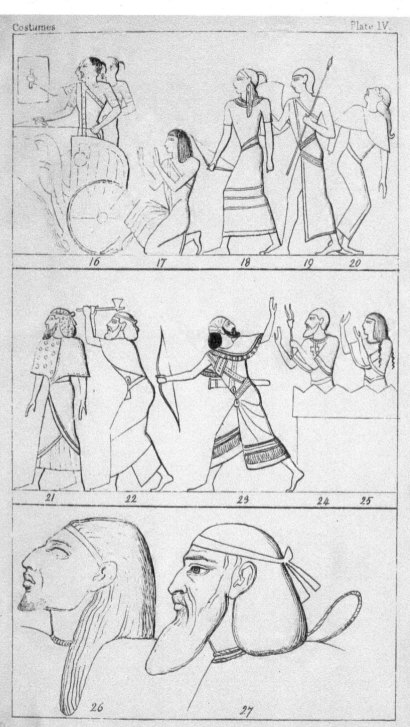

THE REPHAIM